AF412200

Emotion, Politics and Society

Emotion, Politics and Society

Edited by

Simon Clarke, Paul Hoggett and Simon Thompson
University of the West of England, Bristol

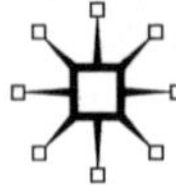

First published 2006 by
PALGRAVE MACMILLAN
Houndmills, Basingstoke, Hampshire RG21 6XS and
175 Fifth Avenue, New York, N.Y. 10010
Companies and representatives throughout the world

PALGRAVE MACMILLAN is the global academic imprint of the Palgrave Macmillan division of St. Martin's Press, LLC and of Palgrave Macmillan Ltd. Macmillan® is a registered trademark in the United States, United Kingdom and other countries. Palgrave is a registered trademark in the European Union and other countries.

ISBN-13: 978–1–4039–9681–7 hardback
ISBN-10: 1–4039–9681–4 hardback

This book is printed on paper suitable for recycling and made from fully managed and sustained forest sources.

A catalogue record for this book is available from the British Library.

Library of Congress Cataloging-in-Publication Data
Emotion, politics and society / edited by Simon Clarke, Paul Hoggett, and Simon Thompson.
   p. cm.
Includes bibliographical references and index.
ISBN 1–4039–9681–4
1. Political psychology. 2. Emotions. I. Clarke, Simon, 1962–
II. Hoggett, Paul. III. Thompson, Simon, 1962–
JA74.5.E57 2006
320.01′9—dc22   2005057507

10 9 8 7 6 5 4 3 2 1
15 14 13 12 11 10 09 08 07 06

Printed and bound in Great Britain by
Antony Rowe Ltd, Chippenham and Eastbourne

Contents

Acknowledgements

We would like to thank Jill Lake and the publishing team at Palgrave Macmillan for their help in the production of the book. It was developed within the vibrant research cultures of the Centre for Psycho-Social Studies and the Centre for Critical Theory which together provide a base for interdisciplinary theoretical and empirical social research at the University of the West of England. Our special thanks go to Julia Long for her invaluable support throughout this project. The origins of our idea to publish this volume lay with a conference we organized in 2004 entitled "Politics and Emotions" for which we are grateful to the British Academy for providing financial support.

Notes on Contributors

Jack Barbalet was, at the time of writing, Professor of Sociology at the University of Leicester, UK, where he is Head of Department. He has previously held positions at the University of Papua New Guinea, the University of Adelaide and the Australian National University. Jack's interests include political sociology and sociological theory. Over the past decade he has made substantial contributions to the sociology of emotions. His publications include *Emotions, Social Theory and Social Structure* and an edited collection *Emotions and Sociology*.

C. Fred Alford is Professor of Government and Distinguished Scholar-Teacher at the University of Maryland, College Park, USA, where he has taught since 1979, when he received his Ph.D. from the University of Texas at Austin. Author of over a dozen books in moral psychology, his three most recent books are: *Why Freedom Has Lost its Meaning and What Can Be Done To Save It, Levinas, Psychoanalysis, and the Frankfurt School, Whistle-blowers: Broken Lives and Organizational Power.* Professor Alford is President of the Political Psychology Section of the American Political Science Association, and Executive Director of the Association for Psychoanalysis, Culture, and Society. He sits on the editorial boards of five professional journals, has received three senior Fulbright Fellowships, and has published over fifty articles and book chapters in the field of moral psychology.

Simon Clarke is Reader in, and Co-Director of, The Centre for Psycho-Social Studies at the University of the West of England, UK. His research interests include the interface between sociological and psychoanalytic theory; identity and conflict and the psychoanalytic sociology of the emotions. He has published widely on the psychoanalytic understanding of racism and ethnic hatred and is author of *Social Theory, Psychoanalysis and Racism* and *From Enlightenment to Risk: Social Theory and Contemporary Society*. Simon is a member of the Board of Directors of the Association for the Psychoanalysis of Culture and Society. Formerly he was an Associate Editor of the *Journal for the Psychoanalysis of Culture and Society* and Editor of *Psychoanalysis, Culture and Society*.

Nicolas Demertzis is Professor at the Department of Communication and Media Studies, Athens University, Greece. He studied political science and in 1986 he received his Ph.D. degree in Sociology from the University of Lund, Sweden. His major works are: *Cultural Theory and Political Culture. New Directions and Proposals, Culture, Modernity, Political Culture,* co-authored with Thanos Lipowatz, *Essay on Ideology. A Dialogue between Social Theory and Psychoanalysis, Local Publicity and the Press in Greece, The Nationalist Discourse. Ambivalent Semantic Field and Contemporary Tendencies, Political Communication. Risk, Publicity and the Internet.* Also, he published in English and French Reviews and collective volumes on political culture, nationalism and the media. His current research interests focus on the realms of political sociology, political communication, and the sociology of emotions.

Paul Hoggett is Professor of Politics and Director of the Centre for Psycho-Social Studies at the University of the West of England, UK. His research interests have focused on the changing nature of the welfare state and the state/civil society interface. He also has a long-standing interest in psychoanalysis and politics, is a psychoanalytic psychotherapist and the co-editor of the journal *Organisational and Social Dynamics.* Previous books include *Partisans in an Uncertain World* and *Emotional Life and the Politics of Welfare.*

James M. Jasper is an independent scholar living in New York City, USA. With degrees in economics from Harvard and in sociology from the University of California at Berkeley, he has taught at Berkeley, Columbia, Princeton, and New York University. He writes about politics, culture, and morality. His works include *Nuclear Politics, The Animal Rights Crusade* (coauthored with Dorothy Nelkin), *The Art of Moral Protest* and *Restless Nation.* Edited volumes include *Passionate Politics, The Social Movements Reader* and *Rethinking Social Movements.* At the time of writing, he was currently at work on a social theory of strategic action.

Simon Thompson is Senior Lecturer in Politics, and Director of the Centre for Critical Theory, at the University of the West of England, UK. His research interests include the politics of recognition, models of deliberative democracy, and the relationship between politics and the emotions. He is author of *The Political Theory of Recognition: A Critical Introduction* (2006), and co-editor of *Richard Rorty: Critical Dialogues* (2001). Simon has also written for a number of journals including *Constellations, Contemporary Political Theory, Critical Review of International Social and Political Philosophy, Critical Social Policy* and *Policy and Politics.*

Part I
The Foundations

1
The Study of Emotion: An Introduction

Simon Clarke, Paul Hoggett and Simon Thompson

Two views of emotions

Emotions occupy an ambiguous place in the popular imagination. Sometimes they are regarded as irrational passions which threaten to destroy our calmly ordered lives. Emotions, from this point of view, are located in the body. When people feel emotions, a violent energy arises within them which compels them to act in ways they may later regret. Emotions are regarded as forces beyond our control for which we cannot be held responsible. They are disruptive forces that may even threaten the rules and regulations on which civilization itself depends. In this account of emotions, road rage can be seen as a typical case in point. A driver believes another road-user has acted in a selfish or stupid manner. He suddenly feels a surge of anger which leads him to want to take violent revenge. It seems as if this rage has derailed his reason and taken him over. If he does take revenge, he may well bitterly regret his action once he has calmed down. Where this view of emotions predominates, the inference likely to be drawn is that we should be guided by our powers of reasoning, thinking through the consequences of our actions. We should stay calm, retain our self-discipline, keep our cool. Thus it would be best if anger and rage were effectively restrained, disgust and hatred diminished, fear and anxiety brought under control. In short, reason should master emotion. Indeed, adapting Freud (1930) a little, it could be said that civilization rests on the repression of emotion.

At other times, however, emotions occupy a quite different place in the popular imagination. Here they are regarded sometimes as desirable, at other times as regrettable, but always as unavoidable aspects of our lives. We distrust and pity people who are only ever calm and logical.

We regard them as cold and unemotional, lacking in the warmth and spontaneity that makes us properly human. Our attitude to the characters of Dr Spock and Lieutenant Commander Data in the Star Trek television series encapsulates this feeling. We know full well that Spock and Data, in spite of their infinitely superior reasoning ability, often make elementary mistakes or serious misjudgements since without emotions they lack a capacity for intuition vital to human life. Thus while emotions may be located in the body, they are not merely brute sensations like toothache. Instead they may be sources of valuable information about us and the world around us. Thus it is that we adore love, revel in joy, feel we can have a right to be angry and a reason to sorrow. Importantly, emotions are not opposed to reason. Indeed the idea of emotional intelligence (Goleman, 1996; Szczurek, 2005) suggests that, if humans have self-awareness, empathy for others, and the ability to love and be loved, they will be able to lead more successful lives. From this account, then, whilst analytic and reasoning capacities are rightly prized, it is recognized that they are not enough. Emotions have an important and valuable part to play in our lives. They are, amongst other things, important indicators of our needs, and vital guides to how we should live. In short, what is needed is not the replacement of emotion by reason, but an understanding of the place of emotion in reason.

The ambiguous place that emotions occupy in the popular imagination influences our attitudes to the role of emotions in the world of politics. According to one view, emotions should play no part in politics. Following on from the first account sketched above, it is felt that if political actors, groups and institutions are influenced by emotions, then they will take irrational and unjustifiable decisions. For instance, politicians who cannot control their emotions are regarded as a liability. They could lose their tempers at crucial moments in delicate negotiations, or could be paralyzed by fear when decisive action is required. For this reason, we have good reason not to rely on them. We also distrust those political actors who try to whip up the emotions of the masses in order to try to attain their own ends. The boundary between this kind of populism and more extreme forms of politics such as fascism is very fluid (Fieschi, 2004). The image of the Nuremburg rallies comes to mind as a vivid example of how a political demagogue can manipulate the emotions of a crowd in order to get them to do what they otherwise would not. From this perspective, then, emotions would have no part to play in politics. In an ideal world, politics would be a matter of rational argument and calm deliberation. Expert knowledge would be used to identify optimal solutions to collective problems. Guided by reason, we would either come to agreement or find a way to live with our differences. In short, reason and not emotion should rule the political realm.

It is possible to find another view about the role of emotions in politics. According to this rival view, it is obvious that in the world as we know it – rather than in the world as we might like it to be – emotions cannot be wished away. We understand the necessary part that emotions play in a whole range of political processes and events. The mobilization of gay men and lesbians under the banner of gay pride, for example, involves a strategic deployment of emotions in which shame and fear are converted into dignity and pride (Gould, 2005). Humiliation seemed to play a key role in the breakdown of recent talks about the next stage of IRA weapons decommissioning in Northern Ireland. Ian Paisley's insistence that the decommissioning process be photographed led Sinn Féin's president, Gerry Adams, to reject what he referred to as the 'politics of humiliation'. At another level, we believe that the world of politics should not be stripped of emotions. We look favourably on politicians who speak from the heart. While we might not agree with what they say, we respect the passion with which they say it. We want our politicians to be energized by their hatred of injustice and their desire to see it ended. This view holds moreover that even in the world of politics emotion is not opposed to reason. In a world threatened by ecological disaster and violent terrorism, there is good reason to be anxious and afraid; such emotions are appropriate responses to the world in which we find ourselves and they can motivate action to address the danger. In this sense, such emotions are entirely rational. According to this second view, in short, the world of politics is inevitably and rightly a world full of emotions.

Academic analysis of emotions

It is probably fair to say that emotions also occupy an ambiguous place in academic accounts of human life. It may be thought that in the natural sciences a strongly negative view of emotions would be found. After all, science is supposed to be the human practice which best exemplifies the application of rationality to our attempts to understand the world around us. The scientist is the archetype of a human being governed by reason rather than emotion. It is not surprising, then, to find that the study of emotions has generally been highly marginalized. In recent years, however, emotion has become a 'hot topic' in science (Evans, 2004, p. xiii). In part, this is because recent developments in neuroscience have facilitated a number of important advances in the study of emotions. Amongst other things, it is now possible to associate different sorts of emotions – and different versions of the same emotion – with different parts of the brain. For instance, fear of a dog straining at its leash to attack you works through the limbic system of the brain, whereas fear of the consequences of global warming also involves the operation of the brain's neocortex. It is important to note that these neuroscientists do not reproduce the popular contrast between reason and emotion. Rather they accept, in Dylan Evans' words, that 'emotions are vital for intelligent action' (2004, p. 33). It is argued that at least some emotions are the product of evolutionary adaptation. Anger and fear, for instance, underlie the fight/flight mechanism which is designed to try to ensure an organism's survival. Thus people are smarter if they are animated by emotion as well as reason (Damasio, 2000; Le Doux, 2002).

Emotions have also been a subject of abiding – if somewhat sporadic and marginal – interest for philosophers, from Aristotle to the present day. While none of them would attempt to deny that some emotions seem 'wild' and irrational, they nevertheless argue that other emotions have significant links with cognition and judgment. Philosophers maintain that emotions are 'intentional' – that is to say, they are about some object in the world. To be fearful is to fear *something*; to be angry is to be angry about *something*. It follows that each of these emotions is bound up with a number of beliefs about the nature of the object that the emotion is about. I fear the tiger since it presents a real and present danger to me; I am angry about my situation since I believe that an injustice has been done to me. What this means is that philosophers, like neuroscientists, do not starkly oppose emotion to reason. While very few of them would claim that emotions are always rational, most would accept that they are 'not *non*-rational' (Calhoun and Solomon, 1984, p. 31). Martha Nussbaum makes the stronger claim that emotions are 'appraisals or value-judgments, which ascribe to things and persons outside the person's own control great importance for that person's flourishing' (2001, p. 4). For Nussbaum, emotions are complex evaluations of the things that these emotions are about. Thus, like the neuroscientists, philosophers do not draw an absolute distinction between reason and emotion.

Within the social sciences, it is sociologists who have shown the greatest interest in emotions in the last decade or so. Here the primary concern is not whether emotions are rational or irrational but whether they are a product of nature or nuture. At present, the dominant view is some form of social constructionism. This holds that emotions are not subjective inner states but rather aspects of social relations. Mary Holmes, for instance, characterizes a 'sociological definition' of emotions as 'one which avoids seeing emotions as "inbuilt" mental or bodily reactions or instincts'. Rather an emotion is 'something we do (or do not do) as part of our interactions with others' (2004, p. 123). Rather than being hard-wired into the brain, they are the products of culture, learnt in what Rom Harré calls a 'local moral order' (1986, p. 6). This means that emotions are not universal constants of human nature but rather vary from place to place and from time to time. In Arlie Hochschild's well-known analysis (1983), such emotions are governed by local 'feeling-rules' which are normative expectations about how to feel in different social contexts. For example, particular rules specify that we should feel joy at the birth of a child, and sorrow at the death of a loved one. At the same time, there is a second sociological approach to the emotions which does not deny their visceral embodiment and their affective power. Simon Clarke, one of the editors of this volume, defends a 'psychoanalytical sociology' which seeks to combine a sociological understanding of 'the structures of modern life that uphold and facilitate phenomena such as racism, social exclusion and inequality' with a psychoanalytic understanding of 'the powerful affective forces, and the embodied, and visceral nature of these phenomena' (Clarke 2003, p. 159). From a social constructionist viewpoint we have a number of conditions which affect emotional response. In the broadest sense (after Harré, 1986) they are, first, the local moral order. Second, the historical context of an emotion in a given culture and in particular the local language. Finally, there is an emphasis on political economy, and in particular the socio-economic position of a group. In other words our emotional feelings are a cognitive response to how we would be expected to feel in a given situation. The problem with this view is that there is little recognition of unconscious motivation behind response, and, as Sabini and Silver (1998) acknowledge, it is difficult to say the least, to pin point why some people are, for example, more envious or more prone to envy than others. Clarke argues that a psychoanalytic sociology which incorporates a recognition of the powerful affective forces that underlie emotional response in tandem with constructionist ideas can give us a better understanding of emotion. Unlike social constructionism, this approach assumes 'some innate, or biological basis for emotion' but still acknowledges the importance of 'the social world' (2003, p. 159). For Clarke, in other words, while at least some emotions may be universal, they are always mediated by particular social contexts.

In this book, it is our contention that, with regard to the emotions, the academic study of politics is rather less advanced than these other disciplines. Despite the growing public consciousness of the importance of emotions in social and political life, the study of the relationship between emotion, power and politics within academia has lagged behind practice. In political analysis, we do not find philosophy's nuanced understanding of the role of emotions in understanding and evaluation; nor do we find sociology's mediation of unconscious affects and social contexts. Instead the academic study of politics is for the most part firmly attached to narrowly rationalist models of explanation and justification which split off head and mind from heart and body. In his chapter in this book, Jack Barbalet suggests that politics is understood 'in terms of one of three possible constructions': 'calculations of interest', 'structures of opportunity for action' and 'norms, mores and values'. On the first account, political action is seen as the result of individuals' reckoning of their best interests. Various forms of rational-choice theory would fall into this category. On the second account, political action is channelled into certain paths by already existing social institutions. On the third account, it is patterns of cultural value which channel action in particular directions. In none of these cases is it acknowledged that, as Barbalet puts it, underlying interests, structured inhibitions and inclinations are emotions.

It should be said that over the last five years there have been some signs of change. Much of this recent work has been undertaken by political sociologists such as Jeff Goodwin and colleagues (2001) and Sheldon Stryker and colleagues (2000). This body of research has largely focused on political mobilization and social movements. The work of another political sociologist, Jack Barbalet (2001), offers insight into some central aspects of political behaviour and political theory. Nevertheless contributions from writers from within the discipline of politics itself are still few and far between. Three recent exceptions are the book by George Marcus (2002), which draws on recent developments in neuro-psychology, the book by Susan Mendus (2000), which investigates the role of love in moral and political philosophy, and Cass Sunstein's (2005) analysis of democracy, risk and fear. There is a stronger tradition of political theory drawing upon psychoanalytic perspectives (Flax, 1993; Alford, 1994) in the USA.

This book seeks to add its voice to this small but growing chorus. It critically addresses the intersection between power, politics and the emotions by arguing that emotions are central to our understanding of the social and political world. They are important at all levels, from international relations and the global political system, through nation states and national political parties, to social movements and groups in civil society. Indeed they are important not just for those engaged in the academic study of politics, but also for political actors themselves. In order to make this case, the contributors to this book combine theory building with empirical case study. They are committed to both illustrating theoretical arguments by using 'live' examples and illuminating 'lived examples' by recourse to theory. Thus the book will address substantive questions in this new field, including the paradoxical and ambivalent contribution of emotions to everyday political behaviours such as the secret ballot (Barbalet), the role of envy in racism and other political hatreds (Clarke), the place of envy and resentment in populism (Demertzis), the relationship between love, hate and the desire to know otherness (Alford), the role of love and hate in pity and compassion in a 'post-emotional' society (Hoggett), and the role of negative emotions such as anger in progressive struggles (Thompson). In this way, the book aims to develop a more nuanced theorization of emotion in politics, one which will help us to understand emotions in contemporary social and political life.

Four general themes

In order to show that that emotions are central to our understanding of politics, the chapters that follow this will develop a number of inter-linked themes. To give some indication of their character, it will be useful to sketch the principal features of four general themes here.

First, it will be necessary to establish what emotions are, and what sort of feelings and experiences they encompass. At one extreme, do they include what Jasper calls 'urges' or 'physical impulses'? At the other extreme, can dispositions like scientific curiosity or love of the truth be considered emotions? Deciding what is to count as emotions will strongly influence an account of what they are. According to one account, emotions are merely physical sensations of which one may become conscious. A second account holds that they can be understood simply in terms of the behaviour of the individual experiencing that emotion. A third account, already hinted at above, contends that since emotions stand in a complex relation with our beliefs and values their rationality can be evaluated. The contributors to this book tend to the last of these accounts. They challenge the traditional dichotomies which counterpose rationalist to non-rationalist epistemologies, and explore instead the interpenetration of reason and passion, thought and feeling. In doing so, they do not advocate the abandonment of reason for emotion, but instead make the case for a more complete and integrated rationalism.

A second theme is closely related to the first. It will also be necessary to determine whether there are different sorts of emotions, whether they can be placed in different groups. For instance, some commentators focus on the different durations and intensities of particular emotions. Consider the difference between powerful but fleeting emotions such as mass grief and more enduring but less perceptible sentiments which may strongly colour a society's culture for decades. Barbalet distinguishes between relational emotions, iterated emotions and programmatic emotions. Into the first group fall emotions which characterize all human relations; hence it could be said that these are universal emotions. However, since humans live in many different social and political worlds, there are a second group of 'iterated' or 'nested' emotions particular to these worlds. Finally a third group of emotions are involved in processes of institutionalization; hence, for example, love is associated with marriage. Jasper offers an alternative fivefold system of classification. Physical urges including lust and hunger may disrupt people's projects. Reflex emotions such as disgust and surprise flare up quickly and just as quickly subside. Affects including love and hate 'are normally tied to elaborate cognitions' and can underlie political solidarities. Moods, which lack an immediate object, 'operate primarily as *filters* for perception, decision, and action'. Finally, moral sensibilities, including compassion and forms of anger, are related in complex ways to our moral perspectives.

A third theme concerns the way in which emotions are related to politics. According to Jasper, emotions are an important microfoundation upon which more complex political processes and outcomes depend. For Barbalet, particular political institutions and practices can be associated with or are accompanied by certain distinctive patterns of emotions. Here Barbalet draws upon the well-known 'social interactional' theory of emotions of Theodore Kemper (1978). Kemper's position is that emotions are experiences which result from particular sorts of social relations so, for example, he contends that excess status leads to shame and insufficient status to depression. Yet others believe that emotions are features of particular human groups (e.g. Bion, 1961). Here a connection is made between collective emotions and group identities. This third theme will also involve determining how emotions compare to other possible *explanans* for political actions, such as interests, opportunities, norms and institutions. Do, for instance, emotions sit alongside, give rise to or energize interests?

Fourth, it will be necessary to distinguish the different levels at which emotions play a part in politics. Here it may be useful to think of emotions operating at the following five levels:

1. They can be regarded as a part of the human condition, providing part of the base material of society. It is here that basic emotions – such as fear and aggression – are located. To focus on emotions operating at this level is to remind ourselves of the psychosomatic soil of the emotions. It is also to accept that there are certain dynamic qualities to such emotions which operate irrespective of the particular shape and meaning that the emotion might assume in a particular culture.

2. Emotions also operate at the organic or epochal level, characteristic of an 'age' or 'period'. At this level we find what Raymond Williams calls 'structures of feeling', regarded as means of understanding 'the particular quality of social experience and relationship…which gives the sense of a generation or a period' (1977, p. 131). The idea of 'structures of feeling' refers to enduring configurations of affect which give expression to an era or epoch, where this is regarded as something which stretches beyond the contingencies of a particular regime, nation or class but which may nevertheless find exemplification within a regime or nation at a particular time. One thinks of obvious candidates such as fin de siecle Europe and, in a more contemporary vein, a cogent case could be made for arguing that anxiety has, to use a Chomskyian metaphor, become the affective deep structure of late modernity. The particular social forms that this gives rise to, such as the American culture of paranoia (Clarke and Hoggett, 2004), then have to be understood in terms of the articulation of this deep structure through the particularities of national histories and traditions.

3. Emotions can take the form of what Jasper elsewhere (1998) refers to as 'abiding affects'. Here emotions are conjunctural phenomena, organized and enduring but more specific to the experiences of a particular social grouping. At this level, emotions are less an expression of fundamental changes in economic and social structure and have more to do with the particularities of social formations within the boundaries of the nation. At this level, once could include states of terror to be found, for instance, in Stalin's Russia (see Overy, 2004). In this book Nicolas Demertzis provides an analysis of ressentiment and populism in post-war Greece which can be considered as an example of an abiding affect.

4. Sometimes emotions can be seen as strategically organized responses to political predicaments, what Barbalet calls 'programmatic emotions'. 'Structures of feeling' and 'abiding affects' draw our attention to the way in which economic, social and institutional forces give rise to enduring configurations of emotion, emotional cultures if you like. But these configurations are not just expressions of structural forces;

they have a dynamic quality of their own. They do not just set 'effective limits on experience and on action' (Williams, 1977, p. 132) but also provide the energy which galvanizes new cultural and political interventions. Thus political actors can seek to harness particular emotions, using them to achieve their own ends. Gail Holst-Warhaft's study of the Mothers of the Disappeared in Argentina (2000) shows how their refusal to mourn helped them to achieve their political purposes.

5. Finally, emotions can be regarded as more fleeting reactions, typified by the phenomenon of moral panics. This is the way in which Gustave Le Bon understood emotions, in his famous study *The Crowd* (Le Bon, 1952). Today it is important to understand the vital role that the mass media play in the development of moral panics. Indeed the role of the media in constructing citizens' emotional responses is now so considerable that it has led some critics such as Stjepan Mestrovic (1997) to speak of 'the post-emotional' society, one where the simulation of feeling has become increasingly confused with 'the real thing'. In this context, it can be argued that the management of citizens' emotional reactions has become one of the key strategic objectives of what has been called the modernized political party (Swanson and Mancini, 1996).

Structure

The book is divided into two parts, conceptual foundations and applications to political theory and action. The *Foundations* chapters both provide a critique of existing rationalist models of political action, and address normative and epistemological questions about the emotions in the light of an explanatory model that integrates reason and passion. James Jasper explores *Emotions and the Microfoundations of Politics*. He argues that political analysts need new microfoundations upon which to construct more realistic explanations, as the building blocks provided by both traditional psychoanalysis and rational-choice theory have reached their limits. Cognition has provided a range of additional foundations, but emotions promise an even broader set of conceptual tools for understanding action. Yet in exploring this new area, we need to recognize that there are disparate types of feelings that most languages lump together as 'emotions'.

In Chapter 3, Jack Barbalet proposes an approach to the role of emotions in politics that indicates both the indispensability of emotions to political analysis and the key role of particular emotions in different types of political practices. This perspective corrects a number of conventional misapprehensions concerning emotions in political processes and sets out a way of incorporating emotions in methodologies for understanding political processes. The chapter then applies this approach to two case studies at opposite ends of the spectrum of possible political practices, namely the electoral ballot and suicide terrorism. In accounting for each of these different types of political processes in terms of the emotions that animate and characterize them, this chapter not only enhances our understanding of emotions but also contributes to a broader theoretical grasp of voting systems and political institutions and also a highly significant but under-explored form of extremist political activism.

The second part of this book addresses the practical application of the study of emotions in everyday life through the work of Alford on hate, Clarke on envy, Demertzis on ressentiment and populism, Thompson on anger and finally Hoggett on compassion. This part of the book has its own introduction which pulls together the various theoretical and methodological perspectives on the practical application of the study of emotional life and politics.

2
Emotions and the Microfoundations of Politics: Rethinking Ends and Means

James M. Jasper

> Only the love of honor is forever young, and not riches, as some
> say. Honor is the delight of men when they are old and useless.
>
> Pericles

For at least 2400 years observers of the human condition have debated whether humans were rational or irrational, which itself is a variation on the question of whether we are basically good or evil. We cannot be good if we are irrational, although being rational does not guarantee that we will be good. In fact, part of the genius of modern economics is to insist that we are rational and selfish (although economists notoriously save the game by arguing that the invisible hand of the market balances selfish *individuals* to make for a good *society*). Thanks to economics, images of rational calculators have recently triumphed over images of irrational crowds in this age-old clash of political theories. Emotions have always been at the heart of these controversies.

Students of politics have recognized the central influence of emotions but usually dismissed them as a diversion from rational purposes. This "disruption" view has taken diverse forms (Marcus, 2000). One, which reached its apogee in psychoanalysis, sees characteristic emotional reactions as expressions of character or personality – which meant they interfered with more objective adaptations to external circumstances. At the opposite extreme, emotions cause individuals to do things they normally would not, giving in to the immediate situation in ways that undermine longer-term projects. Gustave Le Bon perfected this tradition, formulating a theory of crowds – almost universally accepted in the late nineteenth and early twentieth centuries – as imposing a kind of madness on participants (McPhail, 1991). A third tradition, under the influence of modern science, has linked emotions to evolution or to physiology – again suggesting that emotions are not part of rational, conscious projects. (Extreme biologism naturally inspires its opposite, a cultural constructionism that denies biology a bit *too* thoroughly: Armon-Jones, 1986.)

Only recently have approaches developed that link emotions to cultural and social processes more permanent than crowds. One links them to positions in social hierarchies, so that interactions with superiors, with subordinates, and with equals tend to arouse different emotions (Kemper, 1978, 2001). A similar view highlights the strategic display of emotions, usually as commanded by employers (Hochschild, 1983). Finally, a cognitive approach sees emotions as evaluations of the world in terms of how well things are going for oneself (Nussbaum, 2001). As a result, attention to emotions in politics is expanding rapidly (for an overview, see Marcus, 2000; on international relations, Crawford, 2000; on social movements, Goodwin *et al.*, 2001, 2004, and Jasper, 1998).

Today one obstacle to understanding emotions in politics is that our natural languages class numerous phenomena under the same term. "Emotion" is an enormous, heterogeneous category. Depending on what emotions we take as exemplars, we arrive at different visions of emotional processes. Crowd traditions favor eruptions of anger. Psychoanalysis adds anxieties and other behavioral neuroses. Cultural constructionism often prefers complex moral emotions such as compassion or jealousy.

As a way out of this seeming morass, in the next section I follow Griffiths' (1997) lead in distinguishing several basic types of emotion (although my list is not quite the same as his). I then attempt to distinguish the ways that emotions are related to ends of action and means of action, accepting these as basic components of purposive action. In some cases emotions *are* ends or means of action, in others they *affect* ends or means. I also address the ways in which emotions of solidarity help to form and maintain the collective political players who are capable of having ends and means in the first place.

Part of the allure of understanding emotions is that they are an important microfoundation upon which more complex political processes and outcomes depend. They could enhance the current search for causal mechanisms to replace unrealistic general theories (Hedström and Swedberg, 1998; Elster 1999a). Researchers in the rational-choice tradition have clearly specified the micro-level foundations upon which they build: self-interested and normally materialistic individuals. Critics of this tradition, in both structural and cultural versions, have simply not presented the same kind of detailed microfoundations for their work. The results are often vague concepts, metaphors without clear or observable empirical referents. Emotions are clearly a promising category of microfoundation, in that they are easily seen as interpersonal rather than individual and subjective. They are also compatible with recent research in cognitive psychology and behavioral economics that is (despite last-ditch efforts to label it "behavioral game theory") rapidly undermining rational-choice and game theory. This new vision is comfortable with emotion, cognition, and morality, and therefore may be able to reach out to more cultural traditions of research on politics.

Types of emotions

I have found it useful to distinguish several types of emotion, which may operate via different neurological and chemical pathways (Griffiths, 1997, Goodwin *et al.*, 2004, Jasper, 2006b). They run, roughly, from the more physiological end of a continuum to the more cultural end. I have been unable to find a theory of emotions that deals equally well with each of the categories.

Urges are physical impulses that demand our attention and crowd out other goals until they are satisfied. Jon Elster (1999b), who calls them strong feelings, includes addiction, lust, fatigue, hunger and thirst, and the need to urinate or defecate. Urges such as these derail political projects, for instance under conditions of extreme deprivation, but otherwise they have relatively little relevance to politics.

A second category near the physiological end of the continuum are *reflex emotions*, quick to appear and to subside. Inspired by Darwin, Paul Ekman (1972) has described these as universal and hardwired into us, sending quick signals through the hypothalamus and amygdala to set off automatic programs of action – facial expressions, bodily movements, vocal changes, hormonal discharges such as adrenalin. His list includes anger, fear, joy, sadness, disgust, surprise, and contempt. Although reflex emotions often seem to trigger actions we later regret, Frank (1988) has argued that they may send important signals about our character. Being prone to anger may encourage compliance from others; disgust and contempt may encourage humans to keep their commitments. And if nothing else, an important part of politics consists of efforts to elicit reflex anger in others, who may in the heat of the moment do things that discredit or disadvantage them. Our opponents' blunders are often our greatest opportunities (Jasper and Poulsen, 1993).

Affects last longer and are normally tied to elaborate cognitions more thoroughly than urges or reflexes are. They are positive and negative clusters of feelings, forms of attraction or repulsion. Examples include love and hate as well as respect, trust, ressentiment (see Chapters 5 and 7 in this book), suspicion, and perhaps dread. They are felt orientations to the world that we go to great lengths to maintain (Heise, 1979). Affects include the solidarities behind collective identities, as well as the negative emotions toward outsiders that are often equally important (Polletta and Jasper, 2001).

Moods typically last longer than reflex emotions but not as long as affects, differing from other emotions in not having a definite source or object (Clore *et al.*, 1994). We frequently carry them from one setting to the next – although in some cases they are relatively permanent aspects of temperament or personality. They have a biochemical basis, one reason that drugs affect them so directly. Most esthetic responses, which have puzzled many students of emotions, seem to fall in this category, as we *try on* feelings such as sadness or joy with art replacing the usual triggers for these moods. In my view, moods operate primarily as *filters* for perception, decision, and action – especially by giving us more confidence or less.

My final category consists of complex *moral emotions* such as compassion, outrage, and many forms of disgust, fear, and anger. These latter three, although they have their counterparts in reflex emotions, appear here in more cognitively processed forms: the fear we feel about an automobile suddenly veering toward us is more automatic than the fear we feel about a hazardous waste dump down the road. Shame, pride, and jealousy are also complex results of our moral visions of the world (although evidence of something like shame in primates suggests that it too may have a counterpart in reflex emotions, upon which the more complex forms possibly build).

In addition, acting morally carries its own feelings of satisfaction, perhaps a special form of pride and also relief at overcoming temptation. (Spinoza was right and Kant wrong about this.) Moral emotions may express explicit principles that we hold, or mere intuitions that we have never fully articulated. Note that a great deal of politics is aimed at articulating or appealing to those inchoate moral intuitions (Jasper, 1997).

Not all emotions fit neatly into these categories, in part because we frequently use the same term to connote very different feelings. The gag reflex we suddenly feel has little to do with the more abiding disgust and contempt we feel for certain groups. Fear and shame, too, come in both sudden reflex forms and more abiding, cognitive, affective forms. (Although drive theories would claim, implausibly in my opinion, that more complex emotions are built upon and can be explained by a small number of basic impulses.) Any feeling that persists well beyond its initial stimulant can have the effects of a mood, especially pride. Nonetheless, I think a typology of this sort offers some analytic advantages, so that we no longer need to lump so many different processes together simply as "emotions." No single theory will explain them all.

Emotions and ends

Much human action has purposes, goals toward which we strive. When these goals require interaction with others, especially through coercion but also sometimes through persuasion or payment, these actions are political in the broadest sense (or "strategic," as I suggest elsewhere: Jasper, 2006a). Too many political analysts have either ignored the many goals humans pursue or assumed they knew the most important ones. Worst of all, they have assumed that one goal (either wealth or power) inevitably dominates the rest. Understanding emotions as ends suggests ways to avoid this kind of oversimplification.

Urges are immediate-term goals of action, not usually interesting for politics, except that their urgency suggests conditions under which humans are distracted from political goals. We are near the bottom of Maslow's famous hierarchy of needs, and urges prevent us from moving up to other needs until the basic urges are satisfied (Inglehart, 1977). A king or politician may take enormous risks to longer-term projects to satisfy his lust of the moment. Those suffering famine or other deprivation will not devote time and resources to political organizing.

But not all urges are unforeseen. We may go to great lengths to set up the conditions to satisfy them or to prevent painful urges. We make elaborate plans, often over a long period, to satisfy our lusts. We work especially hard to avoid severe deprivation, for ourselves and others. These projects are sometimes political.

Individuals can be taken over by particular urges, especially addictions and lust, so that these become part of their personalities: Scrooge, who cares only about money; Don Juan, obsessed with sex. We may pity such stunted personalities, but we cannot deny that they pursue clear goals in a rational – all too rational – manner. Any kind of goal, not simply urges, can become an obsession.

Even the most immediate, unforeseen urge can have long-term consequences. At least in the case of lust. Homer portrayed the greatest war of all time as the result of Paris' simple, perhaps impulsive choice of love (in the shape of Helen) over wisdom or power. The resulting war was an unforeseen consequence of his urge, not one of Paris' ends. In the traditional disruptive view of emotions, unforeseen consequences are especially likely to result from emotional choices – and urges and reflexes, being so short-run, are especially likely culprits. But these are only a small number of emotions, and unforeseen consequences can also follow from the most carefully calculated, emotionless actions.

Reflex emotions will prove more important as means than as ends, with one important exception. Sudden anger is capable of derailing any number of political projects, and our opponents are forever trying to goad us into losing our tempers for this very reason. But the public figure who lashes out, physically or verbally, can be viewed as satisfying an immediate-term goal at the expense of longer-term goals. She is also pursuing her own personal satisfaction at the expense of her broader team. From their point of view, she has made a mistake. From hers, she has gained one satisfaction at the expense of others. (I assume here that the anger discredits her, but in many cases angry intimidation is effective in the short and the long term.)

Affects provide some of our most basic goals. Melanie Klein believed that love and hate are the basic categories of human existence, a position compatible with Carl Schmitt's analysis of politics as dividing the world into friends and foes (Schmitt, 1932/1976; Alford, 1989). To the extent we love other humans (or places, organizations, or other species), their well-being becomes one of our goals alongside our own well-being. And we take satisfaction in harming those we hate. As the well-known fable of the prisoner's dilemma shows, it may be impossible to compare or rank-order personal and group goals. Certainly, there are times when the group goals are so important that individuals are willing to sacrifice their lives for them. We cannot understand zealots and martyrs unless we can grasp love and hatred for groups. Abiding affects can be pleasurable in and of themselves – and thus can be a goal – but more often they suggest goals for our actions (harming foes, helping friends).

Hatred for others should never be underestimated as a human motive. *The power of negative thinking*, as I have called it (Jasper, 1997, p. 362), captures our attention more urgently than positive attractions, most of the time. Blame is at the center of much protest, requiring that protestors identify the humans who have made choices that harmed others. In any political engagement, it is possible that players begin to concentrate on harming opponents rather than on the original stakes available in the arena. Mutually destructive polarization then occurs, in which each side is willing to bear enormous costs to harm the other side. Disgust, normally a reflex gagging, reappears as part of the bundle of negative images and affects humans can develop toward others, usually highly stereotyped categories of others. (Debates have raged over whether disgust can be rehabilitated, redirected from prejudices about out-groups to outrage over human rights abuses, in other words to buttress empathy: Nussbaum, 2004, argues not.)

Basic affects can cause individuals to defect from group projects by providing alternative goals, such as rebels who go home to protect their families or couples who fall in love and retreat into their own little world. Goodwin (1997) has detailed this issue in the revolutionary Huk movement in the Philippines, whose leaders denounced participants who withdrew to be with their spouses and children. This is a recurrent dilemma for any collective effort: affective ties to the group aid cooperation and persistence, but those loyalties can attach instead to a small part of the broader whole. I call this the *band of brothers dilemma*, which applies not only to comrades who fall in love but to soldiers who care more about their immediate buddies than the broader war effort, and to any movement with small cells or affinity groups (Jasper, 2004, p. 13).

Like reflex emotions, *moods* are probably more important as means than as ends. But there are some moods we seek out as directly pleasurable. We feel a surge of self-confidence and power when we are on a winning team, for instance. Or a kind of joy when we lose ourselves in crowds and other coordinated, collective activities such as singing, dancing, and marching (Lofland, 1982; McNeill, 1995). A great deal of political mobilization is aimed at transforming debilitating moods into assertive ones. Nationalism, which combines affects and moods, developed in large part when political elites needed to mobilize populations for war without wishing to share decision making with them: a belligerent mood of pride, combined with hatred for others, was sufficient.

Drawing on Durkheim and Goffman, Randall Collins (2001, 2004) has analyzed the *interaction rituals* that create collective effervescence when groups come together and share a focus of attention. Individuals crave the emotional energy that comes from being a focus of attention, and thus they enjoy the mutual attention from interactions. But this satisfaction, while an end in itself, also provides the confidence and energy for further action and participation, partly independently of the craving for more attention. By examining chains of interactions, Collins sees the microfoundations for broader structures.

Finally, the special satisfactions of *moral emotions* generate many important goals, especially when they are feelings about ourselves rather than about others. Foremost, we feel pride in doing the right thing, and in being the kind of person who does the right thing. In part, this is an elated mood similar to that when we participate in a crowd activity – which itself is satisfying in part because we are giving voice to deep moral commitments. Moral pride also involves our success at acting like the kind of person we want to be, mixed with some relief at having done the right thing when we had a choice. (Just as we feel guilty when we fail to do the right thing.) Thomas Scheff (1990, 1994, 1997) views pride and shame as the basic drives of human action, especially in that they attach us to or detach us from (respectively) human relationships.

Honor is the form pride takes in societies where there is agreement over the moral rules that determine pride and shame. As Pericles recognized, it was more important in ancient Athens than wealth, and even today reputation ranks as a goal far higher than most political theory recognizes. Reputations are fundamental human values. As with affects, pride is satisfying in itself, but it also generates goals concerning one's reputation.

Other moral emotions include pity and compassion, the emotions that victims are supposed to arouse. These are a kind of empathy, in that we feel pain at the plight of others. This displeasure moves us to try to remove the sources of pain. Photographs have proven an especially good means for arousing gut-level empathy, especially for suffering children or animals who are easily portrayed as victims. As the philosopher Richard Rorty (1993, p. 118) put it, "The emergence of the human rights culture seems to owe nothing to increased moral knowledge and everything to hearing sad and sentimental stories." Social-movement organizers frequently aim to expand public compassion, building a case for victimhood, blame, and pain. At first it seems that compassion is a means, leading us into actions, but I see it as adding a goal to our repertory. Like affective bonds, we care directly what happens to others; their suffering makes us suffer. Empathy for strangers is a recent triumph that it took humans a long time to accomplish – and which remains all too fragile.

In addition, morals help shape our affects, which in turn restructure our goals. We admire those who embody our moral principles, including large collectives to whom we attribute (accurately or not) moral virtues. The charisma of leaders comes from the moral (and practical) virtues we admire in them.

In a variety of ways emotions make us care about the world around us, so that it is hard to imagine goals of political action that are not shaped by them. Even apparently objective goals such as material resources are not exempt: some crave them passionately, others do not. Love of money must be explained, not taken for granted.

Emotions and means

Emotions permeate our political tactics as thoroughly as our goals. Frequently, an emotion tied to ends for a voter or grassroots participant is a means for the politician or organizer who tries to arouse that emotion in her. It was in this rhetorical context – in which a creator of meanings aims at effects on audiences – that Aristotle discussed emotions and what causes them in the fourth century BCE.

It is probably rare to find *urges* used as means in democratic politics, but they may appear this way in cases of coercion. In war, commanders have been known to encourage their troops to rape civilians (although criminologists debate whether rape is a matter of lust or violence). Interrogators often use fatigue to pressure their subjects or to catch them in a lie. But in such cases, we manipulate other people's urges as our own means. For those feeling fatigue or lust, these remain ends more than means (although soldier-rapists may combine the two, using their own lusts as means to terrorize).

Reflex emotions are similarly open to manipulation. The classic (and overused case) is to goad opponents into anger so that they make mistakes. Or we may try to startle or frighten them in order to paralyze them. Whoever or whatever causes the reflex emotion, once in motion it certainly affects our ability to act. Evolutionary theorists believe that these deeply programmed emotions developed precisely to launch us into actions that we needed to undertake immediately, without thinking, typically as a way of moving us out of harm's way. In other words, they are pure means packaged in an automatic, preprogrammed sequence unavailable to conscious thought. For instance the adrenaline that accompanies reflex emotions may propel us into action more quickly and more forcefully. But the accompanying actions may be relatively short term and not typical of political action.

Anger can be a carefully cultivated performance as well as a direct reflex. Mediators "lose" their temper to gain compliance from recalcitrant parties, just as diplomats often do in the hope of intimidating others. Medieval aristocrats, at least the men among them, were known for quick tempers and angry outbursts, which often yielded advantages in social relations (Barton, 1998). It is not that people in these examples do not feel anger, it is that they have considerable control over how to express it, following cultural scripts that advance strategic projects (just as Japanese cultural scripts regularly dampen the expression of anger).

In the case of *affects*, some appear primarily as ends, others as means. Love and hate are basic loyalties that are hard to see as mere means (again, organizers arouse these in followers as means, but for the followers they become ends). But trust and respect for others are means that allow many actions to be fulfilled at lower costs, as "social capital" theorists emphasize (Paxton, 2002; Putnam, 2002). At least, the trust I feel for you allows us to interact more easily. In addition, it may give me confidence in my own actions, especially as they relate to you.

Perhaps the clearest case of affects as means lies in followers' feelings toward their leaders. Love, trust, and respect for leaders ease a great number of activities carried out for the larger group. Attention to emotional dynamics may allow us to revive the concept of charisma, now out of favor, as a way of understanding the psychological benefits that leaders offer their followers (Madsen and Snow, 1991). More generally, organizations devote considerable resources to making others trust them, through a number of symbolic activities and promotion (Meyer and Rowan, 1977).

Moods clearly affect our means for carrying out political ends. Self-confidence aids any player, from the soldier in combat to the prime minister making a speech (Jasper, 2006a). Moods of resignation or cynicism, on the other hand, can cripple anyone's willingness and ability to pursue her goals. The extreme is depression, a sadness which robs us of both goals and means to act. Some medium-term types of fear operate as moods, which can be manipulated to inspire or to freeze action – much like anxiety. In many cases shame must be reworked into pride for action to occur or be sustained (Gould, 2001).

The effects of moods can be complex, often forming a u-shaped curve. Hope, for instance, like other forms of confidence, stimulates action because we think it can be successful. But too much hope may undermine realistic assessments of a situation and discourage information gathering (Lazarus, 1999). Similarly, a sense of threat can spur action, but if that threat is seen as overwhelming it can discourage action. Anxiety, too, stimulates action at low levels but cripples it at high levels. There is some evidence that bad moods improve decision making – by increasing attention to detail and improving analysis (Schwartz and Bless, 1991).

Whereas *moral* emotions we have about ourselves seem best classified under goals, those about others are probably better described as means (although the distinction blurs somewhat in these cases). Outrage and indignation are the emotions associated with blame: not only do we pity victims, but we identify a perpetrator responsible for the suffering. Pity for victims by itself does not lead to action, until we also feel outrage toward the villain. Compassion provides the goal, outrage the spur to action.

Affect-control theorists have argued that the basic dimensions of emotions are whether they are associated with dominance or vulnerability, whether they are associated with activity or passivity, and whether they are pleasant or unpleasant (Morgan and Heise, 1988). Emotional states that are dominant and active, such as outrage, anger, and excitement, are presumably better spurs to political action than those that are vulnerable and passive, such as sadness (Lively and Heise, 2004). Both moods and morals fit well in this picture.

Enormous effort has gone into the study of cognitive dimensions of decision making, and the many ways that our worldviews and other cultural filters shape what we perceive and do. But many of these dynamics have as much to do with emotions as with cognition. Our moods, preexisting affects, and past emotional experience heavily shape what information we accept and what we do with it (Nygren, 1998). Although traditional views saw emotions as derailing rationality in decisions, Blight (1990) has argued that the presence of fear during the Cuban missile crisis focused the attention of Kennedy and his advisors and prevented their being distracted by nonrational factors. Emotional tags may also help us sort and recover memories more rapidly (Derryberry, 1991; May *et al.*, 1995).

David Hume carved out a large role for emotions when he portrayed them as the source of human goals, with rationality as mere means for attaining them. But we can also see emotions as deeply permeating our means as well. Indeed, some have argued that emotional displays are signals to others about our intentions – and may even have been the source of symbols in early primates and humans as well as providing an infant's first experience with expression (Greenspan and Shanker, 2004). By connecting us to a number of social and physical contexts, and providing immediate evaluations of those contexts, a number of different emotions are crucial means in political action.

Interactions

Emotions interact with one another in devilishly complex ways. For one, not every party to an event or activity feels the same emotions; as I have said, organizers may consciously manipulate others' emotions – through maneuvers such as relabeling the emotion, reinterpreting its causes, or changing the accompanying facial and gestural expressions. Those who feel pride in a rights march hope to influence those who still feel shame (on transformations of shame into pride, see Gould, 2001; Scheff, 2001). There is an *asymmetry* to many emotions in politics: very often, the emotions I hope to arouse in you are *purely means for me but closely tied to ends for you* – the reason that rhetorical approaches to politics need to take their place alongside economic traditions that rely on objective interests. We devote enormous energy to trying to shape others' goals.

There is also interaction between short- and long-term emotions. Political organizers try to rework reflex emotions such as fear and startle into more abiding moods or affective loyalties. I have tried to get at this interaction between short term and long term through the concept of *moral shock*, in which fear, surprise, and outrage are used to articulate new moral principles and reasons for acting politically (Jasper, 1997). Whistleblowers are a common example, as they are morally disgusted by what they experience. As Fred Alford (2001, p. 20) puts it, "The greatest shock is what the whistleblower learns about the world as a result – that nothing he or she believed was true." Similarly, we will see, political intellectuals try to spin actions into the essences of players, in the form of ongoing characters, making an action into a symbol of some permanent trait. Often, an emotion is used to transform people's cognitive understandings, for instance by drawing attention to symbolic events or characters.

There is often an element of moral end in the most quotidian political means. We develop *tastes in tactics* so that we find virtue in certain kinds of activities and vice in others (Jasper, 1997). The most striking case is possibly nonviolence, in which a strong moral end is placed at the center of a set of strategies meant to accomplish other ends. But this interweaving of means and ends does not wash away the distinction itself, only the overly simplistic versions of it such as those found in game theory.

The role of intimidation and fear in politics, still poorly understood, involves transformations of emotions. To prevent their partisans or troops from being paralyzed in the face of repression or other intimidation, a leader must rapidly change terror and perhaps shame into anger and outrage – emotions that help rather than hinder action. Electoral defeats can be transformed into additional mobilization if they are attributed to skullduggery or treachery. Revolutions succeed through indignation over state repression. In response to repression in 1978, Iranian revolutionaries fabricated a tape in which the Shah himself was heard ordering his generals to shoot demonstrators in the street (Kurzman, 1996).

The Freudian emphasis on our need to manage internal conflicts is also a form of interaction between means and ends. Our compulsive behaviors come to take on the quality of ends, which we need to repeat over and over, but these interfere with other, more externally oriented projects. In this way, past experiences have too great an influence over us, preventing the most effective adaptation to present circumstances. In the gentler light of the cognitive revolution, we can see this as simply working with the psychological and cultural tools we have, in a web of meanings that we cannot do without: an inevitable part of the human condition rather than a pathology to be overcome. But pathologies remain. As Martin Seligman showed in his famous concept of learned helplessness (1975), repeated events can affect how we interpret and act in the world, in this case robbing us of a sense of mastery (I would label this a "mood").

Emotions in collective identity

Despite efforts in rational-choice traditions to define strategic players on the basis of objective interests, collective players are more an accomplishment than a given. This is best seen for social movements, where organizers must work hard to promulgate a collective identity that can draw potential participants. Considerable research has shown how collective labels are necessary for action, even though they are largely fictional (Gamson, 1995). The same efforts to achieve a collective identity are necessary to create and sustain other political players: states (Ringmar, 1996), nations (Anderson, 1991), perhaps even formal organizations (Meyer and Rowan, 1977). And what is party loyalty other than – as the authors of *The American Voter* put it 45 years ago – "affective orientation to an important group object" (Campbell *et al.*, 1960, p. 121)?

Although most commentators have viewed collective identities as cognitive boundaries between insiders and outsiders (Polletta and Jasper, 2001), such boundaries have no bite without positive emotions toward fellow insiders (I have called these *reciprocal* emotions: Jasper, 1998), shared emotions about outsiders and the state of the world, and – frequently – negative emotions toward some perceived threat or opponent. (In Chapter 6, Fred Alford emphasizes that our hatred for others helps define us.) Drawing on Collins, Erika Summers-Effler (2005) shows how collective solidarities are built emotionally, especially through ritual and shared laughter.

Collective identity neatly demonstrates the interplay between one person's means and another's ends. Someone promoting collective identity is trying to arouse loyalties in others that will be ends for them but are means for the organizer. This is true even if the organizer fervently believes in the good of the collective (although more obviously so if she does not). Organizers are well aware of the rituals that build emotions of solidarity (Epstein, 1991).

It is almost universally assumed that shared structural positions – economic activity, legal and political status, strong cultural expectations – make it more likely that a group will develop a shared collective identity. Potential members of the group will have had the same experiences, and through consciousness raising of some sort will come to realize this. Rarely made explicit are the shared emotions that arise from those positions and experiences that make the identity possible and motivating. Sociological research has shown that characteristic emotions arise from dominant or subordinate positions in hierarchies, and from changes in those positions and the power and status that accompany them (Kemper, 1978; Hochschild, 1983; Morgan and Heise, 1988). For instance we are contemptuous of those who claim more status than we think they deserve, angry at those who do not grant us the status we think we deserve (Kemper, 2001). When political players interact in the context of ongoing hierarchies, characteristic emotions will arise that may advance or hinder collective identities and the accompanying programs and actions.

Let me mention one aspect of collective identity that receives little attention: the characters that collective players create for themselves and others (part of the content of those identities). By this I mean the work of characterizing, often relying on traditional literary *character types* of hero, villain, victim, and (to fill in the 2 by 2 table formed along the dimensions of strong versus weak and good versus bad) sidekick or clown. To initiate political action, it is often useful to present yourself as a victim who is becoming a hero, to triumph over a villain and his minions. This mini-narrative encourages audiences to take sides, expressing sympathy for the victim, admiration for the hero, and hatred for the villain and his sidekicks. Other potential plots include the conversion of villain into hero (whistleblowers, for instance), and the martyrdom of a hero who sacrifices herself. Characters like these almost demand certain feelings toward them (although it is possible to play against type; for instance there are lovable villains and feared heroes). Even though flat characters like these have fallen out of favor in serious fiction, as a form of epideictic rhetoric they live on in political propaganda as efforts to shape our understandings of and feelings about the world. (For this reason they are aimed at affects and moral emotions, I suspect, more often than at reflexes, urges, or moods.)

Affect-control theory, by the way, shows why characters are important, as emotional reactions depend partly on role expectations. If you have successfully negotiated a clown role in the past, you will be less devastated by events that make you look foolish – and can sometimes turn them to your advantage. You will not lose confidence to as great a degree, and those around you will not change their opinions of you if outcomes are consonant with your character. (Plus, we all work hard to make them consonant with our roles or characters.)

As Schmitt pointed out, the construction of friends and foes – and the demonization of the latter – are the heart of politics. Not only political parties and protest groups, but nations themselves craft images of competitors that motivate considerable mobilization (Volkan, 1988). In international relations, realists assume fear and hate to be omnipresent and powerful – but perhaps for that reason they give them little theoretical attention. But without strong emotions, their elaborate cognitive and strategic models collapse.

Emotions as disturbances

Having examined some of the many roles of emotions in politics, we can return to the traditional image of emotions as bumps in the path of rationality. We can see some truth in this image and yet still see how small a part of the picture it is. We can see that anger is only one of several reflex emotions, and that reflex emotions are only one of several types of emotion. Yes, urges and reflexes can cause players to do things they later regret, concentrating on momentary satisfactions that undermine broader ones.

But we need not see even these actions as irrational. I would prefer to view them either as an extreme privileging of the short run over the longer run, or as mistakes later recognized as such. Lust may lead us to sleep with someone we know we should not, but the subsequent costs of doing so may range from nonexistent to devastating. The greater the resulting costs, the more we are tempted to call it an irrational act, but there is no clear cutoff point. For me, irrationality lies in an inability to learn from our mistakes – perhaps for psychoanalytic reasons such that we are trapped in reactions that do not change as our environment changes.

If, as I hope to have shown, emotions are an integral part of both our ends and our means in politics, then they are a fundamental part of rational action, not a diversion from it. This is especially true in that emotions entail processing information and appraising the world. They cannot be fully distinguished from cognitions, much less contrasted with them. They are no more or less likely to be irrational or lead to mistakes than cognitions are.

Building back up

If emotions such as I have described are to be microfoundations for political explanations, how can we build back up to entities such as states, parties, social movements, and international relations? After all, one of the problems with rational-choice traditions is that they have never satisfactorily made that transition from individuals to complex entities. And the recent wave of behavioral research examines only individuals, never larger entities. The behavioralist revolution in political science, in the late 1950s and early 1960s, had similar limitations in its view of individuals – as well as attaching its microfoundational approach to an overly strict positivist methodology. And older traditions, often under Freudian influence, have merely treated complex players as though they had minds and feelings like individuals, which can hardly be the case. Can we do better?

First, emotions are not the only microfoundations. A number of cognitive processes, from symbolic carriers of memory to biases in decision making, have been well documented by cognitive and political psychologists. Strategic decisions themselves, whether taken by individuals or collective actors, are also important building blocks for political explanation (Jasper, 2004, 2006a,b). It is the interactions among decisions – and the resulting outcomes – that have made game theory a lively approach, for all its limitations. These various sorts of microfoundations need to be used together, not artificially contrasted and segregated.

But how do we put these pieces together? One possibility is to aggregate across large numbers of individuals, through traditional survey methods designed to produce representative samples. If we know how large numbers of voters are feeling as well as thinking, we may be able to understand how they act, which symbols will appeal to them, and so on. Getting at their emotions may not be any harder than getting at their beliefs – although the difficulties of doing that are notorious enough.

In political and other strategic engagements, however, not all individuals are created equal. Some have more influence on events than others, whether this is in a local interpersonal network or in geopolitics. Tony Blair's emotions, thoughts, and choices have broader ramifications than mine do. Scholars have long studied "leaders" from a variety of perspectives that incorporated their emotions and recognized that these individuals matter. Too many of these studies, perhaps, have been done from a single point of view, namely psychoanalysis. And they inevitably focus on top leaders, rather than influential individuals at various other levels of politics. Worse, the rest of us have found few ways to incorporate their insights about individuals into research that examines political structures and outcomes. But that could be done. Individuals at many levels have emotions and cognitions, which enable them to make strategic choices, which in turn interact to form the larger entities we are accustomed to calling "structures."

Both these approaches, one of which looks for a large sample of representative individuals and the other for a small number of influential ones, are needed in political research. They are rarely combined, since they draw on very different research techniques. But they each get at important ways that emotions form the building blocks with which we can understand political actions and outcomes. Emotions are generated by characteristic interactions in social structures (Kemper, 1978; Barbalet, 1998), but at the same time they help reproduce or transform those structures.

Emotions have returned to political analysis, to take their place alongside more cognitive and more structural factors so favored for a generation now. In our enthusiasm for incorporating them, we should avoid overextending them to cover too much. I hope that distinguishing among several ways they matter will help us avoid that. Modesty will be a better long-run strategy for rehabilitating the study of emotions than overextension.

3
Emotions in Politics: From the Ballot to Suicide Terrorism

Jack Barbalet

Introduction

Politics and emotions have always gone together. The German sociologist, Max Weber, famously observed that action in a political community is 'determined by highly robust motives of fear and hope' (Weber 1970, p. 79). It is of interest that almost identical statements were expressed at the very beginning of the period of early modern politics. The English statesman and philosopher, Francis Bacon, wrote that 'civil states' offer bribes and punishments, 'employing the predominant affections of *fear* and *hope*', a possibility that arises from the fact that the 'government of states' relies upon 'the government within' (Bacon 1905, p. 145; emphasis in original). Similarly, the French writer, Jean-François Senault, in *De l'Usage des Passions* first published in1641 and translated into English only a short time later, wrote:

> Policy seems to have better intentions than Rhetorick; for when she excites fear or hope in man, by promises or by threats, she endeavours the welfare of particulars (Senault 1671, p. 174).

Indeed, the archetypical political instruments of persuasion remain the carrot and the stick. It is the really astute politician, however, as we are reminded by such otherwise dissimilar figures as Weber, Bacon and Senault, that has no need of either carrot or stick in the knowledge that particular emotions – hope born of a promise and fear spurred by a threat – are sufficient to get the job done.

While politics has always had an emotional element, the emotionality of politics has typically been seen as applying to a segment only of political populations. That is, political emotions are largely held to be characteristic of those subjected to political rule, namely the political masses, rather than elites. Given that masses are usually regarded as only subordinate and therefore without significant political initiative, it follows that emotions (located in the masses but not elites) are unnecessary to take into consideration in serious political analysis. Political elites have always regarded their own enthusiasms as rational, which they hold in stark contrast to the emotional enthusiasms of the political mass. Conventional political analyses similarly tend to operate without acknowledging the importance of the underlying emotions of political elites.

Political analysis and commentary typically operate in terms of three possible constructions. The first of these centres on the calculations of interests of political actors in the allocation or competitive distribution of resources. Second, there is focus on structures of opportunities for action by political actors within institutional frameworks. Third, there is regard to persistent norms, mores or values within cultural systems that influence the inclinations and propensities of political actors. It is necessary to add that underlying each of the key categories of such accounts, namely interests, structured inhibitions, and inclinations, are emotions. Indeed, it should be unexceptionable although it is seldom acknowledged that a leading function of the political state is to legitimate some emotions and differentially encourage, contain and dissuade others. All political organizations in fact, and not just the state are engaged with emotions in the promotion of various dispositions, actions and inhibitions. Before developing this theme it is necessary to say that if we are to take emotions in politics seriously we shall have to go beyond simple mechanical statements of the type we find in Weber, Bacon and Senault, as insightful as they are, which leaves the emotions category itself unexplored and untheorized.

Associated with the neglect of emotions as a category of serious political analysis is the practice of referring to political emotions in general as a level apart from and opposed to political rationality. Such a distinction is in fact self-defeating: to simply privilege emotions against another party that privileges rationality offers no analytical advantage. The opposition between emotion and rationality is internal to our language, certainly; but we should not let the words we use do our thinking for us. The supposed opposition of emotion and reason collapses under scrutiny, and as various philosophers, sociologists and even neurologists have shown, reason and rationality requires emotions: the separation between them has to be replaced with an understanding of the facilitation of reason by emotion and the continuities between the two (Barbalet, 1998, pp. 29–61). Neither should we simply use conventional emotions terms, like hope and fear, without being aware that their received sense and meaning comes from a usage that may not properly serve political analysis. An interest in understanding politics in terms of its emotional processes requires an appreciation of emotions that reflects appropriate research methods and purposes. This point can be demonstrated by considering such dissimilar political means as the ballot and also suicide terrorism in terms of emotions. But before doing so it is necessary to say something about the types of distinctions that might profitably be made when treating emotions in political and social life.

Conceptualizations of emotions

The ideas that persons have about emotions do not necessarily arise from their own direct experience of them, but rather from the work of people whose job it is to develop and circulate ideas about emotions. These have included psychologists and, more recently neurologists. It goes without saying that their purposes are not the purposes of political analysis, and their methods may not, indeed are unlikely to, elicit the emotional experiences in their experimental subjects that occur in everyday and even exceptional political and social circumstances. While some emotions may rise and fall within a short time frame, for instance, it is not a necessary characteristic of emotions that they are of short duration, and many politically relevant emotions are frequently experienced over long periods of time. Yet psychological experimentation, for instance, chiefly studies reactive and highly visceral emotions readily elicited from experimental subjects, and discharged and dissipated during the brief course of a bench-work exercise, as established by pioneering psychological experiments (Garrett, 1941, pp. 317–45). This has coloured conventional understandings of emotions and expectations concerning their operations. Many politically and socially important emotions, however, are not brief and episodic but enduring and ongoing.

The evolutionary perspective that informs much psychology and neurology has been used to support a distinction between basic and non-basic or primary and secondary emotions that characterizes emotions in terms of the presence or otherwise of species-general biological survival. This distinction is held to be fundamental by its proponents, but readily shown to be inadequate for an understanding of a range of particular human emotions (Solomon, 2002). While there may be a meaningful history within the development of natural science that supports such a typology, the resulting understanding of the differences between distinct emotions has little value for political research and cannot be sustained in terms of the social experience of emoting human subjects. The reflexive, historical and culturally diverse nature of the human condition requires a further set of distinctions in addition to those drawn from evolutionary premises in order to adequately characterize human emotions experienced in social interactions and political practices. A rather different set of distinctions, more fitted to social and political research, can be indicated here. This is the distinction between *relational* emotions, *iterated* emotions and *programmatic* emotions. These are not three different types of emotions so much as distinct conceptualizations of emotions.

Relational emotions are those emotions that arise in persons as a result of their relations with others. Psychologists and neurologists are largely concerned with what goes on within the body and brain. The psychological and physical processes of feeling state, autonomic arousal, motor expression, cognitive stimulation and so on – which these disciplines typically treat as the emotion – are at best regarded as so many internal indicators of emotional experience. Emotional experiences typically arise through the emoting subject's relationship with the world and in human subjects that world is essentially social and political. It is necessary to say, then, that emotions may be conceptualized for our purposes in terms of interactions or relations between persons. In their interaction with others persons find that their participation invariably generates a sense of involvement. This involvement may be positive or negative, strong or weak, but in any event it includes an evaluation of the other and the relationship with the other that registers in the person's physical and dispositional reactions and inclinations. This is what is properly meant by an emotion. As Klaus Scherer has put it, 'one of the major functions of emotion consists of the constant evaluation of external and internal stimuli in terms of their relevance for the organism and the preparation of behavioural reactions which may be required as a response to those stimuli' (Scherer, 1984, p. 296).

Given the significance of emotion in evaluating the situations persons experience it is unavoidable that a very large proportion of emotions will 'result from real, imagined or anticipated outcomes in social relationships' (Kemper, 1978, p. 43). In terms of their formal properties, social relationships can be understood as containing at least two significant dimensions. First is the dimension of coercion and domination in which a relationship can be characterized in terms of the assertion of one participant over another. This dimension is that of power. Another dimension of social relationships is found in the provision of support, sympathy and regard between participants such that one participant accords a certain standing or status to the other. This is the status dimension of social relationships. It can be shown that these formal properties of social relationships are the basis of a comprehensive account of a large range of particular emotions (Kemper, 1978). This can be demonstrated with a few simple examples.

Assume the two dimensions of power and status in social relationships and the participation of self and other. The outcome of any social relationship may be an increase, decrease or absence of change in the power of each participant and similarly for the status of each participant. On this basis there are twelve possible outcomes of any episode of a social relationship. Each of these possible outcomes gives rise to a particular emotional experience. For instance, if a person's own power decreases in an interaction or the power of the other increases, then it is likely that that person will experience fear. If a person enjoys an increase in the regard of another, an increase in status, they are likely to experience happiness, while a decline in a person's status is likely to lead to depression. This very simple model can be made a little more complex by acknowledging the significance of perception of responsibility for an outcome of social relationships. Consider a case of status loss. If the agent of a loss of status for a person is impersonal and unavoidable – fate or chance – then that loss will be emotionally experienced as depression. If the agent responsible for the loss of status is the person himself or herself, then it is likely that loss will be emotionally experienced as shame. If the agent of status loss is the other person in the relationship, however, the loss may be emotionally experienced as anger. In addition to the question of agency is evaluation of whether the power or status acquired or lost in a social relationship is appropriate to the relationship itself. For instance, a person may experience an increase of power that they evaluate as in excess of what is required for the relationship. In that case the emotional feeling generated in the relationship is not satisfaction but guilt.

It is clear in all of these examples that emotional experiences can be accounted for in terms of the formal properties of social relationships. As these latter are ubiquitous so in that sense such an account is universal and applicable across cultures and through historical time. The social and political world, though, is paradoxically plural not universal, and therefore local or cultural considerations must be given their due. This is the domain typically occupied by doctrines of social or cultural construction. But it is necessary to move away from such formulations because they leave the impression that emotions are reducible to cultural cues and mores and it is appropriate to give more room to the shaping power of emotions themselves in the formation of cultural differences. Indeed, cultural distinctions can be marked by differences in particular emotional reactions to relational emotions. In this way relational emotions and culturally specific emotions can be conceptualized as continuous and not opposed or alternative formulations.

Because cultural distinctions can be marked by differences in particular emotional reactions to relational emotions they can be characterized as iterated or nested emotions. Jealousy, for example, seems to be a universal emotion. But in 'traditional' or 'Mediterranean' societies people are proud of feeling jealous, whereas in 'modern' or 'western' societies people may be ashamed of their jealousy. The difference between cultures, in this sense, is in the distinct emotional apprehension of relational emotions. This may be particularly evident in the cultural formation of collective personae, such as masculinity or femininity, in which young males, for instance, may feel proud of being angry or may be afraid of experiencing or at least expressing fear.

This account of cultural difference in terms of (local) emotional reactions to (universal) relational emotions must meet two types of objections; first, that some emotions are only ever located in a particular culture, without broader representation and, second, that cultural difference can be located in the absence of particular emotions in one culture that are present in another, as in Briggs' ethnography which reports an absence of anger in Utku society (Briggs, 1970). A frequently presented example of a culturally local emotion with no universal elements is that of *amae*, widely treated as an exclusively Japanese emotion in which there is a feeling of pleasure in helplessness conjoined with satisfaction in indulgent dependence on another's kindness or affection (Morsbach and Tyler, 1988). While the adult desire for dependence on others has to be appreciated in terms of particular aspects of Japanese society, the emotion amae is arguably a local elaboration of the universal emotion of a child's pleasure in dependence on a parent (Bowlby, 1978, pp. 393–423). Finally, those emotions that are simply unknown in certain cultures although unavoidable in others are also likely to be a consequence of iterated or nested emotions. In historically modern Western experience a hallmark emotion is the 'blasé feeling', identified in Georg Simmel's classic account, which is the emotional antidote to self-regarding emotions under conditions of metropolitan life (Simmel, 1971). Indeed, the apparent absence of an emotion in one culture acknowledged in another is *prima facie* evidence of emotional suppression of an emotion, a clear variant of an iterated emotion.

The question arises, then, concerning the mechanism or determination of iterated and nested emotions: what particular local conditions produce the emotion that modifies universal or relational emotions? A predominant culturalist explanation is in terms of 'feeling rules' as described by Arlie Hochschild (1979), for example. Such feeling rules, as far as I am aware, have never been satisfactorily located and operationally described. There are a number of reasons why this is so. First, as Pierre Bourdieu has shown, cultural regularization is a consequence of practice, not its cause (Bourdieu, 1992); feeling rules arise out of emotional experience and its preconditions, they do not determine emotional experience. Indeed, a close reading of her classic paper on emotion work and feeling rules reveals that Hochschild in fact demonstrates that feeling rules do not do what she claims for them. While Hochschild shows that two respondents consciously engaged in emotion work, the evidence she provides indicates that their endeavours to effectively change their emotions failed (Hochschild, 1979, pp. 561–2). Similarly, in her account of 'rights' in the context of feeling rules, Hochschild confuses rejection of a right with refusal to lay claim to a right (Hochschild, 1979, p. 565). A corrective reformulation of her argument would be to say that a respondent's mixed feelings may be resolved by what Hochschild calls 'emotion work'. Although Hochschild claims that emotions are induced in the subject or constructed through emotion work, it is more likely that when mixed emotions – or more properly, a mix of emotions – are experienced through complexity of situation or circumstance, particular emotions are backgrounded while others are foregrounded. In this way contextual practices in which this occurs are generative of cultural mores.

Rather than focus on culture as an independent variable in explaining what emotions predominate, what emotions predominate is the basis for characterizing or explaining culture. The latter largely derives its quality from what are called here 'programmatic emotions'. In their laboratories psychologists work on subjects who are experimentally induced to experience reactive emotions of short duration, as suggested above where it was held that the correlative type of emotional experiences are commensurate with the methods and purpose of psychology rather than revealing something about emotion in general. Yet the psychological construction of the emotions category has led to a theoretical supposition, namely that expression of emotion dissipates or discharges the emotion. Freudians encourage this view by holding that non-discharged emotions lead to neurotic symptoms. These claims may be true of some emotions, such as shame (Lewis, 1971) but many emotions and possibly some of the most important for human sociality are not discharged through expression, but expression of them reinforces and intensifies these emotions.

These latter are the emotions that William James, for instance, says endue the world with value, interest and meaning (James, 1902, p. 150). These are the emotions that sustain our commitments (Frank, 1988). In providing examples of emotions that give direction to a life that otherwise would not arise, James mentions love, fear, indignation, jealousy, ambition and worship (1902, p. 150). The list is neither definitive nor exhaustive but it does indicate some key emotions that lead those who experience them to accept courses of action that are unlikely to be engaged by persons who did not share such emotions. This is because such emotions encourage a behavioural disposition that is distinct from and may indeed be contrary to a person's narrowly conceived interests and mundane and routine practices. These emotions and others like them commit those who experience them to act in ways that could not be explained except in terms of the relevant emotions. That is why they are called here programmatic emotions. They are not reactive but sustained and have consequences that are continuous or serial rather than merely episodic. They are involved in processes of institutionalization and organization, as love relates to marriage, vengeance to criminal law, greed to capitalist corporations, and so on. We shall also see that they are implicit in political institutions and practices. This is not to say that programmatic emotions can be politically constructed, for their formation is subject to the causation and constraints of relational emotions in general. But once formed through relevant social relationships, programmatic emotions are potentially available to be used strategically by activists, as we shall see in the discussion of suicide terrorists.

With these types of distinctions in mind, between relational, iterated and programmatic emotions, it is possible to discern the operations of particular emotions where it is often denied that emotions operate at all in political processes. This will be demonstrated in what follows by beginning with a consideration of voting and the ballot before moving on to consideration of an arguably polar opposite form of politics, namely that of suicide terrorism.

Voting systems and emotional patterns

There is broad agreement that of all political institutions the ballot is the least interesting. This is because functionally it appears to be a means of keeping elections free of corruption and intimidation, and historically it seems to be a result of a process of political rationalization through which working-class voters were not only isolated from their class organizations, but also from each other. Indeed, the ballot neutralized both the threat of working-class electoral solidarity and the formation of working-class crowds that became a problem in England during the nineteenth century, for example, with the registration of new voters through expansion of the franchise with each successive political reform, embodied in the Acts of 1832, 1867 and 1884. Before the advent of the secret ballot in 1872 with the passage of the Ballot Act, open voting, in which electors at large gatherings publicly indicated their preference for one candidate over others, generated carnivalesque if not riotous gatherings of voters. At the time open voting involved not simply nominations and speeches at open hustings, but also the provision of entertainment, food and especially drink in order to influence the vote (see Barbalet, 2002).

While secret voting may be thought to be devoid of emotions, such a view will be dispelled by an account of the history of the introduction of the ballot that requires an understanding of the riotous and rebellious emotions of open voting on the one hand, and ruling-class fear of the disruptive influence of an enlarged working-class electorate on the other. It is not my purpose here to depart from the argument that ruling-class fear led to the containment strategy of legislative reform of electoral procedures. At the same time, an explanation of the advent of the secret vote in England in 1872 in terms of emotions should not lead to a conclusion that secret voting was itself devoid of emotions.

During the nineteenth century, European ruling classes faced a serious dilemma: the demands of the masses for wider participation, which was destructive of established order, could be contained only by extending to them formal political incorporation. Such an enlargement of the political community threatened to endanger the very institutions that supported ruling-class privilege. Thus nineteenth-century political elites experienced a dual fear: fear of emergent working-class power and fear of loss of class privilege. The fear of the masses by political elites was sublimated in a perception that the masses were driven by uneducated passion or emotion. Thus the fear of the one was explained by the emotionality of the other. Nineteenth-century ruling classes attempted to remove the source of their fear by extending the franchise in a manner that, among other things, suppressed and rendered politically irrelevant working-class emotionality. Indeed, this was the principal result of introducing secret voting, an institution largely ignored in historical, political and sociological accounts, but crucial for an understanding of modern politics, and the modern constitution of emotionality.

It is possible to gauge how the emerging working classes were regarded by political elites with reference to contemporary documents such as Walter Bagehot's 1872 'Introduction to the Second Edition' of his classic text, *The English Constitution*, that includes a projection of the consequences of the Second Reform Bill of 1867, brought down just after *The English Constitution* was first written. In this 'Introduction' Bagehot warns of the dangers inherent in giving the vote to workers who are not only propertyless but also prone to excitement and emotion. It is this that Bagehot fears for himself and the class he addresses. He was unrestrained in expressing his own feelings about the new political agenda when he wrote 'I am exceedingly afraid of the ignorant multitude of the new constituencies' (Bagehot, 1964, p. 281). This 'multitude' is a source of fearfulness for a number of reasons. Most superficially is the fear that in seeking the vote of the newly enfranchised worker existing political parties would compete to satisfy the worker's ignorant desires (Bagehot, 1964, p. 277). This is the fear that working-class votes would change the quality of politics. Of greater concern was the fear that the working class would combine to form a solid political block. Bagehot does not treat this in terms of a working-class political *interest* but in terms of the possible realization in the political system of *ignorance*:

> a political combination of the lower classes, as such and for their own objects, is an evil of the first magnitude; that a permanent combination of them would make them (now that so many of them have the suffrage) supreme in the country; and that their supremacy, in the state they now are, means the supremacy of ignorance over instruction and of numbers over knowledge (Bagehot, 1964, p. 277).

The solution to this problem, which Bagehot immediately goes on to indicate, is to prevent the working class acting together, a thing which will require 'the greatest wisdom and the greatest foresight in the higher classes'.

The 'supremacy of ignorance' that Bagehot fears is not an absence of knowledge but an opposition to reason through emotion and passion. This is the most significant fear Bagehot has of the working class, namely its emotionality. He writes: 'democratic passions gain by fomenting a diffused excitement, and by massing men in concourses', which means a real danger of 'a wild excitement among the ignorant poor, which, if once roused, may not be easily calmed' (Bagehot, 1964, p. 282). Bagehot directly links open voting with destructive passions. The solution to this problem is obvious and clear: disaggregate the mass politically, and thereby dissolve its emotionality. This can be achieved by electorally isolating each voter from the other, which is a key function of secret voting or the ballot.

The attitudes and feelings described here were not unique to Bagehot but current in nineteenth-century European political elites. Fear of the masses is the constitutive emotional basis of a large reactionary literature that began in response to the French Revolution, most notably in the work of Edmund Burke and Hippolyte Taine in the late eighteenth century and which continued into the late nineteenth century with Gustave Le Bon's *The Crowd*. But not only reactionary and conservative writers feared working-class emotionality; the progressive liberal reformer and champion of the extension of the suffrage, John Stuart Mill, agreed that while 'everyone ought to have a voice' the idea 'that everyone should have an equal voice is a totally different proposition' (Mill, 1960, p. 283). This claim is part of a discussion in which Mill expressed an interest in the 'education of the intelligence and of the sentiments' of the 'lowest ranks of the people' (1960, p. 277), and asserted that democracy would increase both intelligence and patriotism. Patriotism in particular is able to 'educate' sentiment or emotion, because those who experienced patriotic feelings would be integrated into the national political community (1960, pp. 277–78). Indeed, Mill defended plural voting based on occupation and education on the grounds that it would over-come the dangers of a situation in which the majority of voters are manual labourers (Mill, 1960, p. 283).

Mill changed from an earlier position of supporting the ballot to opposing it. He came to believe that the vote was not a right, and there-fore not an individual possession, but a trust for the public. As a public duty, voting should be 'performed under the eye and criticism of the public' (Mill, 1960, p. 300). Public voting, Mill continues, leads the voter to have 'sure grounds of their own', because it is performed under the scrutiny of others (1960, p. 305). He goes on to say:

> People will give dishonest or mean votes from lucre, from malice, from pique, from personal rivalry, even from the interests or prejudices of class or sect, more readily in secret than in public (1960, p. 306).

Thus Mill's argument, like Bagehot's, hinges on the fact that secret voting separates or cuts off electors from their relationship of duty to the community. Their different attitudes to the ballot do not arise from different assessments of the nature of the working class, but from the fact that Mill but not Bagehot believed that sufficient defence against working-class emotionality could be found in patriotism sponsored by democracy and plural voting. Additionally, Mill valued the educative potential of voting as a public responsibility, which, according to him, can only be achieved with open not secret voting.

A description of the advent of the ballot as part of a process of political rationalization does not mean that this process led to the expulsion of emotion from politics. Rather, it is necessary to appreciate that the process is one of eradicating a particular set of emotional patterns from political life and replacing it with another set. To put the matter this way raises questions not adequately treated in the standard accounts. Indeed, an acknowledgment that '[in] secret voting the individual adult is cut off from all his roles in the subordinate systems of the household, the neighbourhood, the work organization, the church and the civil association and set to act exclusively in the abstract role of a citizen of the overall political system' (Rokkan, 1966, p. 117), while insightful of the structural change brought with the introduction of the ballot, makes no reference to the mechanisms through which the voter is alienated from non-electoral roles. These mechanisms are the emotional transformations that underlie the organizational changes Rokkan refers to. It is typically assumed that rationalization entails an elimination of emotion, not the generation of a particular set of emotions commensurate with it. In fact, though, emotions cannot be eliminated from social and political processes, and even rational activity has a necessary basis in particular emotions. What is important, then, is to show which emotions in particular operate under conditions of open voting, and which emotions operate under conditions of secret voting.

Secret voting or voting by ballot is the norm in modern electoral systems. It is part of an organization of political practices in which voting is seen as an instrumental act, expressive of an interest and registering a preference for one candidate, or policy, over another. This is its rationale. A cognitive consequence of this rationale is an awareness on the part of the voter that no single vote can determine an electoral outcome and therefore that the voter's individual preference cannot in itself be politically effective, let alone decisive. That electoral choices are seldom between different policies but rather between unreliable and promise-breaking politicians simply exacerbates this problem. The emotional dimensions of the ballot must include, then, a feeling of impotence and loneliness. Indeed, the emotional pattern of political rationalization in the practice of voting is the same as that of religious rationalization, classically captured by Max Weber in *The Protestant Ethic and the Spirit of Capitalism*, especially the feeling of inner loneliness and the subsequent feeling of distrusting others (Weber, 1991, pp. 104, 107).

These consequences of voting by ballot have not been highlighted in the relevant literature. Voting studies typically examine the behaviour of electors, and the degree of relationship between their social background and party preference or allegiance. While familial influences on voting behaviour has long been established, the difficulty in attaining high voter turnout for all polities, which rely on elections as a legitimating mechanism, suggests not voter sociality but indifference and alienation from the electoral process, and elector powerlessness.

The feelings of loneliness and impotence inherent in secret voting are associated with, if not symptomatic of, the emotions of depression and shame. These result respectively from loss of regard or standing (Kemper, 1978, pp. 225–36) and loss of self-efficacy (Scheff, 1990, pp. 71–5), which loneliness and impotence describe. It is not being suggested here that people who vote are themselves necessarily depressed and ashamed, but rather that these are the emotional patterns that emerge from the institution of the ballot. While this institution does not absorb the social universe, and the voter is therefore involved in a number of other institutions, relations and interactions that have their own concomitant emotional patterns, the point is that in the act of secret voting the emotions of depression and shame are implicit, and the situated actions of voters tend to reflect the fact.

The behavioural consequence of depression and shame is withdrawal, and it is therefore possible to understand major components of the syndrome of modern politics in terms of the emotional pattern established by the institutionalization of the ballot. In particular, voter apathy, cynicism, low registration and turnout are each predicted in terms of the emotional pattern implicit in the ballot. This is particularly interesting in the light of the fact that studies typically account for these things in terms of ideological convergence of political parties, the behaviour of politicians and other external features of the system, not the structurally contexed emotions of voting. Presented here, on the other hand, is an approach that indicates the inherent susceptibility to political alienation in the emotional pattern associated with the ballot itself.

It is important to emphasize that the point being made here is that the institution of the secret vote or ballot has an accompanying emotional pattern associated with depression and shame. To reiterate, this is not to say that voters are necessarily depressed or ashamed. This is because voters as persons are involved with many more institutions and relationships than the ballot and each one of them will have its own emotional concomitants. Indeed, it is important to add that within the political process are constraints and opportunities that carry their own emotional complexions that at any given election may predominate for an individual elector so that in particular cases those latter emotions will override the affective structure of the ballot. Previously excluded groups new to the formal political process, for instance, may be elated in exercising their vote. Strategically organized voters may similarly experience emotions that arise from the purposes they strive to achieve that are quite unlike the depression and shame argued here to be concomitant with the ballot. It is treatment of the ballot without regard to extraneous patterns of involvement that is required to construct a model of the emotional pattern it produces. Under these conditions the emotional complexion of the ballot itself are readily identified as depression and shame.

An obvious difference between the ballot and open voting, implicit in Mill's description of it as indicated above, is that whereas the former is non-interactive the latter encourages interaction. This is not a superficial difference but points to the fact that voting under open conditions may be 'consumatory', to use a term drawn the work of the American philosopher John Dewey, as opposed to 'instrumental'. Mill's opposition to the ballot was supported by the proposition that voting 'performed under the eye and criticism of the public' (Mill, 1960, p. 300) leads the voter to be more sure of their grounds (1960, p. 305). While this latter requirement might mean, as Mill no doubt meant it, that the open voter's decision will be based on evidence and argument, sociologically it would mean that the open voter's decision would be taken to avoid social rejection, or, to say the same thing positively, to lead to social acceptance. These two possible meanings of Mill's thesis are not opposed.

As a consumatory and interactive activity open voting carries its own emotional pattern. A key element of this pattern is trust, the feeling that one can be dependent on others. Dependency's illegitimate side is corruption and blackmail, the likelihood of which diminishes as the size of electorate increases. Associated with trust are feelings of duty and belonging. These are essential in organizational growth and operations, as is embarrassment, a social emotion that facilitates interaction by allowing those who perform unacceptably to indicate remorse and therefore signals their continuing suitability for social acceptance.

These remarks are not designed to endorse open voting against secret voting, but to emphasize the different emotional patterns associated respectively with open and secret voting and thus appreciate that they imply different types of politics, based on the contrasting emotional patterns each sponsor.

Terror and suicide terror

At the furthest polar end of the spectrum of political means from the ballot is terror, especially suicide terror. Terror is essentially an instrument of social and political practices. These practices themselves require particular conditions which, when met, make available a means, namely terror, which can be applied to a number of possible ends including economic as well as political purposes. Terror can be characterized as violence or the threat of violence enacted to contribute to achieving some extrinsic purpose by inculcating fear of violence in persons other than the immediate target of the (threatened) violence. In this broad sense terror is not only a political instrument but at the core of protection rackets (Gambetta, 1993; Volkov, 2002), for example, and similar economic extortions, possibly including certain forms of tax collection especially colonial imposition of head or hut tax. It is also a means that can be applied to political purposes by groups that are not conventionally called 'terrorist', such as political states or their agents (Stohl, 1983; Stohl and Lopez, 1984).

The basis of the efficacy of terror as a means of controlling persons is the fear of violence inherent in terror that is experienced beyond the direct targets of violence. Fear is typically understood as an emotion of displeasure about the prospect of an undesirable event (Ortony, Clore and Collins, 1990, pp. 112 ff). But the emotion provoked by terror and necessary for its operation is not merely fear of an event in this narrow sense. Because the fear essential to terror is of the possibility of violence beyond the direct target of threatened violence, the audience emotion is more undifferentiated than fear of a discrete event and constitutes also reactions to possible or potential agents of terror. This means that the victim of terror, that is any potential victim of the violence of terror, is angry with those who cause their fear. This combination of anger and fear produces a hate type of emotion (Kemper, 1978, pp. 124–5). It is not difficult to understand, therefore, why in an era of fear of terror identifiable sections of the population thought to have some quality in common with known terrorists (such as religion) are subjected to public hatred.

The nuances presented in the previous paragraph are well understood by the sixteenth-century Florentine writer Niccolò Machiavelli. When considering whether it is better for a prince to be feared or loved, Machiavelli famously counselled 'that one ought to be both...but...it is much safer to be feared than loved, if one of the two has to be wanting...Still, a prince should make himself feared in such a way that if he does not gain love, he at any rate avoids hatred' (Machiavelli, 1950, p. 61). The difference between a strategy provoking fear as opposed to hatred, Machiavelli goes on to show, is whether the violence and its effects are confined to the immediate targets or generalized to a larger population. Machiavelli's advice is very much against the use of terror even though he endorses the use of violence. This is because the prince must remain on good terms with his subjects, the distance between the prince and his subjects must be contained within a particular range. A corollary of this proposition is that terror becomes available as a means of control in social relationships when the social distance between those applying it and those subject to it is very great.

The first social condition that must be met if terror is to be applied in social relations as a means of social control, then, is 'social polarization' (Senechal de la Roche, 1996, pp. 115–22). Indeed, most instances of collective violence of any sort involve groups that have different collective identities, based on religion, ethnicity, region, nationality, or some other basis of significant cultural distance, including economic inequality. In the case of criminal protection rackets social polarization is achieved, independently of those factors already mentioned – which may or may not apply – by the cultural qualities of criminal gang membership and criminal activities which place the racketeers at considerable social distance from their victims, who are typically shopkeepers, householders and mundane industrial or bureaucratic workers.

The archetypical condition of social polarization is to be found in medieval estate society, for instance, in which the cultural formations of the different estates share very few common elements even though there is functional interdependence between them. Under these circumstances the different social groups fail to share common reference points cognitively and affectively, that is to say they literally live in different worlds. As a result they fail to satisfy the conditions that the eighteenth-century Scottish writer Adam Smith (1976), for instance, sets out in his account of a theory of moral sentiments, namely sympathy. We are sympathetic with another when we can imagine ourselves in their circumstances and therefore imagine the emotions they might experience. This is the basic condition for what George Herbert Mead calls 'role taking', on which is based his account of sociality (Mead, 1934). The emotional dimension that is absent under conditions of social polarization, then, that would otherwise give access to a sense of the emotional feelings of the other, means that the humanity of the other is simply not accessible under conditions of social polarization. It is for this reason that in estate society it is possible for one group to inflict the most horrid cruelty on the other: in the absence of sympathy or fellow feeling it is not possible to form a sense of the other's emotional feelings and therefore of their suffering in particular or their humanity in general.

While social polarization is necessary for terror to occur in situations of both criminal economic extortion and political duress, a difference between them, in addition to social polarization, is that in the political but not the economic use of terror social polarization is overlain with 'moral polarization'. Terror becomes a means of social control in political situations when those who apply terror and their victims are not only at great social distance but also at great moral distance. The perpetrators of political terror typically regard their victims as responsible for or implicated in some serious moral transgression, including theft of a national territory, threat to the integrity of national or international organization, despoliation of the religiously sacred, serious social and cultural dislocation, or some other significant moral transgression. While social polarization operates in terms of the absence of the emotional elements of sympathy and fellow feeling, moral polarization involves an intense but negative emotional engagement. Those who are held to be responsible for the suffering of the other are hated, the sufferer both fears those responsible for their suffering and is angry with them. The victim of terror and the perpetrator of terror are involved in a hate–hate relationship in which anger and fear intermingle.

The significance of moral polarization is essential in understanding the etiology, incidence and level of the application of terror in political contexts. First, in overlaying social polarization, moral polarization intensifies the distance between perpetrator and victim, increasing the likelihood of application of terror in any conflict involving the polarized groups and accounting for the level of ferocity in any violent conflict between them. Second, the substance of the perceived moral transgression is the basis of an articulated discontent that takes the form of a principled position which functions as a means of mobilization, converting a grievance into a movement. Third, the perceived moral transgression legitimates with a wider population the movement formed to address it, so that terrorists have a support population from which they draw comfort and recruits.

To summarize the discussion so far: Terror is a means to achieve some extrinsic purpose, and is a means of social control in which violence or threat of its use creates fear or anxiety and also anger in a target population larger than the immediate victims of violence. Those who apply such a means are typically socially polarized from those who are subject to it, and in the case of its application in political disputes social polarization is typically overlaid with moral polarization.

In the simplest terms, 'suicide terror' is a form of delivery of a means of terrorist violence that in order to succeed requires the death of its immediate operative. What is being referred to by this term, then, is not in the first instance a type of terrorist nor a form of terrorism, but a mode of delivering violence, or more properly terror. The proliferation of this means to terror since the 1980s is an index of its efficiency. The tactical advantages of a bomb attached to a human operative are that it (1) decreases the possibility of detection – a suicide bomber appears to be like any other person and the bomb to which he or she is attached is ostensibly indistinguishable from any jacket or car or truck or fully fuelled Boeing 767, as the case may be; (2) it increases the possibility of positioning a bomb for effectiveness – a bomb attached to a person can be manoeuvred to a difficult-to-reach or moving target in a way simply impossible for inanimate bombs; (3) it eliminates the most difficult part of any clandestine operation – there is no need to devise an escape route; (4) it enhances security – the risk of capture or some other breach of security is significantly reduced.

Suicide terror has been used by a number of quite different groups. These include Hezbollah in Lebanon during the 1980s; the Liberation Tigers of Tamil Eelam (LTTE) in Sri Lanka from 1990 to 2002 and possibly continuing; Hamas in Palestine–Israel intermittently from 1994; the Kurdistan Workers Party (PKK) in Turkey during 1996 and 1999; al-Qaeda from 1996; Kashmiri rebels from 2000; Chechnyan rebels from 2000; and various insurgent and foreign groups in Iraq since 2003. This list should quickly dispel one popular explanation of suicide terror, namely that it is a consequence of Islamic religious peculiarities, especially associated with heavenly rewards of martyrdom. Other frequently expressed popular explanations of suicide terrorism can also be quickly dispelled: neither depression or other mental illness, nor despair, poverty or lack of education, is a characteristic feature of suicide bombers (Hassan, 2001, p. 3; Atran, 2003, pp. 1535–7).

The classic account of altruistic suicide by the French sociologist, Emile Durkheim (1970), contributes to an explanation of suicide terrorism, for it refers to a commitment on the part of the individual to kill himself or herself in order to satisfy a collective need, either by way of obligation or by encouragement through acquisition of prestige

(Durkheim, 1970, pp. 221–2). It is appropriate to mention that organizations that engage in suicide terror also have activities that contribute to the generation and dissemination of collectivist values and beliefs that enhance the type of social integration that Durkheim refers to here. Both Hamas and LTTE, for example, have extensive involvement in provision of educational, welfare and recreational services. These function, among other things, to disseminate a collectivist ideology in which altruistic suicide has salience and also to legitimate organizations practicing suicide terrorism and enhance recruitment to them.

The type of social structure in which an individual's identity is defined in terms of their positive obligations to the collective, sociologically summarized as 'traditional', can be explained not only in terms of historically enduring structures and cultural patterns but also in terms of a society's more recent experience, as in Georg Simmel's account, for instance, of the consequences of a conflict of a group with another group on the former's inner structure. Simmel describes this as 'centralization of the group' in which 'individual deviations from the unity of the coordinating principle' is not tolerated (Simmel, 1969, pp. 87–94). Indeed, the galvanizing quality of the social structure that supports terrorist organizations is primarily its conflictual subjugation to an external power and only secondarily its 'traditional' form. In this sense any religiosity in terrorist groups is as likely to be a consequence of the social conditions facilitating their engagement in terrorism as its cause.

The density of social solidarity through conflict, as background to the advent of suicide terror, is insufficient to account for the incidence of suicide terrorism but its veracity is enhanced by a common feature of suicide bombers, namely that they had lost a family member or close friend through the military action of those they oppose. This is the singular basis of recruitment to the Chechnyan Black Widows suicide squads, and it is also reported as a feature of recruitment of Hamas suicide bombers (Ganor, 2000, p. 4; Brooks, 2002). Also frequently reported is the intense loyalty of the bomber to organization and cause. The qualities of loyalty may be appreciated by comparing it with trust. Whereas trust, which is a commitment to rely on another, preserves individual prerogatives and a sense of individual benefits, loyalty, on the other hand, is a commitment to subordinate individual prerogatives and benefits for the sake of a collective entity (Barbalet, 1996).

Yet none of this in itself explains the genesis of suicide terror. This is because suicide terror is a technique not a movement. It is not the result of individual attributes (mental disorder) or social conditions (poverty, oppression, social solidarity), but of a political decision to use it. Once that decision is taken, then certain social or organizational conditions are required to operationalize it, that is to select, train and control suicide bombers, and each of these also involves particular emotions.

The Palestinian case

There is a literature that discusses the selection, training and control or running of suicide bombers. It shows how the relevant organizations attempt to select able, competent and reliable persons who are already motivated for such operations and it shows how, in addition to providing technical training, the organizations use various methods for maintaining commitment (Hassan, 2001; Davis, 2003). The emotional elements of these matters are clear and readily understood. Rather than focus on this aspect I want to consider to what ends or purposes suicide terror might be put in order to understand the programmatic emotions at work.

Like all political activity, suicide terrorism has to be understood in its context. Although suicide terror is not a unique feature of the Palestinian–Israeli conflict, this conflict does provide a particularly well-documented case study. The Palestinian organization, Hamas, commenced a suicide campaign in late 1993 in an endeavour to sabotage the Oslo accords signed between the late Yasser Arafat's Palestine Liberation Organization (PLO) and Israel. In its founding charter Hamas was committed to the replacement of Arafat's government with an Islamist state in the West Bank and Gaza, and the destruction of Israel. The suicide bombing of this period, conducted by Hamas and to a lesser extent Islamic Jihad, was relatively light with 9 incidents from April 1994 to August 1995, 4 in 1996 and 3 in 1997. Although the victims of Hamas and Islamic Jihad terror were Israeli citizens, the campaigns of this period must be seen as directed against the PLO and its agreement with Israel on a peace settlement. The use of suicide terror in intra-movement differences should not be overlooked as a significant factor in Palestinian politics. The suicide campaigns of this period were not widely supported within the Palestinian population.

While there was much support in principle for Oslo in the West Bank and Gaza, conditions in these regions deteriorated significantly after the Oslo agreement was signed. Economically, the standard of living declined 30% and the unemployment rate went to 50%. At the same time Jewish settler populations increased and the protective buffer zones around Jewish settlements were enlarged without compensation. Israeli restrictions on trade, investment and water resources added to

Palestinian concerns. Finally, in its endeavours to enforce Oslo the Palestinian Authority behaved increasingly harshly, closing independent media and jailing opponents. The prevailing climate that dominated the Palestinian areas was fear and despondency.

In late September 2000 the then Israeli opposition leader, Ariel Sharon, visited Temple Mount, which led to large riots in Jerusalem and to Sharon's victory in a general election in February 2001. This exacerbated the despondency among Palestinians. These events initiated a new campaign of suicide terror by Hamas and Islamic Jihad. The following year groups that had not previously been involved in suicide terror, namely the Popular Front for the Liberation of Palestine (PFLP) and the Al-Aqsa Martyr Brigade, joined the new campaign. The incidence of suicide attacks is summarized in Table 1.

The involvement of the Al-Aqsa Martyr Brigade in suicide terror began in 2000 in response to the Israeli assassination of its commander, but its operations were limited to military targets. It attacked civilian targets with suicide missions from 2002 in response to Hamas operations, but unlike Hamas was prepared to run female bombers.

The use of suicide terror in this campaign has been difficult to explain strategically: targets are typically civilian rather than military, and when military personnel have been targeted they have not been strategic in either rank or function. This has led commentators to argue that these suicide operations within Israel are retaliatory against Israeli incursions into territory controlled by the Palestinian Authority. Additionally, it has been argued that to the degree that Hamas suicide terror is strategic it has been used to disrupt negotiated outcomes it considered unsatisfactory or inadequate. But neither of these accounts can explain the suicide campaign of 2001–2004.

Table 1 Incidence of suicide terrorism by organization

	2001	2002	2003	2004*	Total
HAMAS	10	13	9	2	34
IJ	6	6	5		17
AL AQSA		10	3	3	16
PFLP		2	1		3
UNATTRIB	4	7	2		13
Total	20	38	20	5	83

* up until March 14
Source: Israel Ministry of Foreign Affairs.

As we have seen, terror functions by generating fear in the target population. The 2001–2004 suicide terror campaign does that, but it does something else in addition. Unlike other terror campaigns it generates high levels of anger against Israel in the Palestinian population. It is able to do this because the suicide campaign has reliably been able to provoke Israeli reprisals. Before discussing the details it is necessary to say something about the differences between fear and anger.

While both fear and anger share an element of distress, displeasure about an undesirable event, they have quite different, even opposite dispositional consequences. This is because anger includes an element of reproach, absent in fear, that is disapproving of someone else's blameworthy action (Ortony, Clore and Collins, 1988, pp. 112, 147). Fear in times of civil unrest and military oppression tends to politically isolate individuals and contract their activities. While fear tends to deplete a person's power of assertion, anger, on the other hand, increases it (de Rivera, 1977, p. 89; see also Holmes, 2004; Ost, 2004). De Rivera points out that the 'most evident [physical] effect' of anger is to 'increase [a person's] volitional capacity' and that anger functions 'to strengthen the person's will', and anger is therefore:

> necessary for the maintenance of will in the face of the opposition's position and possible use of retaliation. If the anger is unavailable, or insufficient, the person folds and fails to assert himself (de Rivera, 1977, p. 87).

Thus it was necessary for Palestinian political organizations to produce anger in the face of objective conditions post-Oslo leading to fear and despair. This has been the purpose and outcome of the suicide campaigns of Hamas, Islamic Jihad and the al-Aqsa Martyrs Brigade from 2001. Expression of such anger does not dissipate the emotion but intensifies it.

Palestinian anger is provoked by the structure of social relationships that characterized life in Gaza and the West Bank. But this anger is enhanced by wrapping the terror campaign against Israel in a mantle of martyrdom through suicide bombings. In Arabic the suicide terrorist is known as a *shahid*, a martyr. To suffer and indeed to die for a cause as a martyr attributes the responsibility for the death neither to the person who dies, nor even to the cause for which they die, but to the force opposed to that cause. The cause itself is seen in terms of the *shahid's* representation of the community from which they are drawn. The martyr's act is blameless; those whom the martyr opposes are reproachable. Palestinian reproach against Israel fuels Palestinian anger and energizes the Palestinian movement. In addition to the cultural element another necessary component of the suicide campaign productive of Palestinian anger is the provocation of Israeli retaliation, upon which these suicide campaigns are dependent if they are to produce the requisite anger.

Israeli policy requires demolition of the suicide bomber's or their family's house. There is also usually arrest of family members, friends and associates. In addition there are targeted killings of Palestinian militants. The geometry of suicide attack and reprisal can be seen in a single case. A Hamas suicide bombing occurred at a pizzeria in the centre of Jerusalem on 9 August 2001. Fifteen people were killed, including 7 children, and about 130 were injured. Israeli reprisals included a humiliating confiscation of a Palestinian building in east Jerusalem, a strike by F-16 fighter jets firing 3 missiles at the Ramalla Police Station causing damage to about 80% of the building, and a Palestinian security position shelled in Gaza in which 27 people were killed. The suicide raid itself was in retaliation for Israeli-targeted killings or decapitations of Palestinian militants in preceding months through which Hamas lost 9 activists (Malakunas, 2001).

If we consider the death rates from Palestinian suicide bombings and Israeli reprisals for the period 2001–2004, as in Table 2, we can see that it averages out to just over 5 Israeli deaths and 30 Palestinian deaths for each suicide mission. The terrorist organizations and the Israeli authorities know this ghoulish proportionality. And so does the Palestinian population: It is a further source of the anger of ordinary Palestinians.

It is interesting to note that suicide bombing had a quite different structure and effect in the first historically recent instance of its widespread use, by Hezbollah in the early 1980s. Here suicide bombers were directed against military and diplomatic targets to remove American

Table 2 Numbers of deaths associated with suicide bombings.

	Number of suicide bombings	Number of Israeli deaths	Palestinian deaths through IDF actions
2001	20	81	577
2002	38	197	1068
2003	20	139	664
2004*	5	33	187
Total	83	450	2492
Ratio	1	5.4	30

* to April
Sources: Israel Ministry of Foreign Affairs; Palestinian Red Crescent Society.

forces from Lebanon. The most extensive use of suicide missions has been by the LTTE. Their use of suicide bombers has been against military targets and also in assassination attempts against prominent military and civilian leaders, practically all successful, the best known being the assassination of Rajiv Gandhi by belt bomb in May 1991. Similarly, Iraqi insurgents and foreign fighters have targeted military and police patrols and installations with suicide bombs, although increasing numbers of civilian victims are reported. The Palestinian suicide campaign of 2001–2004 had the particular purpose of generating anger in its support population.

Conclusion

In a pioneering work of political analysis, *The Process of Government*, first published in 1908, Arthur Bentley (1949) devoted nearly a hundred pages of the first chapter, 'Feelings and Faculties as Causes', discrediting the idea that emotions can be of primary importance in political processes and therefore of interest to political analysis. Having dispelled emotions from explanation of political events and organization, Bentley returns to the question of emotions towards the end of the book. He now writes that his argument of the first chapter contained 'certain exaggerations' and 'shades of overemphasis' (Bentley, 1949, p. 443). While he still wishes to insist that feelings or emotions have no 'independent existence' his revised position is that 'they do indicate a very important part of the social activity' (Bentley, 1949, p. 443). The reason that exclusion of emotions can only compromise the explanatory capacity of accounts of social and political phenomena is that emotions are essential to the values, interests and meanings of those who have any social and political involvement. To leave emotions out of an explanation or account removes the agent responsible for an outcome and also the consequences of an agent's actions. As we have seen when considering voting, for instance, it also leaves out a full understanding of organization and institution.

While emotions are essential in political explanation, a common sense or popular understanding of emotions is inadequate. Like all concepts, the meaning of the notion of emotions derives from the theory of emotion within which it operates. It has been proposed that aspects of some conventional understandings of emotions are less useful in political analysis than a more self-consciously sociological approach to emotions, briefly outlined in the first section of this chapter. In particular, it is important to keep in mind that some emotions, and especially emotions relevant to significant political processes and organizations, endure over long periods of time and that expression of emotions does not necessarily mean their dissipation but their possible reinforcement. Also, the distinction between relational, iterated and programmatic emotions was proposed. The importance of relational emotions in indicating the difference between open and secret voting, for instance, has been demonstrated in the discussion above. Similarly, the relational emotions generated in social and moral polarization that is the basis of adaptation of terror as a means in political conflict has also been demonstrated. The role of iterated emotions in the construction of martyrdom in the campaigns of Palestinian organizations was noted, and the importance of anger as a programmatic emotion in the Palestinian suicide campaign of 2001–2004 has also been discussed in the case study above.

No aspect of the social and political worlds is free of emotional involvement and any explanation of those things that ignores emotions is to that extent of limited utility. Norbert Elias warned that 'any investigation that considers only people's consciousness, their "reason" or "ideas", while disregarding the structure of drives, the direction and form of human affects and passions, can from the outset be of only limited value' (Elias, 2000, p. 408). But to this caution must be added another: it is not sufficient to simply refer to 'emotions' as a generic capacity or faculty. Only particular emotions are real and in their reality are responsible for quite distinct dispositions, inclinations and outcomes. As we have seen, the difference between open and secret voting, for instance, is not that one is 'emotional' and the other 'rationalized'. Emotions are inherent in both; the difference lies in the distinct specific emotions of each. Analysis of emotions and explanations that draw upon them must always refer to and contribute to our understanding of particular emotions, be it fear, anger, shame, contentment or any one of the vast number of emotions of which humans are capable, indicating the detailed particulars of their specific involvements in all aspects of politics.

Part II
The Applications

4
Applying Theory in Practice: Politics and Emotions in Everyday Life

Simon Clarke, Paul Hoggett and Simon Thompson

Introduction

Now we have established some of the microfoundations of emotion in the previous two chapters we want to turn to the practical application of the study of emotion in everyday life. To reiterate some of the themes thus far, we have argued that emotions occupy a place of ambiguity in the popular imagination or consciousness. Emotion is often seen as an eruption of the irrational, for example, of a rage where the individual is unable to contain his or her feelings and act in a rational manner. We tend to see eruptions of such 'negative emotions' as bad or destructive whereas it is quite all right to fall in love. Academically, there has always been a tension between what we might call a social constructionist view of emotions and that of a biological standpoint. In other words are emotions part of cultural socialization or are they an innate part of the structure of our biology? At times the counterposition of social constructionism to biological reductionism, the nature-versus-nurture debate if you like, has detracted from their study. Several of the chapters in this second part of the book take a far more reconciliatory view. They carve a path between what we might term 'learnt behaviour' and the idea that we may also have certain innate predispositions and reactions that are driven by our unconscious mind.

The foundations of modern research into emotion can be traced back to three people: Charles Darwin, William James and Sigmund Freud. As Jenkins *et al.* (1998) note: 'Darwin founded ethology with his observation of emotional responses in natural settings. James emphasized physiological changes in the body...(and) Freud offered the method of listening to what people said about their emotional lives' (Jenkins *et al.*, 1998, p. 8). For Darwin, emotions are innate and derive from primitive states of physiological being. Emotion is somehow to do with our instincts, and emotional response is a reaction which is central to survival, a reaction to threats and dangers. In James' model, emotion is initially a bodily experience that becomes cognate in the sense that it is evaluated and assigned a specific label. In other words, it is not the cause of anything, it is an effect. So for example, we feel sorry because we cry, afraid because we tremble. This biological basis in human emotion has put it at odds with sociological and political thinking. But also, we have the idea that we intimated in the introductory chapter of this book that the emotions have been seen as something that need taming or harnessing, preferably by the hand of reason. The emotional is always the antithesis of that which is calm, controlled and scientific. In his early work *Sketch for a Theory of Emotions* Jean Paul Sartre (1939, 2002) argues that emotions are intentional and a way of coping with difficult situations, emotions do not control us, we control them. We tend to aim at changing the world but if we cannot we change our own behaviour. Sartre gives the example of fainting, in which we magically annihilate the world by severing our consciousness with it. Emotion arises as the world of rationality disappears and the world of magic comes to the fore (Sartre, 1939, p. 57). Simon Williams (1998) argues that we have to rid ourselves of the idea that emotions are the poor relation to reason – 'without emotions, social life, including our decision making capacities and our ability to make informed choices amongst a plurality of options, would be impossible' (Williams, 1998, p. 761).

In some sense this dichotomy between constructionist and innate accounts of the study of emotion reached an impasse in sociological research in a debate through a series of papers in the journal *Sociology* in the mid-1990s. This debate between Ian Craib, Simon Williams and Gillian Bendelow largely centre around the neglect of the study of emotions in British sociology. Craib's (1995) paper argued that the sociological study of emotions might restrict, rather than further our understanding of emotional life. In it he argues that men and women are engaged in interlocking forms of emotional work and that there is no simple relationship between the experience and the expression of emotion. Craib is pointing to the complexity of emotional states of being in which he argues that no one form of knowing, in this case sociology, is sufficient for us to understand the complexity of emotional life. Craib argues for a psychoanalytic rendition of the explanation of emotion, but in a far from reductionist form. Rather, in understanding emotion we need to draw on both social and psychological aspects of culture and society. Williams and Bendelow (1996) are quick to point out that Craib's charge that sociological commentaries on emotions are crass and insensitive is not only an overstatement but neglects much of the good work done by sociologists. After all, many of the founders of sociology have touched on emotion in their work: in the *Protestant Ethic* Max Weber (1978) describes the emotional powerhouse that is the basis for development of the modern Western world and politics. Scheler (1992) provides a rich source of material in his writing on empathy and emotion. Simmel (1950) analyses the emotional life of the city. In Marx and Durkheim we see the analysis of feelings of alienation and solidarity. So, sociology has touched on the emotional and political in society. In 1997 Craib launched his fiercest attack on the sociological tradition by arguing that social constructionism is a manic psychosis which is unable to recognise the limits of its own discipline, unable to take on the ideas of other disciplines and therefore unable to discover anything new. These are strong words, and there is much irony in Craib's paper, but what he is arguing is that we need to take a multidisciplinary stance if we are to understand the basis of emotional life. In *The Managed Heart* (1983) Arlie Hochschild posits a theory of emotion which manages to synthesise all these positions. Her model of emotion oscillates between biological, interactionist, or social constructionist and psychoanalytic approaches to emotion in three theoretical currents:

> Drawing from Dewey, Gerth and Mills, and Goffman within the interactional tradition, I explore what gets 'done to' emotion and how feelings are permeable to what gets done to them. From Darwin in the organismic tradition, I posit a sense of what is there, impermeable, to be 'done to', namely a biological given sense related to an orientation to action. Finally, through Freud, I circle back from the organismic to the interactional tradition, tracing through an analysis of the signal functions of feeling how social factors influence what we expect and thus what feelings signal. (Hochschild, 1983, p. 222).

Thus we have the idea that we can have an interactional view of biologically derived emotion, but far from reductionism, Hochschild posits a dynamic model in which the biological or innate is a potentiality which is shaped by the social. This is similar to Eric Fromm's thesis – 'Man's nature, his passions, and anxieties are a cultural product' (Fromm, 1942, p. 11). Fromm does not reject Freud's ideas, but turns them on their head. Man's nature, the emotional self is neither a result of innate biological drives nor a 'lifeless shadow of cultural' patterns, but a product of the tension between the two. In other words a tension between outer and inner worlds, between social and political structure and society. Joanne Brown and Barry Richards (2000) characterise a psychoanalytic sociology of the emotions which attempts to avoid dualistic thinking: 'we combine psychoanalytic with social theory, as well as some more philosophical discourse lying behind both forms of theory, with observations of social processes ranging from commentary on complex cultural themes to microanalysis of social interaction in specific settings' (Brown and Richards, 2000, p. 31).

It has in many senses been the use of psychoanalysis in tandem with social and critical theory that has led the way in this kind of multidisciplinary approach and this is evident in the first two papers in the second section of this book. Clarke and Alford make use of Kleinian psychoanalytic ideas to make sense of the emotions that we call 'envy' and 'hate', as does Hoggett in his exploration of compassion. This is a tradition that goes back to the early work of the Frankfurt School and in particular in the writings of Max Horkheimer and Theodor Adorno (1947, 1994) in the exploration of the dark side of Enlightenment thinking. Although Horkheimer and Adorno's work did not specifically address emotion *per se*, it did seek to understand the affective and irrational forces behind the development of modern society. Using a critical fusion of the work of Marx, Weber and Freud, Horkheimer and Adorno sought to explain the visceral, irrational and embodied nature of anti-Semitism using psychoanalytic theory. In a later paper Adorno (1991) turned to the political and specifically Fascist propaganda to try and explain the emotional ties that people developed with certain leaders, despite their better judgement. This multidisciplinary approach that leans towards psychoanalysis tends to focus on negative emotions such as hate and aggression. Frantz Fanon (1968) in *Black Skin White Masks* delves into the political economy and psychopathology of colonialism. Again Fanon uses psychoanalysis to understand the position that the black finds himself or herself in the white world. Fanon demonstrates how powerful emotional forces quite literally batter the black person into the stereotypical imago that the white person has constructed. We thus start to see an interdisciplinary approach to the study of emotions that combines ideas from sociology, psychoanalysis, philosophy and cultural studies to analyse socio-political phenomena. In the next section we want to outline some of the key ideas and themes in the second part of this book.

Key themes

The first three chapters of the second part of this book weave together ideas around envy and hatred as an emotion and the idea of *ressentiment*.

Clarke and Alford's chapters complement each other in so far as Clarke's exploration of envy as an emotion lays a theoretical introduction to Alford's analysis of hate as an emotion. Clarke's use of psychoanalytic concepts configures a very different notion of *ressentiment* to that portrayed by Demertzis who takes a philosophical approach to *ressentiment* and populism in a political sociology of emotion.

Clarke's approach to the study of emotion is firmly psycho-social. That is, it contains an analysis of the underlying unconscious dynamics in social life as well as the conscious socio-structural elements that form social interaction and society. Using the work of Melanie Klein (1952, 1957) Clarke explores psychoanalytic renditions of envy as an emotion arguing that although the term is used to mean many different things in everyday language, in psychoanalysis its meaning is far more specific; it is an expression, projection and deflection of what psycho-analysts call the 'death drive' – Thanatos. In Kleinian psychoanalysis envy is an entirely destructive emotion as it blocks the possibility of the greatest passion – love – existing at all, by destroying all that is good. This has serious consequences in social and political life, argues Clarke, as certain types of envy can be seen to form the emotional basis of racism and ethnic hatred. Envy stands as a projective and destructive attack on the processes that underlie many forms of the reconciliation of difference. The racist seeks to destroy all that is good in the Other because he or she cannot have it himself or herself. The Other is envied not only for being sexual and disinhibited, but also for having in phantasy stolen something that rightfully belongs to us. This, argues Clarke, is at the heart of the new politics of fear that is currently sweeping the United Kingdom in relation to asylum seekers and refugees. Unconscious phantasies about the way people are and exist in the world get transferred to mainstream politics through distorted perceptions and fears. After Richards (2000), Clarke argues that it is important that we understand what is *inside* our politicians and leaders in order that we can vote for those leaders who do not contain unmodulated envy and are able to manage the rivalry that exists between groups in a nation. If we do not then psychotic anxieties are mobilised and we spiral into a politics of fear where the other becomes demonised and persecuted. Clarke concludes by arguing that unless envy is modulated it becomes entirely destructive: if excessive envy is allowed to interfere with intergenerational success; that is, if we do not encourage our children to do better than us, then *ressentiment* will damage the future for further generations to come.

Focussing on the case of Sinedu Tadesse, an undergraduate at Harvard University who stabbed her roommate to death while she slept, Fred Alford explores the idea of hatred as an emotion and more precisely the consequences of hatred of thought. In this chapter Alford argues that in order for us to understand the hatred that binds communities and nations together, that is an imitation of love, we need to understand what binds those who hate to their victims. Again, in Alford's paper we see a co-joining of sociological, psychological and philosophical perspectives that give a wider view of social and political phenomena.

For Alford, hate is a relationship both with others and with ourselves; that is, our relationship with others also constructs our own psyche, not as mirror but in more complicated structure of knowing. The crux of Alford's argument is that hatred is more than simple projection or intolerance of others – hatred for Alford is an expression of the death drive in the realm of knowledge, where destructiveness is mobilised against our own thinking capacities. Using the work of Melanie Klein, Alford argues that hate is most frequently encountered as a paranoid fear of aggression; in other words, one's own hatred projected onto the world. In a discussion of envy Alford notes that this was precisely what was reflected in Sinedu's diary, hating her roommate for goodness that she could never enter, let alone possess. In turning to discussion of the nature of evil largely through reference to Arendt's (1965, 1973) work, Alford posits another way of conceptualising different levels – shallow and deep evil – and relates them to thoughtfulness. In discussing the ideas of *thought* and *thoughtlessness* Alford notes that we seem to assume that thought is difficult and we associate it with great thinkers. But what if thought, understood as thinking about what we are doing, is both the easiest and the most difficult task in the world? Using Bion's (1984, 1989) ideas, Alford argues that the reason why some people have trouble in thinking is tied in with Bion's idea of attacks on linking. In other words, it is easy to have thoughts, but more difficult to put them together, to link them. For Alford, attacks on linking are attacks on emotions, or more precisely the link between emotion and its object. If you break the link between emotion and object then the emotion loses its energy. Attacks on linking destroy thought, and it is not difficult to say that Sinedu lost her ability to think, argues Alford; crucially this loss consists of an inability to use symbol instead of object and word instead of deed. Her victim's body not only became a slate on which she inscribed her rage (the victim was stabbed 45 times), but also her longing and desire, what Sinedu could no longer bear to feel. Alford concludes by arguing that there is something doubly difficult in thinking about hate. Not only does the powerful emotion of hate make thinking difficult, the same could be said of love, shame and desire, but also there is a dimension to hatred that hates thought itself. This is the job of us all, to recognise this tendency and avoid the exploitation of the hatred of thought in politics.

The question of *ressentiment* continues in Nicolas Demertzis' chapter, which addresses a political sociology of the emotions in relation to populism. In Demertzis' work we see a shift away from the psychoanalysis of the emotions to a political and philosophical sociology of the interpretation of emotion. Demertzis is adamant that a political sociology of the emotions should differentiate itself from an 'emotive political sociology' because the latter would reduce political phenomena to emotions and feeling whereas the former would explicitly integrate an emotional perspective in the examination of political phenomena. A political sociology of the emotions for Demertzis is political sociology that uses an affective filter to examine the objects of study. In this case Demertzis is using *ressentiment* to analyse Greek populism.

In a comprehensive overview of the concept of *ressentiment* Demertzis differentiates between Nietzschean and non-Nietzschean interpretations. Non-Nietzschean views include those of Strawson (1974) who sees resentment as a negative reactive attitude that someone develops in relation to another negative attitude towards him or her. Rawls (1971, 1991) defines resentment as a moral sentiment, which arises as wrongs are done. Barbalet's (1998) view is that *ressentiment* is an active feeling determined by specific social structures which determine in turn the intensity of class struggle. From these perspectives *ressentiment* is therefore an unpleasant feeling that leads to an active posture. This is in contrast to Nietzschean approaches where *ressentiment* is construed as the morality of weak people, which leads to inaction. For Demertzis the main proponent of Nietzsche's view is Max Scheler who inherits the largely negative view of *ressentiment*. Indeed, for Demertzis, what Scheler means by resentful 'transvaluation' is a substitution where old values stay in the back of the psyche and overcast new ones, what Scheler calls 'value' blindness. Demertzis concludes that *ressentiment* is an unpleasant moral feeling which operates as a reliving of repressed and endless vindictiveness, hostility and envy. In other words, it is the outcome of repetition rather than working through or transformation.

In trying to explain and analyse populism and in particular Greek populism, Demertzis argues that the rise of the Greek socialists (PASOK) in the 1970s was driven by an array of emotions which are typical of populations undergoing rapid social change and mobility. These emotions include vindictiveness, spite, envy and ressentiment. PASOK was heavily supported by new middle strata with its origins in the defeat of the civil war (1946–49). Although they were more or less integrated socially and economically, until mid-1970s they were politically marginalised and dominated. As an effect, for more than twenty years they were resentful against the post-civil war 'establishment'. This resentment came from the conflict between desire (political inclusion) and impotence (political losers with repressed vindictiveness) and served as the social psychological basis for the nurturing of Greek populism in the 1980s. When PASOK took office in 1981, ressentiment led to vengeance because it could be released and acted out publicly. Thus Demertzis gives us an analysis of what happens when emotions are pent up over a number of decades. *Ressentiment* grows and fades and is replaced by other emotions contributing to the formation of collective identities and the consolidation of political institutions.

In his chapter Simon Thompson argues that close attention to the emotion of anger can help us understand the political world. He notes that there are two distinct and closely related ideas in the study of anger in politics. The first is the notion that anger often leads to mobilisation; that is, the idea that anger as an emotion is capable of motivating people into political action and participation. Second, we have the idea that the reason people mobilise is to often to overcome some form of perceived injustice. Indeed, Thompson argues that the study of anger can play a key role in both political science and political philosophy. If anger is something people feel when they experience injustice, then understanding anger may offer some insight into the nature of justice itself. If anger as an emotion motivates political action, then its study may well offer new insights into the character of struggles for power. Bringing these together, argues Thompson, should give us a clearer insight into why people engage in collective action in order to try and achieve justice together.

Using the work of Axel Honneth (1995) on recognition, Thompson explores the notion of negative emotional reactions, such as anger, which Honneth argues provide the motivating force behind recognition. In sketching the fundamental elements of Honneth's account, Thompson concentrates on the links between negative emotions, the consciousness of injustice and the struggle for recognition. He argues that in Honneth's model of recognition negative emotions such as anger perform a twofold function. First, they provide insight into the situation of the people experiencing these emotions. Second, they provide a motivational function for people to break out of the situation they find themselves in. Anger therefore performs both a cognitive and a mobilising role in the politics of recognition. In some sense Thompson presents a positive aspect of a negative emotion that is in some way contra to the *ressentiment* outlined in both Clarke's and Demertzis' work. In comparing and contrasting Honneth's work with that of Aristotle, Thompson highlights some striking similarities and differences in the work of the two thinkers on emotion. Aristotle, argues Thompson, endorses a cognitive account of the emotions which does not oppose emotion and reason; rather, there are often circumstances in which it is entirely rational to be angry or irrational to be unemotional. Similarly Honneth does not oppose reason to emotion; rather, he believes that emotions can give us information about a situation and therefore good reason to act. Aristotle also believes that in some circumstances anger can be justified and in others not. Honneth on the other hand does not consider whether emotions can be more or less justifiable. Both thinkers however seem to agree that emotions have a role to play in the explanation of action and also endorse what Thompson terms an 'ethics of recognition'. Aristotle suggests for example that we become angry when we are not given the respect that we expect, whilst Honneth would argue that negative emotions arise from the violation of our expectations of recognition. Finally, argues Thompson, both thinkers make certain assumptions about the status order which underlies their accounts of emotion. In Aristotle we see an assumption that promotes hierarchy; in other words, we would feel more anger if insulted by an inferior rather than an equal. In contrast, Honneth makes a distinction between pre-modern societies where hierarchy reigns and modern society where we have strong egalitarian principles. This transition for Honneth is a matter of moral progress.

Thompson's rationale for this focus on Aristotle and Honneth is that their work offers the possibility for connecting accounts of everyday suffering, theories of justice and theories of collective action. Thompson outlines the way in which Honneth attempts to combine empirical analysis which seeks to explain the character of social conflicts with a normative theory which aims to describe and justify an ideal society. Thompson considers various ways that this link may fail and highlights the way in which, for example, we could have hurt feelings without injustice just as easily as we can have injustice without hurt feelings. Thompson argues that Honneth finds himself pulled in two ways, either he aligns himself with philosophers who defend a strongly cognitive view of the emotions and thus risks overlooking the importance of the cultural political environment or he takes into account the role that mediation plays in the cultural political environment and thus dilutes his insight into the cognitive and mobilising role of the emotions themselves. Thompson sees no way that Honneth can square this circle. So in this chapter, we see a deeply philosophical eye cast over the role of emotions in political life. In some sense, although Thompson focuses on a negative emotion, his analysis holds out the hope that we can think about anger and its constructive role in the politics of recognition and in collective action. In a similar vein, the final substantive chapter in this book looks at the role of compassion in post-emotional society.

In Hoggett's chapter we see a psychoanalytic and philosophical reading of the notion of compassion which the author also grounds in empirical research. Compassion feels much like a caring emotion associated with love and empathy for the other. Sketching a resounding critique of Martha Nussbaum's (2001) work, Hoggett draws our attention to the psychoanalytic concepts of identification and projective identification to unravel the nature of the emotion we call 'compassion'. For Hoggett, while Nussbaum's project of emphasising rationality in the analysis of emotion is welcome, it tends to underestimate the affective and bodily dimensions of compassion within a narrowly rationalistic framework. Her framework assumes a unitary view of the human subject which, for Hoggett, constrains us from comprehending the full complexity of the human subject.

For Nussbaum we can demonstrate the intelligence of compassion by delineating three cognitive elements of judgement, which are inherent in the make-up of the emotion. First, we have a judgement of size; we feel more compassion if the misfortune of another is greater. Second, there is a judgement of non-desert; in other words, did the person bring the misfortune on himself or herself? Finally, there is a judgement, which is eudaimonistic – is the person a significant element in the feeler of the compassion's project or schema of things? Hoggett argues that Nussbaum resorts to a cognitive framework to analyse the similarity between self and other because she does not understand the concept or mechanism of identification which is both crucial in the development of the infant and can blur the boundary between self and other preventing realisation of both the difference and the separateness of the other. Nussbaum's cognitive view of compassion is confirmed in her discussion of pain which she sees as wholly caused by thought rather than having any causal independence. For Hoggett there is something far more affective about compassion – a tugging of the heart, throbbing and aching – because if we are not affected by the suffering of the other then our response becomes mere duty, compliance or social conformity. For Hoggett, a condition of compassion is that the self is affected, moved or touched by some other, but this not necessarily empathy, and he is careful to distinguish between empathic and non-empathic forms of compassion. In the latter, the suffering other seeks to get through to an often impermeable self. This is evident for Hoggett in the institutions of government where the liberal style of politics protects us from the sufferings of others, particularly the 'undeserving', while seemingly being responsive to the deserving few who are increasingly seen as 'customers'.

It is here that we see a real paradox in Nussbaum's work in that to base compassion on a judgement of non-desert turns the political into the ethical and vice versa, leaving very little protection for those who are increasingly termed the 'undeserving poor' in the modern (welfare) state. On the one hand, we feel compassion for the victims of Chechen terrorism and at a push the Kosovan refugees, but our own poor seem more out of sight than the sufferings of the poor in Dafur if only they could portray themselves as innocent victims rather than troublemakers. Essentially Hoggett is arguing for a durable, less conditional form of compassion, which he illustrates with examples from his own research. After all, argues Hoggett, Nussbaum's tidy distinctions, between innocence and culpability, non-desert and desert break down on the housing estates of Britain's poor.

Thus to conclude this introduction we can see how emotions like envy, ressentiment, love, hate and anger proliferate in political practices and discourse. We can also see how many of these emotions have a double bind: the underlying ressentiment fuelling the Greek socialist party almost certainly took it into office, but the after-effects led to vengeance. We can also see that anger is a double-edged sword: on the one hand it is destructive, on the other it leads to political mobilisation and participation. Compassion too, has a double meaning, the bind often comes between those deserving or not, those recognised or not, and those we are able to feel empathy with. The analysis of these emotions calls for an interdisciplinary approach drawing on sociology, philosophy, and psychoanalysis in tandem with mainstream political studies. The chapters that follow give a broad synthesis of these themes and approaches in the practical application of the study of emotions in social and political life.

5
Envy and *Ressentiment*

Simon Clarke

Introduction

This Chapter explores psychoanalytic renditions of the concept of envy as an emotion. The term 'envy' is used to mean many different things in everyday language but in psychoanalysis its meaning is far more specific – envy is an expression, projection and deflection of Thanatos – the death drive. This is a particularly important concept in Kleinian psychoanalysis as envy blocks the very possibility of love existing at all by destroying all that is good. This can have serious social consequences and the second half of this chapter addresses envy in racism, politics and passion in everyday life, relating the concept to the social arena and social action.

The concept and idea of envy as an emotion is used in everyday life on a daily basis, and often arbitrarily to describe certain social encounters, psychodynamic situations, feelings, which lead to destructive outcomes. Kate Barrows (2002) notes that envy was recognised as a problem long before the invention of psychoanalysis. Paraphrasing Chaucer (1958), Barrows explains that ' envy is full of sorrow in another man's goodness and prosperity, but joyous in another man's misfortune' (Barrows, 2002, p. 3). It is even used in the context of a begrudging admiration for the achievements of others: ' I'm green with envy' said with a smile and clenched teeth. It is often used to describe the less comfortable situation of a grudging contemplation of more fortunate persons. The term 'envy' then has two clear meanings: the first less destructive form in which we have begrudging admiration, and the second form, which Barrows uses Chaucer to illustrate, that psychoanalysts describe as the spoiling destructive attack. The concept of envy has been addressed by social psychologists and psychoanalysts who argue about it from one end of the theoretical spectrum to the other – envy as a reciprocal exchange in a social encounter to envy as an expression of the death drive.

In 1957 the psychoanalyst Melanie Klein put forward a hypothesis that Hanna Segal (1989) argues was to shake the psychoanalytic world. Klein argued that envy is one of the most primitive and fundamental emotions: an expression, projection and deflection of Thanatos, of the death drive; an attack on the life instinct, the wanton destruction of the good object; and the denial of life itself – *ressentiment*. (Nicolas Demertzis gives a very different reading in his contribution to this book.) In this chapter, I want to examine an in-depth Kleinian psychoanalytic reading of envy to show how psychoanalytic ideas can help us understand the social implications of psychic life, in particular the effect that envy can have on the social encounter. This should serve as an introduction to Fred Alford's chapter on 'Hate' in which he looks at the concept in relation to envy using empirical examples. For Alford, hatred is not just about the intolerence of otherness but an expression of the death drive. Envy hates the good because good alone is truly self sufficient, needing and wanting nothing from the envious one. I therefore explore envy as an emotion and argue after Klein that it has devastating social consequences. Envy in its most virulent form undermines the development of one of the greatest passions of all – love. This is not a case of love turning to hate; rather, envy blocks the possibility of love existing at all by destroying all that is good.

Thinking about envy psychoanalytically

If we look at envy through a psychoanalytic lens, rather than restricting ourselves to its everyday usage, we have a rather different *interpretation* of this emotion. As Betty Joseph (1989) has noted, envy has been paid little attention to by psychoanalysts, which is strange given that it is such a widely discussed emotion. Freud talked only about a very specific form of envy, 'penis envy', and it was not until the publication of *Envy and Gratitude* in 1957 that the significance of envy became an issue of debate in the psychoanalytic world. Melanie Klein has written extensively on envy and described a very precise form of it which differs quite significantly from the everyday usage of the term (although related). For Klein, envy is entirely destructive. It is a destructive attack on the sources of life, it is innate, and it is reminiscent of Nietzschian *ressentiment*. It is a primitive raging outburst against all that is good, with the intent to destroy in full the good object.

Klein makes a clear distinction between envy, jealousy and greed (see also Hinshelwood, 1989; Joseph, 1989; Segal, 1989). Jealousy excludes another from good; destructiveness is a by-product of the exclusion and usually involves a second party. Greed operates similarly by taking the whole of the good, regardless of the consequences that others may suffer, and, again, destructiveness is a by-product of the process. Envy, however, 'seeks to destroy the good itself' (Alford, 1989, p. 37). In other words, what makes envy so destructive or dangerous is that it attempts to destroy good rather than bad. The sharpest distinction between envy and greed is that the former is bound up in projection, the latter in introjection. Klein (1997) notes:

> Greed is an impetuous and insatiable craving, exceeding what the subject needs and what the object is able and willing to give. At the unconscious level, greed aims primarily at completely scooping out, sucking dry, and devouring the breast: that is to say, its aim is destructive introjection. (Klein, 1957, p. 181)

There is no triangular social situation in envy as with jealousy. Envy involves two persons, subject and object, in which there is a comparison of the self with another person or object. Objects, for Klein, as Hinshelwood notes, are at least as important as drive(s); in fact, in Klein's notion of phantasy, the object is inherent in the drive.

For Klein, envy is an expression, projection, or deflection of the death instinct – an attack on the life instinct in which there is a primary confusion between good and bad. Hostility is directed at an object that excites a need (the breast). Hanna Segal explains:

> The love, care and food received from the mother stir in the infant two opposite reactions: one of gratification leading to love, a primitive form of gratitude, the other of hostility and envy, based on the realisation that the source of food, love and comfort lies outside one's self. (Segal, 1989, p. 139)

Envy, after Hinshelwood (1989) is therefore the hatred of the capacity to excite, and the satisfaction of the need which is excited. In other words, envy of the breast is stirred by gratification, and the infinite riches of the breast's resources (Segal, 1989, p. 140). Envy involves both life and death instincts: the drive to life in terms of the recognition of a need and the urge towards an object, the drive to death in the form of attacks upon the object. This fusion is persistent in envy. Envy is therefore, for Klein, a constitutional destructive drive.

There is often a confusion between frustration and envy in relation to the breast, but envy is not related to the frustration of instinctual impulses *per se*. It is not the withholding breast that seeks gratification for itself that is envied; rather envy is the spoiling of something good *because* it is good, not because it is frustrating. Klein thought that gratitude was a specific feeling that arose from a sense of enjoyment and satisfaction in relation to the object (breast). Envy is an attack on an object that provides gratification rather than frustration. But as Segal notes, to add a layer of complexity and paradox to this, envy can be stirred by frustration 'since the infant idealizes the breast in his phantasy', and in phantasy the infant may imagine that the nourishing breast is actually being enjoyed by the breast itself (Segal, 1989, p. 140). In an envious state the infant attempts to spoil that which is good. This has a defensive dynamic, in that the infant no longer feels the pain of envy – spoiling is therefore a defence against, and an expression of envy.

Envy is often modulated into jealousy as the depressive position is worked through. Klein is clear that jealousy 'is based on envy, but involves a relation to at least two people; it is mainly concerned with love that the subject feels is his due and has been taken away' (Klein, 1957, p. 181). Jealousy therefore involves at least a triangular social situation – the subject, object and the object that arouses anxiety, and it has something to do with possession. Klein's use of the term 'jealousy' reveals a deeper reading of Oedipus – pure violence and persecution; jealousy emerges out of this as a specific affect that allows admiration of the person towards whom the jealousy is felt.

As Segal (1997) notes, jealousy is a more sophisticated feeling than envy 'belonging to the Oedipal triangle. It is based on love, and the hatred of the rival is a function of the love for the object of desire' (Segal, 1989, p. 141). Greed, that is, possession of all the goodness of the object, may also cover up envy. In reality, for Segal, envy, jealousy and greed are related and interacting feelings. So, in greed we may want all the goodness of the object, but this may be a manic defence against the pain of envy. In *Clinical Klein*, Robert Hinshelwood argues that 'Jealousy, however painful, is a progression towards a state of mind in which appreciation (if not yet love) begins to show itself and grows stronger within the mixture of feelings' (Hinshelwood, 1994, p. 143).

Envy on the other hand seeks to expel, to put bad objects into some other in order to destroy their peace and happiness. Envy is a destructive form of projective identification: to look maliciously or spitefully *into*, 'to produce misfortune by his evil eye' (Klein, 1997, p. 181*n*). Envy, if excessive, becomes part of the basic pathology of the paranoid schizoid and depressive positions. Envy interferes with the introjection of the idealised good breast in the paranoid schizoid position, since the good object has been attacked and spoiled. For Klein this interferes with the creation of the fledgling ego and the transition to depressive functioning. Introjection of a good and trustworthy object is crucial in the development of the child – destruction of the good object leads to a confusion between good and bad. Again Hanna Segal elucidates:

> Envious attacks on the ideal breast preclude the introjection of a good object which would strengthen the ego. This gives rise to a painful vicious circle. The more the good internal object is destroyed, the more impoverished the ego feels, and this in turn increases envy. (Segal, 1989, p. 143)

Similarly, envy in the depressive position leads to a spiralling back to manic defences. An envious attack on a good loving object gives rise to intense feelings of persecutory guilt and anxiety. Envy and anxiety stand as a barrier to the reconciliation of good and bad in the depressive position (the depressive position for Klein is a group of attitudes in which we start to see both good and bad in whole people). Arguably, envy compounds the anxiety associated with reparation in the depressive position as the damaged object remains in a superior position. Envy makes reparation almost impossible as manic defences are reinforced. This instils in the infant (and adult) a sense of hopelessness.

Meira Likierman (2001) untangles Klein's theory to produce two accounts of primary envy. First, there is the destructive form of envy that I have discussed, with its wanton and gratuitous attack on the good object – a senseless emanation of the death instinct. As Likierman argues, if this is taken as the main message of Klein's work, 'it seems to confirm it as the fitting conclusion to a treatise on human negativity' (Likierman, 2001, p. 180). There is, however, for Likierman, another form of primary envy in Klein's work which relates to the unavailable breast – to the pain and suffering experienced by the infant through deprivation. In this context we move away from the idea of envy as an emanation of Thanatos, to envy as an understandable reaction to infantile deprivation. In this form of envy the external environment plays a significant role in Klein's theory. So, if a child is poorly fed, deprived of nourishment, there is an increase in persecutory anxiety, the infant becomes aggressive, and this form of aggression can take the form of envy. Thus for Likierman:

> Klein's ideas on deprivation fit into her views on primitive psychic life in a much more logical way, and represent the strand of 'Envy

and Gratitude' that is in continuity with a central aspect of Klein's lifelong work that portrays early life as a struggle to establish a core of goodness and security in the personality. (Likierman, 2001, p. 181)

As Likierman notes, for Klein, early life experience and deprivation amount to far more than mere vague experiences of pain; they shape the way in which the child develops and copes in later life. What Klein actually says, though, is that deprivation increases *greed* and *persecutory anxiety*. There is in the infant's Phantasy an inexhaustable breast – the good object of its greatest desires. When deprived of this, the child hates the good object, it becomes the mean and begrudging breast – envy spoils the primal good object (Klein, 1957, pp. 183–186). Thus we have the second constitutional agent that Klein describes in *Envy and Gratitude* – that of the fragile ego. Put quite simply, some people are better predisposed to deal with life's ups and downs than others, to deal with everyday deprivations and experiences – some people need more comforting and nurturing than others.

Thus we have a move from a primary destructive force, the death instinct, towards the hatred of all that is good in others, a constitutional drive as Klein would put it. This is envy. Envy can arise from Thanatos, from absence which evokes the death drive and from the effects of deprivation on a fragile ego. This destructiveness can soon be placed in others and manifests itself in jealousy. Jealousy is distinct from envy in that it does acknowledge that a rival possesses good; destructiveness is a by-product of the jealous person's attempt to try to attain the good object, not destroy it. Thus, as I noted earlier, however painful, jealousy is often a positive step from envy in which positive feelings are inter-twined with destructiveness. There is a spectrum from the wanton invasion and spoiling of the good object (envy) to healthy competition and admiration as we move to or attain depressive functioning. This, Hinshelwood argues, is complimentary to the progress of projective identification, the modification from violent expulsion to a form of communicative empathy.

The problem of envy

Criticisms of Klein's concept of envy are numerous. Segal (1989) notes that the publication of *Envy and Gratitude* and the paper which preceded it caused a storm of controversy (Segal, 1989, p. 147). It was thought that the young infant simply was not capable of having such sophisticated feelings and emotions, that envy is too complex a state of mind for the young infant: 'rage and frustration were conceivable, envy aroused by good experience, was not' (Segal, 1989, p. 148). Klein was accused of blaming the infant, reverting to a doctrine of original sin and renaming it as envy. Segal notes this debate about envy was also in some sense a continuation of the controversy about how much ego and object awareness there is at birth. Klein is clear about this: the ego functions from the beginning of life, object relations exist from the very earliest post-natal experience, from birth. The emphasis for Klein is on unconscious forces. She concludes the short paper *The Mutual Influences in the Development of the Ego and Id* (1952, 1997) with the following comment:

> I shall end by restating a well-known fact – one of which, however, we become more and more convinced the deeper we penetrate into the mind. It is the recognition that the unconscious is at the root of all mental processes, determines the whole of mental life, and therefore that only by exploring the unconscious in depth and width are we able to analyse the total personality. (Klein, 1997, p. 60)

Hinshelwood (1989) provides a useful commentary on some more contemporary criticisms of Klein's concept of envy. First, Kleinians have failed to respond to general criticisms of the death instinct and therefore envy, and the failure of this response indicates either their inability to do so, or their dogmatism (see Kernberg, 1980). Likierman notes, 'to attribute destructive impulses to the infant was one thing; it was quite another to propose a curious anti-life tendency which underpins attacks on the very mothering resources that are essential to mental growth' (Likierman, 2001, p. 177). Second, there is Joffe's (1969) critique in which he misreads the Kleinian concept of envy in an ego psychological framework. Joffe assumes that envy is related to the frustrating breast, and the frustration of instinctual needs. As we have seen, this is not the case; envy is the spoiling of something good because it is good, not because it frustrates. Hinshelwood argues that Joffe has merely shown that the Kleinian concept of envy is not compatible with the ego-psychology framework. Indeed, for Hinshelwood, 'it becomes merely a choice between two whole frameworks. In fact, since 1946 Kleinian theory has moved so far away from ego-psychology that it is hard for those of one camp to grasp the important features and nuances of the conceptual framework of the other' (Hinshelwood, 1989, p. 176).

The final criticism that Hinshelwood draws our attention to is that the Kleinian concept of envy supports the view that Kleinian psychoanalysis is pessimistic in the extreme, focusing on aggression and the wanton destructiveness of human nature. This may be true to a certain degree, and it is also true that Klein always stressed the role of both love and hate from the earliest years of our life. I would argue that in the context of looking at and addressing social issues and social justice Klein's view on human nature is more realistic than pessimistic. We all tread this tightrope, as Robert Young (1994) has stressed, between love and hate, between the paranoid splitting of good and bad. One only has to look at reactions to world events over the past 50 years to witness the denigration of others and the idealisation of *us*. This is characteristic of the totalitarian and dominating impulses of Western civilisation, of imperialism, and marked by the psychotic anxieties generated by leaders and groups and the paranoid splitting between *us* and *them*. Much of this is underpinned by a modulated form of envy and destructiveness which I want to address in the next section of this chapter on envy in relation to racism, politics and everyday life.

Envy in racism, politics and everyday life

How do we relate the concept of envy to the social arena and to social action? Previously (Clarke, 1999a, b, 2003) I have outlined what I believe to be a Kleinian psychoanalytic sociology of racism. I want to reiterate some of those themes later in this chapter to ground my argument empirically in social behaviour, as racism is fuelled by some of the most powerful emotions that we can know and perhaps not know about. So, for example, we may perceive others as possessing something good that has been stolen from us: jobs, cultures, ways of life. We try to take it back, but we cannot have it all (greed), so we destroy it (envy). In seeking ethnically to cleanse 'others', we are in fact cleansing ourselves, ridding ourselves of the discomfort of envy. The racist in envy seeks to destroy the good that he cannot have. The racist, unable to enjoy cultural difference is a manifestation of envy, making bad and spoiling what is good and destroying what he cannot have.

As I have noted, envy stands as a barrier to reparation in the depressive position and often leads to a spiralling back to manic defences, not the least of which are splitting, denigration and virulent projective identifications. In order to understand the role that depressive anxiety plays in the explanation of racism it is necessary to elucidate Klein's notion of positions. The paranoid schizoid position is characterised by a splitting of difference. Good and bad objects are split, the good introjected, the bad projected outward into someone or something else. Persecutory anxiety stems from the fear of internal and external attack. Gradually the tendency to split good and bad lessens as the fear of bad objects diminishes; the child's world becomes less polarised and both good and bad are seen in whole objects. Thus we have the transition to the depressive position. Klein (1997) identifies the depressive position as an integration of experience. Rather than a split there is a perception of whole people containing both good and bad. Conflicts within the self are no longer split and pushed into others; recognition of both good and bad within the self allows recognition of this in others. The depressive position can be viewed as a recognition of the plurality of difference, in which the individual hates the hating self and tries to repair, to make reparation for the damage that has been done. Care for others develops as does guilt, as one realises that the attacked 'other' contains both good and bad. Thus, depressive anxiety fuels the need to make reparation. The depressive position involves fear, anxiety and despair about the ability both to make reparation for those destroyed in phantasy and to overcome one's own destructiveness. The anxiety generated may be so great that it leads to the employment of paranoid schizoid defences.

To apply this to the analysis of racism, we note that anxiety is not created by acceptance and celebration of difference. Rather, the individual's doubt of his ability to accept difference leads to the employment of paranoid schizoid defences. Envy is therefore a projective and destructive attack that stands as a barrier to reconciliation in the depressive position. The racist seeks to destroy the good that he cannot have. Excluding and persecuting others alleviates the discomfort of not only envy but also guilt and depressive anxiety. The urge to make reparation, in itself, as I have argued, perpetuates and justifies racism for the racist. When depressive anxiety invokes schizoid defences, what ensues is a vicious and destructive envious attack on others.

Farhad Dalal (2002) has also seen envy as a precipitator of racism. Dalal argues that the Kleinian concept of envy adds a new twist to the death instinct, reminding us that the intention behind envy is not to appropriate goodness, but to destroy its source. Dalal raises some problems in the psychoanalytic analysis of racialization. So, for example, for envy to be the precipitator of racism, the attack on the racialised Other must be because the Other has some perceived goodness. The problem, for Dalal, 'is that the hated racialised Other is more often than not the more deprived of the two' (Dalal, 2002, p. 44). I think Dalal hits at the very heart of the psychoanalysis of racism here, in that while the breast is envied by the infant because of its real goodness, nourishment, fullness and ability to deprive and cause pain, the racialised Other is attacked in envy because of its *phantasised* goodness, potential, potency and fullness. Racism and processes of racialization are, as I have previously argued (Clarke, 1999a, 2002), steeped in phantasy, imagination and uncanny strangeness (Clarke, 2003b). For Dalal, a possible explanation for what amounts to the projection of good onto a bad object, into what should be a safe space, (after all, the racialised Other, by definition cannot be this safe space), is as follows:

> The amalgam of various psycho-social tides (two of the most important being Christianity and the Enlightenment), inculcated the repression of the passions (particularly sex and aggression) in the European Christian. These repressed elements are bound to be split off from consciousness and into a territory which is designated as similarly repellent in some way (enter the racialized Other). The racialized Other is now experienced as containing not only something desirable, but being desire incarnate. (Dalal, 2002, p. 45)

This whole process, for Dalal, leaves the conscious mind feeling perturbed and disgruntled. Hence, my emphasis in other papers on the Freudian uncanny and its relationship to the colonial condition (Clarke, 2001; Clarke and Moran, 2003). The uncanny stranger, the aborigine can evoke feelings that are long-lasting, but strikingly familiar – as Dalal notes, the racialised Other is not only envied for being rampantly sexual and disinhibited, but also for some vague recollection, or realisation that the thing that resides within them rightfully belongs to us. The issue of asylum, and asylum seekers in the United Kingdom has seen the growth of a new politics of fear in which the Other threatens to not only engulf us but destroy us from within. In a dangerous political amalgam, the asylum seeker not only has become a popular folk demon in the media but is now being equated with terrorism. Thus the dispersal of refugees from Kosovo and Somalia, North Africa and the Middle East around the country has, if we were to believe the media, planted a stranger within our community who lives off of us, whilst returning nothing. It is no wonder that media coverage has concentrated on policies for sending 'them' home, rather than understanding the position that another human being finds himself or herself in. They, the stranger, the refugee, represent all our fears of displacement, of chaos, and represent a threat to our psychic stability. This does not seem on first sight to be anything to do with envy, and perhaps to think of this reaction in terms of jealousy is more appropriate as stories in the press focus on taking away and not giving. Certainly the politics of fear has added a new psychodynamic dimension to asylum: the asylum seeker represents not only our own fears of chaos and displacement, but also the possibility of being destroyed from within by both our own phantasies of terror and the terrorist in our midst.

Ian Craib (2001) notes a different intensity or dynamic of envy arguing that while envy or an envious attack can be violent in the extreme, underlying torture and murders that involve mutilation, it operates in everyday social interactions in more subtle ways. Think of the way in which subtle projective identifications often make people feel a particular way in social situations, usually unspoken but often painful. Envy is more outright. There is, as Craib notes, a tendency through envious comments to undermine people's achievements or successes, or something good that has happened to them:

> If my friend tells me that he's off to Switzerland for a skiing holiday, my unthinking response is a half joking 'It's alright for you, some of us have to stay here and keep the organisation going', perhaps half hoping that I might spoil his fun by sending him off feeling guilty. (Craib, 2001, p. 65)

The problem with envy, as Craib notes, is that it is easy to talk about it in a humorous and sophisticated way, easy to see it in others, but very difficult to recognise and acknowledge in oneself. I think this is a problem that Betty Joseph (1989) recognises when she talks of the broader sociological implications of envy. In her paper *Envy in Everyday Life* Joseph relates the concept of envy to our progression through life – to ageing. To age with 'proper resignation' as Joseph describes it, we have to allow our children and the children of others to have things, knowledge, material goods that we have not had access to, we have to identify with and share in their success, we have to make way for them in other words. Life goes on, and we have to accept it. Excessive envy can hinder this process. Just as envy on an individual level is a form of life denial, it can just as easily be applied at a societal level, and our *ressentiment* can damage future generations.

Barry Richards (2000) has used Klein's work in order to situate envy within the social and political world. Envy, in the Kleinian tradition, as Richards' notes, is a direct expression of the death instinct. But Richards also points to a more interesting source of envy, certainly from a social or interactionist viewpoint. In revising Klein, he sees envy as a primary confusion between good and bad, which leads the infant and, presumably, the adult in later life to attack the good object. For Richards:

> Whether we see the primary inability to distinguish the good from the bad as itself a manifestation of the death instinct, or as a separate, though still inherited, component of envy, the constitutional strength of the death instinct and of primary confusion are major determinants of the strength of envy in the individual. (Richards, 2000, p. 68)

This is where the Kleinian view of envy differs significantly from that of the everyday usage of the term, and certainly from a social constructivist viewpoint as expounded by Harré (1986) and Sabini and Silver (1986). For Harré, envy exists as a reciprocal exchange in a social encounter. In other words the emotion that someone would feel in a given situation is a cognitive or a thought response to how they would be expected to feel. What differentiates envy from jealousy, one emotion from another, is the social context in which they are expressed; for example, the moral rights, duties and obligations of the concept of marriage in a given culture. This seems very much a case of 'I expect' because 'You expect' because 'I expect'. Emotion is therefore reduced to a language game, to which Harré gives priority (see Clarke, 2003a for an extended discussion of this argument).

Envy, for Sabini and Silver, acts in service of the self and is a protection against self diminution and denigration; if someone pursues a course of self defence, and in doing so limits the chances of someone else's success, or devalues another, this is likely to be called envy: 'The sexuality in a sin of lust is patent and unavoidable; the self protection in the sin of envy is obscured by envy's secondary but more overt end, the demeaning of another' (Sabini and Silver, 1986 p. 176).

Whereas Sabini and Silver argue that envy is primarily about self-protection, for Klein it is entirely destructive, and ultimately self-destructive. Richards suggests that it might be helpful to think of everyday envy, that is a feeling about one's lot in relation to others, as another way in which primitive envy is modulated and diffused across the social field. For Richards, many feelings that we label 'social envy', when understood psychodynamically, 'dissolve in something more like jealousy, or sibling rivalry' (Richards, 2000, p. 71). In addressing the potential envious consequences of politics for example, Richards argues that the most important thing is that which is *inside* our leaders, and therefore the most healthy electoral choices 'are of politicians who are felt to contain good things, but who do not provoke too much envy of ourselves, and who offer to contain the various forms of modulated envy and rivalry that exist between groups within the nation' (Richards, 2000, p. 74). If we think now directly in terms of social justice then we can see within our own political climate, in which envy is neither modulated nor contained, the direct opposite of this social justice model. The *destructive impulse* is now directed at other groups as our psychotic anxieties are mobilised by political agendas as well as very real and demonstrable fears. This again is apparent in a growing politics of fear where the West and the rest are counterposed and there is an increasing suspicion of those seeking asylum or refuge in the West.

Conclusion

For Klein, envy is innate and the dynamic exists between subject and object; there is no third person. However, we cannot discount the role of social relations in the psychodynamics of emotional interaction. The social world quite plainly has a great influence on the psychic world, and the interplay between the two is not only moderated by psychic mechanisms but by rules, norms, behaviours and morals. As both Klein and Segal have told us, excessive envy in infants can also be accounted for in terms of external factors and circumstances that play an extremely important role. Not the least of these are the socio-economic position of parents and primary carers, the dynamics of groups and organisations, the role of the state and the role of narcissistic leaders. Thus, although Kleinian thinking concentrates fundamentally on the unconscious, it also regards environmental factors as vitally important in the development of the child.

I argue after Klein that envy has far greater social consequences than even constructionists have acknowledged. Envy in its most virulent form undermines the development of one of the greatest passions of all – love. As I have said, but it is important to reiterate, this is not a case of love turning to hate; rather envy blocks the possibility of love existing at all. In relating envy to racism we should not forget that there is both a psychodynamic and a political economy at work. Phantasy and imagination fuel uncanny feelings of that which is old and familiar, which in turn provoke envious attacks on the racialised Other. But also, as we have seen, the socio-economic status of the individual is important if we are to understand the personal expression of emotion. There are huge rifts between those who have access to material goods and riches and those who live in poverty and need, and this is not a case of east and west, or north and south, but on our own doorsteps. Capitalism is as chaotic and schizoid as many of our political leaders, encouraging and indeed creating a wider gulf between rich and poor.

The Kleinian concept of envy is complex, ranging from the wanton destruction of all that is good – an expression of the death drive on one hand, and, as some would argue, the basis of healthy competition on the other. This is further complicated by the idea that envious feeling can arise from both a constitutional drive and an absence or deprivation. There is also the debate as to whether these are largely innate characteristics, or fuelled by psychodynamic processes within a relational context to societal, or psycho-social tides. There is one thing that is absolutely clear however, and that is unless envy is modulated it is entirely destructive. In Betty Joseph's words, life goes on and we have to make way for those who may have better opportunities in life than we. If excessive envy is allowed to interfere with this process then our *ressentiment* will damage further generations.

Acknowledgement

A version of this chapter originally appeared in the journal *Psychoanalysis, Culture and Society*. Vol. 9(1) pp. 105–117, 2003 and is reproduced with the permission of Palgrave Macmillan Journals.

6
Hatred of Thought

C. Fred Alford

On the morning of May 28, 1995, Sinedu Tadesse, a junior at Harvard, stabbed her roommate Trang-Ho 45 times while Trang lay sleeping in her bed in their Harvard dormitory. By the time police arrived, Sinedu had hanged herself in the bathroom. Unlike most killers, the Ethiopian student left a detailed diary of her emotional state in the years leading up to the killing.

Unlike her roommate, Sinedu was not a popular student. She had difficulty finding a roommate and was elated when Trang-Ho agreed to share a suite with her. But they did not get along, in part because Trang's boyfriend frequently slept over, and Trang was looking for another roommate. Sinedu found the humiliation intolerable.

> You know what I fear? I fear that shitty cringing feeling that accompanies me.... Should my rooming thing does [*sic*] not work out in a way that makes me hold my head high and speak of it proudly. (Thernstrom, 1996)

If she could have, Sinedu would have inflicted this terrible cringing feeling on her roommate. Only that, it seems, would have made her feel better, and that, she knew, was impossible. "Our situations would never reverse, for me to be the strong and her to be the weak. She'll live on tucked in the warmth and support of her family while I cry alone in the cold."

It was a situation made worse, or at least more pathetic, by the way so many seemed to confuse them, regarding the roommates as virtually identical non-western exotics. Even at the memorial service, Harvard's minister could not seem to keep victim and executioner straight, referring to both as victims, asking the Lord to forgive them both. "Media accounts made them sound like twins, petite, hardworking foreign-born premed junior biology majors."

Unable to become Trang-Ho, unable to trade places with her, Sinedu decided to kill herself, while taking Trang-Ho with her. Only that would feed her hatred. "The bad way out I see is suicide and the good way out killing, savoring their fear and [then] suicide. But you know what annoys me the most, I do nothing."

In his novel *Immortality*, Milan Kundera (1990, p. 24) has one of his characters say that "hate traps us by binding us too tightly to our adversary." What Kundera (or perhaps just his character) fails to understand is that this is just what is wanted, hatred allowing us to pretend that what we want is to be free, but never giving us the chance. In hatred we transform interpersonal bonds into bondage, and relationships into prisons. For a little while, hate allowed Sinedu to come out of the cold, as she cocooned herself in the warmth of her hate.

Sinedu's strategy did not work for very long; it usually does not. Hatred culminates in violence when the one who hates comes suddenly and late to reality, recognizing that the intensely desired fusion is impossible. By then, however, the one who hates has given up so much of herself to the desire to be the other that there is no going back. The self of the hater has been depleted, and no return is possible, only the perverse satisfaction that the one who is hated will share the annihilation, fusion in the realm of entropy.

In order to understand the hatred that binds communities and nations, the hatred that is the imitation of love, it will be useful to investigate further the hatred that binds those who hate to their victims. Not because group psychology is individual psychology writ large, but because hatred is a relationship on whatever scale it is conducted. Though the importance of hatred is widely appreciated, far too little has been written about it from a perspective that seeks to join psychological insight with social theory.

Hatred is a relationship with others, and it is a relationship with oneself, which is but another way of saying that in structuring our relationships with others we are at the same time structuring our psyches, ourselves. That, I take it, is a non-controversial assumption (at least when stated so generally), the foundation of object relations theory in psychoanalysis. It is not the case that our relationships with others are mirrored, or reflected, in psychic structure; the relationship is more subtle than that. But the principle remains, as intrapsychic relationships resonate with extrapsychic ones.

Today much writing about hatred assumes that what we really hate is the "Other." Unassimilated otherness and difference is almost unbearable to the benighted human psyche, or so it is often argued. Some, such as Elaine Pagels (1995) in *The Origin of Satan*, write as if Otherness itself were the demon.

> Concluding this book, I hope that this research may illuminate for others, as it has for me, the struggle within Christian tradition between the profoundly human view that "otherness" is evil and the words of Jesus that reconciliation is divine. (p. 184)

Other more psychoanalytically astute writers such as Peter Gay (1993, pp. 68–71), in *The Cultivation of Hatred*, write of hatred of the other in terms of denied sameness. We project onto the other what we cannot abide in ourselves. Hatred, I shall argue, is about more than the intolerance of otherness. Hate is an expression of the death drive in the realm of knowledge.

Psychoanalysis of hate

Freud (1915, p. 138) defined hatred as an ego state that wishes to destroy the source of its unhappiness. What Freud calls the death-drive, what has come to be called, following Jung, as *Thanatos*, is not hatred, but something more and less: more destructive perhaps, but less intensely involved with the object, the source of unhappiness. Thanatos is not merely the instinct to destruction. It is the more general impulse to death, which Freud understands as having the quality of Nirvana, total cessation of stimulation. Darkness, night, stillness and death – all are related via the absence of tension and conflict. "All instincts tend toward the restoration of an earlier state of things," says Freud (1920, pp. 30–31), and the earliest state of things is a state of tensionless non-existence: the inertia of non-being.

It is, by the way, not necessary to see Thanatos as a death-drive, that is as an instinct. Thanatos may have more the quality of a raging protest against pain, a protest that makes no distinction between subject and object, cause and effect. As Herbert Marcuse (1961, pp. 119–126) argued in *Eros and Civilization*, his philosophical reinterpretation of Freud, Thanatos is a protest against the agony of existence. The more painful existence, the more attractive the annihilation of death. The mark of Thanatos is that it hardly cares whose death: yours, mine, ours – to Thanatos they are all the same.

To see hatred as rooted in Thanatos, and Thanatos in pain, is not to minimize its destructiveness, but only to point that it is a destructiveness of a certain type, one that would end all tension with the other by obliterating the other along with the self, fusing in the nothingness of the All (Freud, 1920, pp. 32–37). Thanatos is the rage to obliteration: of self, of other, of tension with the other, of tension in the self – among these Thanatos makes no distinction. Thanatos is obliteration as fusion, coming close to what Germans calls *Liebestod*, Romeo and Juliet united for all eternity in death. This is not so far from what Sinedu wanted.

Melanie Klein is one of the few psychoanalysts to take Thanatos seriously, though in Klein's account Thanatos loses its quest for Nirvana, becoming tantamount to primal hatred at the source of our pain. For Freud's Eros contra Thanatos, Klein substitutes love contra hate, the eternal conflict that makes the world go around. Klein rarely, if ever, writes about hate except as it is at war with love. For Klein, hate is most frequently encountered as a paranoid fear of aggression, one's own hatred projected onto the world. The key problem of mental life for Klein is to separate one's love and hate sufficiently in early life to be able to integrate them later. Otherwise we shall be eternally confused as to what is good and what is bad, and so likely to confuse love and hate. For Klein, there is no deeper and more terrifying confusion than this.

While envy is not the root of hatred for Klein, it is hatred's most pernicious expression. Envy hates the good because it is good, because it is separate, whole, and beyond the ability of the hateful one to possess. Envy is hatred of the good because it is good, filled with itself and life, something the envious one cannot bear because it makes him or her feel so empty and cold. Envy hates the good because good alone is truly self-sufficient, needing and wanting nothing from the envious one (Klein, 1975b). Envy is precisely what Sinedu expressed in her diary, destroying Trang-Ho because she was cocooned in a goodness Sinedu could never enter, let alone possess. Envy hates the good because good alone is truly self-sufficient, needing and wanting nothing from the envious one.

A colleague of mine says that Western philosophy would have been spared much woe had Socrates loved Plato back. What he means is that much of Western philosophy is an attempt to create an autonomous self free of the need to be loved by others, but in its heart of heart still enraged that it is not. Fortunately, one need not decide whether this is true of all, most, or some of Western philosophy to understand hate a little better.

Worse than Thanatos?

While both Freud and Klein set Eros against Thanatos, life against death, for Klein there is no Nirvana principle, no connection between the hatred and aggression of Thanatos and the peace and absence of stimulation that Freud writes of in *Beyond the Pleasure Principle* (1920, pp. 34–43). For Freud, the *Todestrieb* ultimately seeks to return to the origin of things, a state of oblivion. There is, in other words, a type of satisfaction inherent in the *Todestrieb*, a satisfaction from which life itself is a long detour. For Klein, on the other hand, the *Todestrieb* is sadism, envy, and destruction. Nothing in Klein's account of the *Todestrieb* suggests she shared Freud's idea that death is the telos of life (Alford, 1989, p. 25).

This might make it seem as if Klein's account of the "death instinct" would be easier to assimilate into mainstream psychoanalytic thought than Freud's. That may not be the case, for Klein makes it clear that the infant and young child hates, envies, and would destroy its mother if it could, regardless of how responsive and loving mother truly is. To be sure, Klein and Kleinians recognize that the mother's response to the child's aggression, how well she is able to contain the child's hatred and envy, will make an enormous difference in how well the child is able to integrate its experiences of loving and hating, and so enter into and remain within the depressive position (Klein, 1975b). Nevertheless, the thesis that the child's hatred and destructiveness is innate, unrelated, at least at first, to the quality of the child's relationship with its mother and others leaves even some sympathetic followers cold. As Meira Likierman puts it,

> To attribute destructive impulses to the infant was one thing; it was quite another to propose a curious anti-life tendency which underpins attacks on the very mothering resources that are essential to mental growth. (Likierman, 2001, p. 177)[1]

If one allows oneself to think about it for very long, Klein's version of the *Todestrieb* is even more troubling than Freud's, as it seeks not even the pleasure of Nirvana, but the destruction of the good that makes even one's own life and growth possible. The only character who comes close to such an awful thesis is Milton's Satan. This is true whether Satan's rage is directed against his benevolent creator God precisely *because* He is generous and kind, asking so little in return (*Paradise Lost* IV, 43–55). Or whether Satan's rage is directed against the mutual love and respect of Adam and Eve before the Fall. Satan is not simply jealous; for he would not have sex with Eve even if he could, eventually procreating Sin and Death out of himself. Rather, Satan simply cannot abide the very existence of such a pure and perfect love as that between Adam and Eve (PL IV, 505–508). What Klein calls envy, the desire to destroy the good because it is good, comes closer to Satan's desire.

Klein draws a sharp distinction between jealousy and envy. We must do the same in order to think clearly about hate. In jealousy, I want to possess goods that belong to you because I do not have them, such as a beautiful spouse, or a lovely house. In envy, I do not want what you have, perhaps because I already have a beautiful spouse and lovely house of my own. Rather, I want to spoil what you have because the very existence of you enjoying these goods makes me feel less good. For me to feel good, you must feel bad. As Chaucer puts it in a passage quoted by Klein (1975b, p. 189), envy is the worst sin because it opposes life and creativity itself.

It is certain that envy is the worst sin, for all other sins are sins only against one virtue, whereas envy is against all virtue and against all goodness. Klein might have continued to quote Chaucer, who goes on the say that envy

> is sorry for all the goodness of one's neighbor, making it different from all other sins. There is scarcely any sin that doesn't have within it some delight, but Envy has within it only anguish and sorrow. (*Canterbury Tales*, "The Parson's Tale," 485–490)[2]

Only Klein, I believe, allows us to fully appreciate the lust to destroy the innocent and good. Only an appreciation of hate that takes this perverted lust seriously has a chance of making sense of this benighted world, for only then do we see why we must put reparation for all the destruction we have witnessed, caused, or imagined at the center of moral life. But perhaps Freud said it best after all, drawing even the ancient gods into this conflict.

> And now, I think, the meaning of the evolution of civilization is no longer obscure to us. It must present the struggle between Eros and Death, between the instinct of life and the instinct of destruction, as it works itself out in the human species. This struggle is what all life essentially consists of, and the evolution of civilization may there-fore be simply described as the struggle for life of the human species. And it is this battle of the giants that our nurse-maids try to appease with their lullaby about Heaven. (Freud, 1930, pp. 121–122)

What it takes to think clearly

In the conclusion I will return to Sinedu and Trang-Ho. I now turn to Hannah Arendt's famous study of the trial of Adolf Eichmann, a study in the banality of evil, as she called it. To be sure, the banality of evil that Arendt discovered in this Nazi bureaucrat is not the same as the vicar's inability to distinguish victim and executioner. Nonetheless, the Reverend Peter J, Gomes' identification of killer and victim reflects a disorder of thought that is widely shared. It is with the inability to think clearly about threatening things that Klein and Arendt, as well as Klein's most independent students – Wilfred Bion and Donald Winnicott – are all concerned.

Arendt covered the trial of Adolf Eichmann in Jerusalem for *The New Yorker* magazine. Though the Holocaust may have been the product of a single evil mind, it required thousands of willing conspirators to carry it out. Few were more important than Eichmann, who organized the transfer of Jews to the death camps. It was Arendt's experience listening to and watching Eichmann day after day that led her to formulate her controversial concept of the banality of evil.

Arendt's report on the trial of Eichmann remains controversial to this day, as Arendt seemed to say that Eichmann was such a banal bureaucrat that he never truly thought about what he was doing, murdering millions of Jews. Indeed, this is what puzzles Arendt so. How could pale little men do such awful deeds, the murder of millions? In coming to terms with this fact, Arendt says that she had to give up her former belief in radical evil.

> It is indeed my opinion now that evil is never "radical," that it is only extreme, and that it possesses neither depth nor any demonic dimension. It can overgrow and lay waste the whole world precisely because it spreads like a fungus on the surface. It [evil] is "thought-defying," as I said, because thought tries to reach some depth, to go to the roots, and the moment it concerns itself with evil, it is frustrated because there is nothing. That is its "banality." Only the good has depth and can be radical. (Elshtain, 1995, p. 76)

Arendt, by the way, never denied the existence of radical evil in the abstract, in theory. If we understand radical evil as malevolence and hate, then Arendt found it in such fictional characters as Iago and Macbeth (Arendt, 1965, p. 229). Not the existence of radical evil, but its absence in Eichmann and his collaborators, is Arendt's position.

Earlier, in *The Origins of Totalitarianism*, Arendt characterized the last stages of totalitarianism as "absolute evil."

> If it is true that in the final stages of totalitarianism an absolute evil appears (absolute because it can no longer be deduced from comprehensively human motives), it is also true that without it we might never have known the truly radical nature of evil. (Arendt, 1973, p. ix)

Though Arendt did not elaborate, the concept of radical evil struck a chord. To be sure, hate and evil are not identical. On the contrary, hate seems to have its own dynamic, a dynamic characterized by Otto Kernberg (1995, p. 69) in terms of structured rage. "The underlying mechanism [of hatred], I am suggesting, is the establishment of an internalized object relationship under the control of structured rage, that is hatred.... Hatred consolidates the unconscious identification with victim and victimizer." Nevertheless, the way in which Klein talks about hatred in terms of the destruction of the good itself because it is good comes so close to Milton's ideal of Satanic evil that it is worth continuing to assume (but not posit) a connection between hate and evil. Not just for literary reasons, but because Klein's thoughts about hatred and death challenge Arendt's concept of the banality of evil. In other words, Klein's account suggests that it is Arendt herself who cannot think deeply enough about hate and evil.

In *Eichmann in Jerusalem*, Arendt (1965) does not change what she thinks about evil. Evil is still defined in terms of its incomprehensibility, what she now calls "thought defying." What changes is her judgment about what makes evil thought defying – that it possesses no qualities to think about. Indeed, one might argue that not even this changed, just the location of evil, so to speak, from deeply rooted to on the surface.

Behind Arendt's reformulation of evil was her determination not to permit Eichmann or any of his fellow Nazis to attain the status of dramatic or romantic demiurges. They must be shown to be who they really were: limited, hollowed-out, pale, and empty men. This is the banality of evil. Especially important for Arendt was to strip evil of its generative power. Above all, evil cannot be creative; evil cannot be allowed to bring anything new into the world (Elshtain, 1995, pp. 84–85).

Surely Arendt is onto something; her program of destroying the legend of the greatness of evil is a worthwhile project. William Blake's *bon mot*, that Satan gets all the best lines in *Paradise Lost*, should remind us that there is something attractive about evil, and that should worry us.

Though Arendt understands something important about evil, aspects of her project are troubling. It is as if the goal of showing that evil cannot be great (even greatly evil and terrible) is so important that something of the horror of the evil gets lost: that behind evil lies the will to destroy the pure, the innocent, and the good because the other is pure, innocent, and good, and the evil doer is not. It is this that Milton's Satan grasps, the same point that Klein knows.

Let me suggest another way of thinking about evil and evil doers, along the lines of the cliché "way down deep he's shallow." Admittedly, the Nazis were shallow men, but that does not mean their evil was shallow. On the contrary, it is because they were shallow men that their evil ran so deep. Evil may be deep even as evil doers are generally (always?) shallow. To make evil deep is not to glorify it, only to suggest that evil is a force that transcends (as the unconscious transcends) the awareness of those who practice it.

At about this point the thoughtful reader may be asking "What is this deep and shallow business anyway? What sort of intuitive but vague distinction does it represent?" One result of the Freudian revolution was to see that even the most ordinary man has a creative unconscious, expressed for example in dreams. Even the most boring bureaucratic may have fantastic phantasies. Phillip Rieff makes this same point when he says "Freud democratized genius by giving everyone a creative unconscious" (Rieff 1961, p. 36). Banal Nazi bureaucrats likely possessed an extraordinary unconscious, filled with phantasies of hate and destruction, as well as perverse urges to purify the world. That these men and women, like Eichmann, may not have been aware of their destructive phantasies, that they may have deeply repressed them, does not mean that these phantasies were not present. On the contrary, the more repressed the phantasy, the greater (not the lesser) power it has over its possessor, as the possessor has no opportunity to exercise rational control over what he knows nothing about. It is incorrect to say that the motivation of someone like Eichmann is shallow. Eichmann may be shallow, but his motivation is deep, as deep as the hating human heart, and the most destructive human phantasy.

Evil may run deep, even as those in whom it runs deep are shallow and banal, unaware of the world of death and destruction that lies within. Perhaps it is the very shallowness of their understanding that makes them more vulnerable to the acting-out of these phantasies when they become socially sanctioned, as was the case under the Nazis. Indeed, in these circumstances we might even be justified in talking about a collective destructive unconscious, though precisely what that might mean remains obscure. Perhaps just that the ideology of the times encouraged and channeled the destructive phantasies of millions in a similar direction, as though to socialize phantasy itself.

Alice Miller gives an example of what this might mean:

I know a woman who never happened to have any contact with a Jew up to the time she joined the *Bund Deutscher Mädel*, the female equivalent of the Hitler Youth. She had been brought up very strictly. Her parents needed her to help out in the household after her siblings (two brothers and a sister) had left home.... Much later she told me with what enthusiasm she had read about "the crimes of the Jews" in *Mein Kampf* and what a sense of relief it had given her to find out that it was permissible to hate someone so unequivocally. She had never been allowed to envy her siblings openly for being able to pursue their careers.... And now, quite unexpectedly, there was such a simple solution: it was all right to hate as much as she wanted; she still remained (and perhaps for this reason was) her parents' good girl and a useful daughter of the fatherland. (Miller 1983, p. 64)

While it may be correct to argue that evil is not creative, reducing the world to the dimensions of pain, suffering, and destruction, one wants to be careful about employing aesthetic categories, such as creativity, to moral debate. Is the good always creative? Sometimes the good itself is boring, and mundane, the tedious work of feeding the hungry, and clothing the poor, including victims who are not always ennobled by their victimhood. Why make creativity the issue one way or the other? Is it not enough to say that evil is bad and should be avoided, whereas goodness is good and should be pursued?

In fact, the deepest anxiety posed by evil seems to be that we shall confuse evil with the good, for they are never so separate as all that. The stories we tell ourselves about good and evil are generally attempts to clarify the borders and boundaries between them, so we never make the terrifying mistake of confusing one for the other. Recall the story of Klein's (1975c) most famous patient, Richard, a little boy who could not keep clear in his own mind whether the cook and the maid were good or bad, to say nothing of his mummy and daddy. He could not do so because of inadequate splitting-and-idealization (Donald Meltzer runs these terms together with hyphens as though they were one process), which fails to protect the good object from the split-off bad parts of the self. The result was confusion and emotional immaturity, as Richard "could not keep the destructive and Hitleresque part of himself from crowding in on and taking over the good part" (Meltzer, 1978, pt 2, p. 64).

Richard is not just a disturbed little boy. He represents the threat faced by us all, that we shall mistake good and bad and so destroy all we love and care about. Culture, institutions, and leaders are generally eager to tell us which is which, and so reinforce paranoid-schizoid defenses against anxiety. From confusion to clarity, but at the cost of dividing the world into two, alienating one's own hatred and aggression in others and fighting it there. Here is a defense that almost guarantees that we shall never arrive at a more complex resolution of our angst, one that sees the good and bad mixed together in ourselves as well as others.

Why is creativity so important to Arendt? Because she sees the act of bringing something new into the world, what she calls "natality," as the only alternative to bureaucracy, totalitarianism, and the banality of evil. Indeed, for Arendt, bureaucracy itself is virtually a form of totalitarianism: in both the individual disappears, or rather becomes superfluous. In a letter written in the month that *The Origins of Totalitarianism* was published, Arendt says "What radical evil really is, I don't know, but it has something to do with [this] phenomenon: the superfluity of men as men" (Young-Bruehl 1982, 255; McGowan, 1998, pp. 30–31). This is also the goal of bureaucracy, what the phrase "like cogs in a machine" means when it refers to bureaucracy: bureaucracy is not that people are not needed to man and woman, but that one can readily be replaced by another as they are all alike. Bureaucracy is the principle of the factory, the division of labor, applied to the manufacture of decisions.

If totalitarianism and bureaucracy are both characterized by the superfluity of the individual, then the link to the banality of evil becomes clear, for that is precisely what characterizes the evil of men like Eichmann, "desk murderers" (*Schreibtischmörder*) as they are rightly called in German. Eichmann was not acting as an individual; he did not even think about himself as an individual, except perhaps when questions of promotion were concerned, and even then it was his place in the system that mattered. Eichmann conceived of himself as superfluous.

Totalitarianism, radical evil, bureaucracy, and the banality of evil are all of a piece: in each of them the individual disappears, and with his or her disappearance comes an inability to think about what one is doing.

Arendt is unhelpful not because she resists psychological speculation (often that is the best course, especially among the psychologically uninclined), but because thoughtlessness, superficiality, banality, and evil come to mutually define each other in a way that is unilluminating. Thoughtlessness is not just the operational definition of evil, so to speak. Thoughtlessness becomes the very essence of evil, at least by default. This does not make Arendt wrong. It means that we must devote more time to thinking about thoughtlessness.

Thought and thoughtlessness

Recall how Likierman (2001, p. 177) characterizes the death drive in Klein: as an attack on those mothering resources (let us just call it mother love, though in some cases it might as well be father love or grandmother love) that makes mental growth possible. Developing this insight at length, it is Klein's student, Wilfred Bion (1970), who made the inability to think the great puzzle of psychoanalysis.[3] Perhaps it should be the great puzzle of philosophy as well. We assume that thought is difficult, the product of great minds. What if thought, understood as thinking about what we are doing and to whom we are doing it, is at once the easiest and most difficult task in the world? Almost anyone can do it, but most people, as well as entire societies, are organized to defend against it. Bion's answer to why some cannot think was what he called "attacks on linking."

It is easy to have thoughts. The trick is to know how to put them together, what is called thinking as linking, without being overwhelmed with terror or despair. Attacks on linking seem to stem from hatred of thought itself, a hatred of knowing what one is feeling. What is puzzling, or at least surprising, is why Bion, and to a lesser degree Likierman, would connect a hatred of emotion with a hatred of thought. Why, for instance, would Likierman say that the death drive attacks the mother love that makes mental growth possible? One might have expected her to say that the death drive attacks the mother love that makes emotional security or autonomy possible. In fact, for Bion, as for many post-Kleinians they amount to the same thing.

Inspired by Bion, post-Kleinians focus on the destruction of thought for reasons that run something like this.[4] What children and adults need, albeit in different degrees and in different ways, is for their unbearable emotions to be held and contained by another. What are unbearable emotions? Emotions that feel as if the self is going to fall to pieces or explode, for the emotions are so intense, unstable, and unintegrated into the self. If mother contains the young child's unbearable emotions ten thousand times, eventually the young child will learn to do this emotional work for himself or herself, a process that might be thought of as internalizing the maternal holding function so as to make it one's own.

At first, mother contains these emotions simply by showing that she can experience them without retaliating or falling to pieces. Later she may help the child put words to these emotions, such as "You look so angry that you're about to burst." This must be said in a way that neither trivializes nor over-dramatizes the emotion, as if to say "but of course you're not going to burst, so let's get on with making dinner."

Attacks on linking occur when there is a failure of containment and holding. The attack on linking is the fragmenting alternative to being held, in which the unbearable emotions are broken into pieces, disconnected from thoughts, so that thoughts become sterile, one-dimensional, bereft of the emotions that would invigorate thoughts and give them life; only in this case life is too terrifying, too close to death. The result of attacks on linking is thinking marked by a lack of curiosity, a hatred of emotions, and from there it is but a short step to hatred of life itself. Emotions are what give life the feeling of living, not just existing. But when emotions are too intense and frightening, such as rage at and terror of abandonment, emotions are experienced as an alien intrusion into the self. An emotion or feeling itself becomes a hostile attacker that – if it cannot be destroyed – must be severed from all meaning.

Why? For the same reason that Milton's Satan would be his own progenitor, wrenching himself from the earth to be born, entirely self-caused. Lusting after Eve, Satan will nonetheless not have intercourse with her, because to do so would be to desire her and so to be emotionally affected (linked) to another, if only for a moment. Instead, Satan procreates Sin and Death out of himself, children of incest and his own imagination (PL IX, 480–495). Satan will not accept the most fundamental reality of all, the emotional reality of others, the emotional claim of others upon our lives: the existence of others whom we want, need, desire, or pity invades the sanctum sanctorum of our inner world, causing us to feel. Attacks on linking are an attempt to protect this inner sanctum from the invasion of feeling that feels as if it cannot be contained.

Attacks on linking are attacks on emotions, or rather on the links between emotions and their objects. Short-circuit this link, and the emotion loses the emotional energy that feeds it. So too does thought, which becomes dry, withered, abstract. It is this state that Antoine Roquentin, the protagonist in Jean-Paul Sartre's novel *Nausea*, longs to recover but cannot, instead feeling overwhelmed by the insistent particularity of the world. "I would have liked [the world] to exist less strongly, more dryly, in a more abstract way" (Sartre, 1964, p. 127).

"Reality" is a suspect term these days. More useful perhaps is to focus on the lie. Lies can be characterized not just by their content, but by their function. Lies are not just attacks on linking. Lies stem from the inability to tolerate not knowing. In order to think and to know, our minds must be able to contain our experiences, letting new experiences in without being overwhelmed and reduced to chaos. For a brief moment we must know nothing at all (what Bion calls "living without memory or desire"), so that the container that is one's mind is open to new experience. Trouble is this synapse between container and contained, this gap in time and space, can be felt like an eternity – that is, like death. We must experience a little death in order to think and to know. For many this experience is unbearable, for it recalls all too many little deaths in our lives – that is, too many failures of containment, what D. W. Winnicott (1965) calls "holding." Holding is the opposite of abandonment.

Bion (1984, p. 94) puts the same idea more cryptically. "Tolerance of doubt and tolerance of a sense of infinity are the essential connective in ♂n [an infinite recombination of thoughts] if K [knowledge] is to be possible." For Bion, linking is always about one thought, what he calls a "preconception," holding another, a conception stimulated by an experience. In order to have experiences that change us, we must have this "tolerance of a sense of infinity," which I have reframed as an experience of a little death, a willingness not to know, and hence to be, for just a moment. There are, as Bion's quote suggests, many ways to explain the same idea, even as there is something about Bion's mode of expression that tends to get lost in itself.

Attacks on linking destroy thought. Idealize the destruction of thought, and the result is contempt for thought, indeed the idealization of stupidity and mindlessness. Now we see why. Thought leads to self-transformation, such as the growth and development that comes from learning something new. The change in perspective that results implies that one was previously incomplete, immature, unknowing in some way. If this possibility is itself unbearable, then not only will learning be impeded, but everything that is the opposite of learning and knowledge will be valorized. Strength, vitality, and self-certainty will be championed as sources of power. Doubt and reflection, including the doubt and reflection that create the gaps that allows one to learn something new, become merely a sign of weakness and impuissance (Bion, 1989, pp. 89–99).

Herbert Rosenfeld (1988) writes about this process as if the Mafia had seduced the self. It is as though the death drive offers the self death-in-life in exchange for protection. Only instead of the Mafia, it sounds like Rosenfeld is writing about Satan. In either case the result is the same. Not only is the death drive directed at good objects outside the self, the sources of life, comfort, and support that Likierman writes of. But the death drive first comes to mimic, and then to attack the life affirming forces in the self, the forces that want to know, and grow in truth and knowledge. By then it is too late. The life affirming forces have surrendered too quickly and completely to the Mafia, as only the destructive forces promise to be powerful enough to keep the dread of annihilation at bay. Søren Kierkegaard (1957, p. 38) called this dread (*angst*) "a presentiment of a something which is nothing," and that seems about right. Better to ally oneself with the devil than to be annihilated by nothingness. Though this experience does not lend itself to words, we can try. Imagine the sudden recognition that in the scheme of things one knows little, and that to learn even a little more one must die a little death (including the death of an image of one's own wisdom), one that anticipates my own nothingness.

Perhaps the greatest contemporary image of the willful surrender to the tyranny of ignorance is George Orwell's *Nineteen Eighty-Four*. Indeed, we can now understand the meaning of that infamous slogan of Oceania, "Ignorance is Strength." Ignorance is strength because we need never admit doubt, weakness, uncertainty, or dependence on others for the help we need to grow in knowledge and understanding. *Nineteen Eighty-Four* is a great example for another reason as well: the distinction drawn between party members who enthusiastically shout the slogans, and the Inner Party members, men like O'Brien, who have become utterly cynical. For such men, there is only power and pain and privilege. O'Brien represents the death drive. Indeed, by the end of the book he has become death for Winston and Julia, torturing them until they are spiritually lifeless.

Though they are both destroyed, Winston and Julia know that the great enemy of the Inner Party, the death drive, is Eros, its only worthy opponent. "What overwhelmed Winston in that instant was admiration for the gesture with which she had thrown her clothes aside. With its grace and carelessness it seemed to annihilate a whole culture, a whole system of thought" (Orwell, 1949, p. 29). Here is precisely what Freud (1930) was so afraid of, and Herbert Marcuse (1961) so longed for, the hope behind *Eros and Civilization* that Eros might overthrow a world.

What would a society look like that failed to contain its members' unbearable emotions, and so encouraged attacks on linking? It need not be as extreme as Oceania, or Nazi Germany. Might it not look like a society that confused its citizens about good and bad, convincing them that this or that injustice is necessary to the smooth functioning of the productivity machine? Would it not, in other words, be a society that encouraged its members not to connect the dots – that is, not to make the links between the prosperity we enjoy, the existence of a permanent underclass in our society, as well as persistent poverty in the third world?

One could read the preceding paragraph as ideological cant. Read it instead in light of George Orwell's comments about the corruption of ordinary human decency by the corruption of language, be it the language of bureaucracy, doctrine, ideology, or academic life. Is it not the function of these languages to shatter the links between knowing and feeling? Anyone who is not corrupted by these languages, anyone who just looks and sees, will know, says Orwell, that kicking a coolie, procuring an abortion, abject and systematic poverty, and the destruction of natural beauty (to use four of Orwell's examples) are wrong.[5] Writing so limpid that it seems to disappear, leaving only its subject, is the contribution intellectuals can make, perhaps their only contribution, to preventing doctrine, dogma, bureaucracy, laziness, and educated stupidity from getting in the way of ordinary human decency.

Trouble is, today we know or think we know, that Orwell's windowpane theory of language, language so limpid it lets us see reality with nothing added or subtracted, is just one more rhetorical strategy, designed to create the illusion of objectivity, when it is of course the author who is creating the frame and form within which an infinitely interpretable reality is seen as objectively present to the reader. While certainly true, this insight hardly matters. The key point is not the windowpane theory, but Orwell's moral particularism. (Orwell, 1953) They are related.

Study what is going on around you, pay attention to details, try to understand what they are, and how you stand in relationship to these details, empirically and morally. That is, make the links, preferably little links not big ones: not "globalization" (which at its worst links every-thing to everything else, which is functionally equivalent to linking everything to nothing), but how do I stand in relation to the person who cleans my house, serves my food, begs on the corner?

There is no reason not to make larger, more encompassing theoretical links as well, but it is too easy to use big abstract links to dissolve little, concrete links, and so feel a little less: less responsible, less engaged – that is, just feel less. Theory too can obliterate the links between thought and feeling. Instead,

> observe closely what's going on around you; pay attention to its particulars and try to understand why they are what they are; you will often know when something you see or have proposed to you is offensive to the natural order; when you know this, protest it, remove your cooperation from it, refuse to listen to those who offer theoretical justifications of it, and do what you can to prevent if from continuing. This won't, thinks Orwell, solve all political and economic problems. Some can only be addressed at the theoretical level. . . . [But] In the kinds of cases that interest him, Orwell thinks that the clear eye can be sure that what is recommended is wrong – surer than the intellect

can be of the upshot of any theoretical argument at a high level of abstraction. This conviction lies at the heart of an Orwellian episte- mology. (Griffiths, 2004, p. 38)

But first we must see, and to see we must feel, and to feel we must repair the links that make knowing and feeling possible in the first place. Since Plato, the image of knowing as seeing has been problematic, but unpacked in this way it makes sense: to see means to do the work, individual and social, that allows ordinary human decency to prevail. Above all, this means allowing the links between knowing and feeling to come into being, and this is best done, or at least begun, at the local level, about particulars.

Emilia Steuerman puts the same point a little more abstractly when she states that the contribution of psychoanalysis to our understanding of hatred and evil "is the recognition that our capacity for thinking and tolerating separateness and difference has to acknowledge an unconscious world that can attack the most basic links that make understanding possible" (Steuerman, 2000, pp. 35–36). Recognizing the reality of these categories is how humans express our love for the plurality of the world, above all the power of the world to surprise us with some- thing new.

Thinking about Sinedu and Trang-Ho

It would be easy to say that Sinedu had lost her ability to think, and that would be correct. However, it is important to be clear in what that loss consists of: in the inability to use symbol for object, word for deed. Trang-Ho's body became the slate on which she inscribed not just her rage but her longing and desire, as though to say "Now you must feel this with me for a moment what I can no longer bear to feel alone before we are both obliterated in the fusion of death." Absent the ability to symbolize, we cannot protect those we love from our wrath, as we cannot imagine, dream, or think our hatred. Janine Chasseguet-Smirgel (1994, p. 235) puts it simply: "Symbol formation derives from the need of the child to protect his object, or parts of the object, from the effects of his attacks."

More puzzling is the Reverend Peter J, Gomes' identification of killer and victim, a tendency in which he was hardly alone, as Thernstrom (1996) makes clear. The first thing to say is that Reverend Gomes, who has been at Harvard for over thirty years, is not a stupid man. His books of religious wisdom for everyday life, such as *Strength for the Journey: Biblical Wisdom for Daily Living* (2004) are a cut above the average. And yet clearly he could not think that hate and evil had occurred in that dorm room, that one woman had been brutally slain by another: separate beings in life; separate non-beings in death. Instead, Reverend Gomes adopted Sinedu's fantasy, transforming it into the fantasy of the warmth of shared victimhood, rather than the perverted warmth of spilled and mingled blood. The answer why, I believe, is distressingly simple. Reverend Gomes, like the rest of us, does not want to think about the terrible hatred that lives under the same roof with us, even in the most loving families. Indeed, the more loving the family, the more terrible the thought.

It is, by the way, no accident that family violence is the theme of almost all the Greek tragedies. Or rather, says Aristotle, it was by chance that the tragic poets stumbled onto that one theme above all others that would cause the audience to tremble in fear and cry out in pity, and so when they found this theme they stuck with it (virtually all the 28 extant Greek tragedies concern family violence). No other theme ever evoked the *katharsis* of pity and fear as did family violence. By katharsis Aristotle meant not purging, but the clarification of these emotions – finding their proper place in one's *psyche*, the Greek term usually translated as self or soul (*Poetics*, c.6, 14). Finding the proper place for pity and fear in oneself sounds a lot like what it takes to contain our hatred: replacing bodies with symbols, and so coming to make finer distinctions. For example, the distinction between the hatred I feel and the hatred I know is justified; or between the hatred I know that is justified, and what I might justifiably do about it.

"You are over-intellectualizing hatred," the reader might complain. No, I would reply, I am only trying to bring to hatred something of the thought that we ordinarily bring to bear on most other areas of our lives. For there is something doubly difficult in thinking about hatred. Not only does the powerful emotion of hatred make thinking difficult, a difficulty shared in thinking about other powerful emotions, such as love, shame, and desire. But there is a dimension of hatred that hates thought itself. Here is the real danger, and it is the task of cultural workers at every level, from analysts to teachers to journalists to professors to be aware of this tendency. Of our political leaders we can perhaps only ask less – that they not exploit the hatred of thought. Those who reach and teach political leaders might remind them of this, their first duty.

Notes

1. Simon Clarke (2004) helped me understand how radical Klein's concept of envy and the death drive truly is, both in his article and in conversation. D. W. Winnicott cannot abide Klein's thesis, writing in "Hate in the Counter-transference" that "the mother hates the baby before the baby hates the mother, and before the baby can know his mother hates him" (Winnicott, 1978, p. 73). If this is so, then we must rethink the "death instinct," seeing it as a response to real relationships, including the relationship of being hated.
2. Klein (1975b, 189) does not give the source for her translation into modern English. Mine is Chaucer. (1993, p. 536).
3. Klein (1975a) first saw psychoanalysis as an account of failed thought and failed symbolism, both the result of the intense aggression associated with the desire to know, the "epistemophilic impulse" as Klein calls it. Bion developed what was begun in Klein. The exact status of Bion among the Kleinians is a subject of much dispute, none of which matters here. R. D. Hinshelwood (1989, pp. 229–234) discusses the issue succinctly and well.
4. My primary sources are Bion's (1984) essays "Attacks on Linking" (pp. 93–109) and "A Theory of Thinking" (pp. 110–119) both in his *Second Thoughts* (1984). "Attacks" was originally published in 1958. Also helpful was his *Learning From Experience* (1989, pp. 89–99), which introduces the minus K, or anti-Knowledge link: not just the desire to destroy the links between thoughts, but the desire to destroy knowledge itself. Among other authors on this topic, Herbert Rosenfeld (1988) and John Steiner (1993) stand out.
5. These are Orwell's examples, and they are (in order) from a newspaper column written in 1940, recalling his first experience of Asia in 1922; *Keep the Aspidistra Flying; The Road to Wigan Pier; and Coming Up For Air.*

7
Emotions and Populism

Nicolas Demertzis

The disciplinary context: Toward a political sociology of emotions

It is strange to think that the political sociology of emotions is quite immature when compared with the enormous growth of the sociology of emotion over the last 25 years or so (Kemper, 1990, 1991; Barbalet, 1998; Williams, 2001). Scholars have only recently brought emotions back in the analysis of social and political movements, power relations and institutions (Goodwin, Jasper and Polletta 2001; Holmes, 2004; Ost, 2004; Marcus, 2002; Berezin, 2002). Even so, a robust political sociology of emotions is far from being to the fore. I could make a claim analogous to a statement made by Jack Barbalet (2002, p. 6) with regard to the sociology of emotions: even before the advent of the term, the *political sociology of emotions*, the centrality of emotion and the role of particular feelings in politics had been recognized. The marginalization of emotions and feelings[1] in political sociology up to now is in a large degree the result of: (a) the stripping of the dimension of passion from the political because it was associated with romantic and utopian conceptions unrelated to the modern public sphere as well as because of the more or less instrumental and neutral-procedural conception of politics, a popular view at the end of the 1960s as well as today (Habermas, 1970; Mouffe, 2000); (b) the supremacy of 'interest' as opposed to 'passion' as an explaining factor of political action, already in effect in the middle of the eighteenth century (Hirschman, 2003); (c) the dominance, for many years, of the rational choice paradigm in a very large number of political science departments in the USA and Europe, in the context of which emotions are either conceived as irrational elements or taken as objective traits which do not affect the actor's, by definition, 'rational' thinking (Barbalet, 1998, pp. 29ff; Williams, 2001, pp. 15–16); and (d) the mistreatment of emotions even in the political culture paradigm, the great rival of rational choice (Barry, 1970; Eckstein, 1988), due to the prevalence of quantitative methodologies according to which the affective dimension has been shrunken into a numeric item or variable.

A possible 'political sociology of emotions' should, however, differentiate itself from an alleged 'emotive political sociology'. This is so because the latter would reduce, in a monistic way, political phenomena to emotions and feelings. By contrast, the former would explicitly integrate the emotional perspective into its examination of political phenomena. But the need to establish a political sociology of emotions is not self-evident, even if the academic community was to make such a demand. This is so because any political sociology of emotions could not possibly break away from the general field of political sociology, as happened in the case of the sociology of emotions. Paradoxically, the 'political sociology of emotions' should be coterminous with political sociology (whatever that might mean). The political sociology of emotions is none 'other' than its original scientific discipline (i.e. political sociology). The difference probably consists in the 'affective filter' through which each political sociology will from now on examine its objects. This is what I will try to do myself in the rest of this article, analyzing Greek populism on the basis of the feeling of *ressentiment*.

On *ressentiment*

As opposed to most other feelings, *ressentiment* and/or 'resentment' has been sufficiently analyzed (Barbalet, 1998, p. 63). Prominent scholars argue that the politics of late modernity is a politics of generalized *ressentiment* as the uncertainties of capitalism and the surveillance of the state create in individuals a diffuse sense of powerlessness, the public expression of which is not positive and self-grounded praxis but a hasty and dependent reaction which usually takes the form of 'identity politics' and ethicism (Brown, 1995, pp. 21–76; Connolly, 1991, pp. 22–23, 207). The concept was introduced by Nietzsche in 1970 (*Genealogy of Morals*) and since then it has found its way into the works of many other philosophers, sociologists and psychologists. It is no wonder then that there is no general consensus as to its meaning. By and large, I would say that in the relevant literature there are two kinds of uses of the notion: the 'nietzschean' and the 'non-nietzschean'[2]. According to the former, *ressentiment* is a feeling of the weak who follow in general the logic of La Fontaine's fox. According to the latter, resentment signifies emotional opposition to unequal and unjust situations.

In this section we will discuss the views of sociologists and philosophers who use the concept in the first and the second ways. Special emphasis will be accorded to Max Scheler's analysis, since in the next section it will be used for the interpretation of Greek populism.

The non-nietzschean approaches

The British philosopher of language Peter Strawson gave particular emphasis to the concept of resentment, placing his analysis within a wider moral approach to human sociability. In their interactions, people make relationships invested with feeling, so that it matters for somebody what someone else's opinion about, and behavior toward, them is. The importance of others for the construction of the self is expressed in emotionally laden 'reactive attitudes'.

In Strawson's approach, then, resentment is the negative reactive attitude that a person develops in the face of another person's indifference toward, and insult and injury of, him or her (1974, pp. 7, 14). Strawson uses a simple example: if someone accidentally steps on my hand as they help me do something, the pain may be no less than if they did it on purpose in a gesture of contempt toward my person. But while in the latter case I would feel deep resentment, in the former I might as well feel gratitude in the light of their good intent. As a negative reactive attitude, resentment implies a disapproval of the injurer who is considered responsible for his actions with good reason. Strawson thinks that toward a small child, a mentally deficient person, a drug-addicted criminal or a sick man, who causes us some sort of injury, we cannot feel resentment. This feeling presupposes moral responsibility.

Ending our analysis of his views on resentment, what puzzles us is his self-confessed looseness in the appellation of the negative and unpleasant feelings he describes as 'resentment' and 'indignation'. Strawson writes (1974, p. 14): 'both my description of, and my name for, these attitudes are a little misleading'. And a bit earlier in the text: 'resentment, or what I have called resentment, is a reaction to injury or indifference'. From what we have seen, the meaning of 'resentment' in his own context comes close to the notion of 'pique', of stubborn anger and indignation.

John Rawls (1971/1991) also uses the concept of resentment, which he defines as a 'moral sentiment', in about the same way. In fact, he incorporates it in an absolutely organic way into his theory of justice, as 'moral sentiments' constitute the necessary condition for every rational individual to realize, behind the supposed 'veil of ignorance', the two basic principles of justice as fairness: (1) every person is to have an equal right to the most extensive total system of equal basic liberties compatible with a similar system of liberty for all; and (2) social and economic inequalities are to be arranged so that they are both to the greatest benefit of the least advantaged and attached to offices and positions open to all under conditions of fair equality of opportunity (1971/1991, pp. 60, 83, 250). These two principles, ranked in lexical order, cannot be applied if individuals are not governed by an immanent, as well as an acquired, sense of justice and moral sentiments. Moral sentiments are defined as families of dispositions and propensities regulated by a higher-order desire (1971/1991, p. 192) which touch on the very sociability of man (and here Rawls is not diverging from the classical philosophical tradition): relations of love and trust between children and parents, trust and sympathy between friends, the love of humanity, adherence to a common good. Moreover, 'they presuppose an understanding and an acceptance of certain principles and an ability to judge in accordance with them' (1971/1991, p. 487).

In line with the above analysis, Rawls, in almost the whole of the eighth chapter of his book, makes distinctions between moral and non-moral sentiments: anger, rancor, anxiety, envy, spite, jealousy, annoyance and grudgingness are *not* moral sentiments primarily because in their manifestation and explanation the individual does not presuppose a binding sense of justice and injustice. Together with guilt, shame, trust, indignation, obligation, infidelity, deceit and sympathy, resentment, for Rawls, is placed among the moral sentiments. He defines it (1971/1991, p. 484), then, as a sentiment which arises when wrongs are done to us.

Jack Barbalet (1998), moving on to the field of the sociology of emotions, handles the concept of resentment with particular care since he links it to wide-ranging social and political phenomena, such as inter-class and intra-class antagonism, social inequality and citizenship. In his analysis he draws many arguments mainly from the work of T. H. Marshall and he points out that the antagonistic context of a class society generates a multiplicity of emotions and feelings, contrasting and/or complementing one another. But he thinks that resentment in particular is a critically important feeling in a class society characterized by horizontal and vertical mobility (1998, p. 68). It is precisely this feeling that allows for the conversion of a structural-class contradiction to a class conflict, to real action in the public sphere.

In a first reading, resentment for Barbalet is the negative and unpleasant feeling that somebody is enjoying one or more privileges in an improper and unequal way. This makes for the accompanying feeling of indignation against inequality, which is the catalyst for the inter- and intra-class antagonism, something which is not sufficiently stressed in the literature on class and class contradictions[3]. Resentment is directed not toward power but toward the normative content of the social order, in the sense that someone: (1) judges unworthy the position that someone else has in the social hierarchy and (2) thinks that someone else – a person or a collective agent – deprives him of chances or privileges that he himself could enjoy (1998, pp. 68, 137).

For this Australian sociologist (class) resentment is an active feeling determined by the specificity of each social structure, determining in its turn the intensity of the class struggle (1998, p. 71).

Nietzschean approaches

In the paradigmatic non-nietzschean approaches I just referred to, resentment is an unpleasant feeling that leads to an active posture. On the contrary, the nietzschean approaches I am going to discuss now, resentment qua *ressentiment* is linked to passivity. Those who subscribe to these latter approaches adhere to the nietzschean view of ressentiment as a morality of the weak creatures 'who have been forbidden of the real reaction, of the act' (Nietzsche, 1970, p. 35). In the German philosopher's thought, the resentful man is governed by a frightened baseness that appears as humility, his submission to those he hates becomes docility, his weakness is supposedly transformed to patience or even virtue. The basic characteristic of Nietzsche's resentful man is a hidden vindictiveness that leads to inaction (1970, p. 133). The main representative of the nietzschean approach is, of course, Max Scheler (1874–1928). Other representatives include Werner Sombart (1913/1998) and Robert Merton (1957/1968, pp. 209–211).

Scheler inherits Nietzsche's negative conception of *ressentiment*, but differentiates himself in a few but crucial points. First, he rejects the nietzschean genealogical explanation. According to Scheler, it is not the Christian worldview, and particularly the Christian notion of love, that fuels the servile resentful attitude. Christian morality is founded on the wealth of the open soul and has nothing to do with the ungenerous and repressed aspirations of *ressentiment*. For him, the genealogy of *ressentiment* is to be found in the bourgeois morality that was gradually taking shape from the thirteenth century onwards and reached its peak in the French Revolution (1961, pp. 81–82).

There are two necessary conditions for the stirring of *ressentiment*, according to Scheler. The first is a not acted out vindictiveness, an unfulfilled and repressed demand for revenge. The second *sine qua non* of *ressentiment* is a chronic interiorized powerlessness, a sense of impotence and the lack of ability to influence the order of things. So, while you want to take revenge you feel that you cannot do anything about it.

Even though Scheler refers to related negative feelings whose manifestation exhibits a climax – malice, annoyance, envy, grudgingness, rancor, jealousy, spite (1961, pp. 46–48) – he does not identify them with (or regard them equal to) *ressentiment*. They may be stages in its progressive formation, but in order to speak of *ressentiment* properly we have to exclude two possibilities: their genuine moral transgression through forgiveness or inner purification, on the one side, and their active expression, on the other. When both of these are absent, then *ressentiment* emerges. This is because it builds upon the intensity of the aforementioned feelings that demand revenge and, at the very same time, upon the catalytic powerlessness of expressing them, due to fear and/or physical or mental inferiority. Scheler, echoing Nietzsche, states openly: '*ressentiment* is chiefly confined to those who *serve* and are *dominated* at the moment, who fruitlessly resent the sting of authority' (1961, p. 48). To be sure, according to Scheler, it is not just repressed vindictiveness that leads to *ressentiment*; it is the repression of the imagination of vengeance too that contributes to this particular state of mind where at the end of the day the very emotion of revenge itself evaporates (1961, p. 49). This is another point where Scheler departs from Nietzsche's conception according to which *ressentiment* characterizes powerless natures who 'compensate themselves with an imaginary revenge'.

His argument (1961, pp. 49 ff) reveals several necessary conditions for the cultivation of *ressentiment*, without however himself naming them thus. The first condition is the gap between the perceived equality of social position and the rights that emanate from citizenship and the real power of the individual to enjoy them. This gap, says Scheler (1961, pp. 50, 69), functions as psychological dynamite since a structural element of modern political democracies is the gulf between formal and substantive equality. This condition would by itself lead to envy, class hatred or moral indignation, if it was not overdetermined by chronic interiorized powerlessness (which is the second condition).

This second condition, which is relevant to the first, states that there has to be a comparison. If you do not compare yourself to others you cannot feel these hostile feelings which make up *ressentiment*. That is, you cannot feel vindictiveness, envy, jealousy or rancor if you do not compare yourself to others. The 'other' could be an individual, or it could well be a reference group, especially so in open societies which are characterized by loose class differentiations and upward social mobility.

Finally, the third condition is the irrevocable nature of the injustice you feel subjected to. Each particular injustice, from which the revengeful attitude begins, has to be experienced as destiny, as something that cannot be changed in any way. So, it is through the combination of these necessary conditions that schelerian *ressentiment* unfolds. When these conditions are absent we cannot speak of *ressentiment* in the proper, technical, meaning of the word.

As to the intrapersonal processes which characterize the resentful man, Scheler's theses follow the nietzschean line, which he extends even further. He believes that the resentful attitude leads to a reversal of values. Since the resentful man does not possess the moral virtues and the psychological abilities (for example, faith, high self-esteem, sublimation mechanisms) nor the social resources to manage the pressure his inferior social position exerts on him – and also the ever present existential anxiety (1961, p. 52) – he proceeds to a chronic withdrawal into himself, thus avoiding acting out his revengeful attitude. In this way, says Scheler, he morally poisons himself. While at first he admires the values and privileges he does not possess (prestige, education, wealth, descent, beauty, youth, etc.), because he cannot acquire them, he goes on to invalidate them, valuing the exact opposites. Since *ressentiment* is not rage or hatred which has an expiry date and a specific addressee, but is instead a chronic and complex emotional disposition with unclear recipients which is molded by the endless rumination of repressed negative affective reactions, it entails a reversal of values, so that the person can bear and handle his frustrations. At first I admire the wealthy, the handsome, the aristocrat, the educated, the famous and so on. But since I cannot become like them or compete with them, there is a silent hostility growing in me, a repressed vindictiveness for something that was unrightfully taken away from me. So I start slowly to undervalue what I once admired. In psychoanalytic terms, we would say that it is a reaction formation, a defense mechanism against pressures exerted on the psyche. Of course, on a purely individual level, this transvaluation is a sort of self-therapy for Scheler[4]. However, the German sociologist focuses on the study of social and cultural phenomena and, because of that, he believes that the resentful mentality (or emotional climate) changes the whole cultural value system as well as the way in which we cope with power, knowledge, historical memory, social evolution, social hierarchy and so on.

Scheler goes beyond Nietzsche in maintaining that the reversal of values does not mean that in real time the resentful man is conscious of the positivity of the values he disputes. It is not about a *'rational* self-interested' attitude. Ultimately, the resentful man is not the rational, and yet impotent, actor who reacts according to the logic of the 'sour grapes' seething with bitterness. But it has nothing to do with cynicism either. It is not as if the resentful man knew and recognized the values but acts as if he did not (i.e. he knows and accepts education as an end in itself, but since he cannot be educated himself he devalues it placing in its stead the spontaneity, let us say, of the common man). But nor is the hypocrite a model for the resentful man, since the latter does not pretend to reverse values (1961, p. 77).

What Scheler means by resentful 'transvaluation' is literally a substitution: the old values stay on the backstage of the psyche, in a misty landscape of the soul, so that the resentful man cannot see them as he operates within another level of values, which he has elevated to a positive normative context. The positive values are still felt as such, but they are overcast by the false ones (1961, p. 60); it is a matter of an obscure awareness of true values which Scheler calls 'value blindness' or 'value delusion' (1961, p. 59). Psychoanalytically, I would say that we are dealing with the result of a 'splitting' due to an intense narcissistic trauma, which displaces and/or negates the object of desire. For Scheler, the resentful man may be honest but his values have been mutated.

Toward an appraisal

In our presentation of nietzschean and non-nietzschean approaches to 'resentment', it was revealed, first, that it is an annoying and unpleasant moral feeling; second, their common reference point was the lived experience of injustice; and, third, their fundamental differentiating element was the articulation of this moral feeling with an active or a passive attitude respectively. It is this difference that determines the gap in the conceptual substance of the term. Linked to inactivity, 'resentment' is defined, *a la* Nietzsche and Scheler, as *ressentiment*. Even if, as Barbalet (1998, p. 63) and Meltzer and Musolf (2002) argue, we do not generally have to hypostasize, freeze and reify the content of the concepts, I do not find reasonable enough causes to abandon the conceptual substance of '*ressentiment*' as a *terminus technicus*. Since we have the concept of moral or righteous indignation (*nemesis*) and rage, linked to activity, already from Aristotle, they could well stay in use in sociological (and ethico-philosophical) analysis without burdening *ressentiment* with a meaning it never had.

Meltzer and Musolf (2002, pp. 242–43, 251) think of *ressentiment* (general sense) as a persistent moral feeling induced by being insulted, affronted, or deprived and linked with vengeful desires that cannot be readily consummated; they differentiate it from 'resentment' (specific sense) which is a transitory feeling caused by relatively minor insults. The difference between the two concepts is, hence, a difference of degree. In their analysis *ressentiment* is not linked to passivity; on the contrary they see it as a potential source of individual and collective action and social change, departing, therefore, from Nietzsche's and Scheler's conceptualization. The problem with their account is that they reify the emotion they deal with; first, they seem to forget that emotions are experienced in flow; they come and go, spark and fade within certain social situations. So it is not *ressentiment* per se that is linked to social action and transformation; it is the transformation of the social milieu which may modify *ressentiment* into anger, rage or any other activity-laden emotion. Second, they understate the role of transvaluation in the constitution of *ressentiment*, especially in its Schelerian version. Yet it is transvaluation itself which makes for the passivity which characterizes the emotion and for the distinction of *ressentiment* from cynicism, envy, and rancor[5].

All in all, then, as the German word *Schadenfreude* cannot be translated to other European languages – except perhaps to Greek, as equivalent to 'χαιρεκακία' (in the sense that someone is glad that someone else rightly suffers)[6] – *ressentiment*, as a technical term, should be kept untranslated and 'resentment' should be taken as synonymous to moral indignation, bitterness, pique, rage and moral anger (Bittner, 1994). Distinguishing thus *ressentiment* from resentment is not merely scholastic but also crucial in understanding and describing different aspects of seemingly uniform social and political phenomena. In the analysis of Greek populism which I will attempt later, this distinction will be put forward.

So, I regard *ressentiment* as an unpleasant moral feeling without specific addressees, which operates as a chronic reliving of repressed and endless vindictiveness, hostility, envy and indignation due to the impotence of the subject in expressing them, resulting, at the level of values, in the negation of what he unconsciously desires.

Populism: A political phenomenon charged with ressentiment

Populism can, on the one hand, be studied as a political discourse, as an ideology, as a movement, as a regime, as a practice, as a code or a syndrome (Wiles, 1969), as a dimension of political culture (Worsley, 1969, p. 245). On the other hand, it can be analyzed together with other relevant political phenomena such as nationalism, fascism, racism, revolutions, revolts, socio-economic development and so on.[7]

Nearly all interpretations of populism include the affective factor only in a disguised or implicit way. Even though none of its interpreters would be willing to neglect this factor, few are those who approached it in a systematic way, the others depending on its 'common sensical', allusive and elusive presence. A concrete problematization of feelings, within the analysis of populism, is almost absent because for many years feelings did not receive particular attention within the general context of sociological analysis.

Often, emotions and feelings are used in a metonymic way. That is, the analysis of each particular populism is carried out through the use of general affective categories and not through the interpretation of concrete feelings. The concrete and particular feelings are hidden beneath the generalities of the 'subjective' dimension of the phenomenon. For example, it has been argued that the 'discontent' of the agricultural and lower-middle-class strata caused by the enforcement of the economic policies and institutions of the political system, as well as by the 'antipathy' and 'alienation' they felt toward the power elites (Hennessy, 1969, pp. 29, 46; Taggart, 2000, p. 43), contributed to the appearance of North American and Latin American populism. But 'discontent', 'alienation' and 'antipathy' are general affective categories, which may cover a wide range of specific feelings such as, for example, hatred, rage, indignation, sorrow, etc.

In the interpretation of Russian populism (but not restricted to it) the romantic idealization of the agricultural community and the myth of 'the people' are referred to as being central analytic categories (Walicki, 1969, p. 79; Taggart, 2000, p. 46). However, these are mechanisms producing imaginary constructions, which only indirectly refer to 'actual' feelings, which are their 'raw material': joy, hope, nostalgia, admiration, pride, exultation and so on. Similarly, when the imaginary element of populist movements is mentioned, in the sense of a collective identification founded on the redoubled multiplication of the subjects' Ego Ideal, or even when what is discussed is the appellation itself, that is the master signifier of 'the people', through which popular-class interpellations are activated (Worsley, 1969, p. 244; Laclau, 1977, pp. 143–198, 2005), we get the impression that the emphasis is placed on the description of the identificatory mechanisms and not on the concomitant feelings supporting them.

As I mentioned earlier, apart from the metonymic there are also incomplete uses of feelings in the analysis of populism. This is the case in the notion of a 'mythical heartland', which Taggart (2000, pp. 95–98, 117) considers to be a necessary element of populism. But apart from its imaginary substance, Taggart does not clarify the affective content of this notion. This is also the case with the notion of a 'populist mood' put forward by Canovan (1999) as a fundamental ingredient of populist movements. For this distinguished theorist of the populist phenomenon, populist politics cannot but be based on 'heightened emotions' for charismatic leaders, 'enthusiasm' and spontaneity. This is so not only for the historical cases of reactionary populism (nazism, bonapartism, etc.), but also for the 'healthy' populisms, which appear in western democracies and aim at the 'redemptive revival' of politics, beyond the managerial and pragmatic style of governing. But apart from this general call, Canovan does not attempt a specification of the populist emotional 'mood'. Recently, in his attempt to encapsulate the populist *Zeitgeist* in contemporary western democracies, Cas Mudde (2004, pp. 547, 557, 560) does not do justice to the affective dimension of populism as he makes only three references to political resentment, charismatic leadership and the growing anger of the silent majority in connection with Taggart's idea of 'heartland'.

Of course, the question that arises is: why is that so? Why is the affective factor in the theoretical analysis of populism barely discussed, while its function is so important especially in the cases of 'protest' and 'identitarian populism' (Taguieff, 1995)? I believe that besides the general negligence of feelings in sociological analysis referred to above, this is due to the fact that many theorists who have dealt and still deal with this issue adopt a more abstract, generalizing and macroscopic level than the micro-scale level of emotions and feelings. Microanalysis, as is well known, may demand qualitative methodological tools as well, but these are different from those of the macroscopic approach: discourse analysis, interviews and so on. So, by studying populism at the level of social structures using a historical sociological approach and comparative analysis, the affective dimension is necessarily put aside. However, the need for closing the gap between the macro- and micro-analytical levels has been long noted (Giddens, 1984, pp. 139–144; Turner 1987) and the study of populism should be no exception. In fact, this closing of the gap is facilitated by the sociological study of emotions since it precisely combines subjective action with social structures. I must say that focusing on feelings *as well* in the study of populism, what is of interest is not the psychosomatic etiology of individual attitudes – something that William James (1902, p. 42) would call 'medical materialism' – but their inter-individual intellectual and moral importance. In other words, the particular interest in the study of emotions lies in the fullest *in situ* understanding of the *meaning* (or meanings) of each populism. Kenneth Minogue underlined this early on (1969, p. 197), without however finding many to follow his example: 'To understand the (populist) movement is to discover the feelings which moved people.'

This means that there is not one but many, though interrelated, feelings in place that permit the existence of populism as a practice, a movement, a party and a regime. All the more so since populist ideological discourse (and/or code/style) is articulated with other ideologies and constantly adapts to various political, religious and social environments (Taggart, 2000, pp. 2–4, 55; Taguieff, 1995). In the context of particular populisms, which flourish in particular national political cultures, then, one can easily find a wide range of feelings, which include nostalgia, angst, helplessness, hatred, vindictiveness, ecstasy, melancholy, anger, fear, indignation, envy, spite and resentment. Minogue mentions some of the above (1969, pp. 197, 206, 207). Edward Shils (1956) used specifically the feeling of resentment in order to interpret the American political scene of the 1950s, which we will also use to explain Greek populism after the political changeover. But the American sociologist's analysis was also aimed at a more general theoretical evaluation of populism as a social and political phenomenon. So one of his points was that populism is 'an ideology of resentment against the social establishment imposed by the long-term domination of a class, which is considered to have the monopoly of power, property and civilization' (Shils, 1956, pp. 100–101). In his analysis, Shils thought of resentment in terms of moral rage and indignation.

In his attempt to explain the emergence and the chances of the far right European populist parties during the period 1990–2000 (i.e. FPÖ, Ny Demokrati, Republikaner, Front Nationale, Schweizer Volkspartei, Lega Nord, Vlaams Blok, etc.), Hans-Georg Betz uses the concept of resentment. He states (2002, pp. 198–200) that in the early phase of their appearance they were greatly buttressed by the defuse grievances of working-class and lower-middle-class electorate against globalization, the immigrants, the fiscal crisis of the welfare state, politicians' corruption and so on. Thus they can be seen as a result of the mobilization of *ressentiments*. Persuasive as his argument may be, however, his use of *ressentiment* is quite inconclusive as he oscillates between a nietzschean and a non-nietzschean conception. *Ressentiment* in the schelerian sense does not lead to mobilization as it explains political inaction rather than political action. It is 'resentment', meaning moral anger and indignation, which may explain better the initial phase of populist mobilization. Contrary to Betz, I think that *ressentiment* can be used not for the interpretation of this phase but for the understanding of the emotional climate, which preceded it long ago.

Greek populism in the constellation of ressentiment

From the end of the 1970s onwards, probably reaching its peak in the five-year period from 1989 to 1993, populism in general and Greek populism in particular began to attract the strong interest of Greek political sociologists. In his well-known text, Wiles isolated 24 elements that, in his opinion, comprise the populist code. These elements stem from the fundamental assumption that 'virtue' is on the side of the traditions of the common people (Wiles, 1969, p. 166). Of course it is not necessary that all these elements should coexist in each and every movement or political project in order for it to be characterized as populist. Particular combinations depending on the circumstances, the political culture and the international environment could well demonstrate the populist nature of a movement, party or project as long as the aforementioned basic assumption is present.[8] From Wiles' 24 ideal-type elements, then, I believe that we can locate 12 of them in the Greek case: *ideological looseness, moralism, instrumental conception and pragmatic use of the state, charismatic leadership, anti-intellectualism, aversion towards the technocrats, opposition to the Establishment* and *avoidance of the language of class*; moreover, Greek populism is *urban, petit bourgeois, racist/nationalistic* and *espouses traditional inequalities*.

All these are inscribed in the wider context of Greek political culture in the *medium* and *long dureé*, as well as in the particularities of the Greek social formation ('spurious modernization', semi-periphery, etc.) and they cannot but presuppose and ignite various feelings. For example, nostalgia is a feeling that causes and is caused by Greek populism. This feeling must be understood in terms of the special relation of populism to tradition. In either case, for developing as well as for developed countries, populism arises as an indirect answer to problems that are the consequences of modernization (Stewart, 1969, pp. 180–81). These consequences involve tensions and/or crises that stem, on the one hand, from the position of a country in the international division of labor and symbolic capital and, on the other, from social, peripheral, inter-class and intra-class inequalities in its interior. This explains why populist phenomena are not only observed in semi-peripheral societies but in the societies of the center as well (Mouzelis, 1985). Sentimentally, crises of this sort are frequently coped with by nostalgic uses of the past.

The Greek case can be easily placed within the context of semi-peripheral populisms where the masses are integrated into the political system through vertical incorporation and mobilization which is based on the logic of equivalence, as opposed to the horizontal (class) type of integration which is founded on the logic of difference and the articulation of various partial interests (Mouzelis, 1985). In this context, *ressentiment* is transformed into a material force, which in post-civil war Greece incited populism as a movement and a discourse. To make this clear, we have to recall some of the structural characteristics of Greek society during the 30-year period from 1950 to 1980.

Post-war populism is, as I said before, a petit bourgeois political phenomenon *par excellence*. The solid presence of petit bourgeois strata has always been a structural feature of the Greek social formation. In fact, during the whole of the twentieth century, due to their social ambivalence and inner dissimilarities, these strata were at one time adopting conservative-authoritarian political attitudes and preferences while at other times they opted for radical alternatives. Immediately after the World War II and the Civil War, there was an increase in the number and special social significance of the petit bourgeois strata. Within 15 years a rural exodus of enormous proportions toward the great urban centers took place, especially toward Athens and Salonica, which together absorbed the 65% of the transferred population (Karapostolis, 1984, p. 109). A very significant, if not the most significant, proportion of the transferred farmers was absorbed in the wider public sector. Many manual laborers were occupied in the construction industry, others were incorporated into 'free' retailing professions and relatively few into the productive economic sectors (Lyrintzis, 1987, 1993). For most of them, then, the rural exodus meant upward social mobility, since the place of the poor farmer was exchanged for that of the 'multivalent' petit bourgeois, often implicated in networks of political patronage.

But all this came with a price. The rapid geographical and social mobility, as the one that happened in the particular context of 'deformed capitalism' and 'authoritarian modernization', made social identities fluid and strengthened traditional, pre-modern, individualism as well as the informality of the institutional and normative environment (Karapostolis, 1987, pp. 38–40). If the petit bourgeois strata in general experience a floating social identity anyway, the newly formed petit bourgeois strata in Greece of the 1950s and 1960s in particular, precisely because of their rapid emergence and the malfunctioning of the political and economic systems (state of emergency, clientelistic networks, gray-economy, etc.), experienced even more pressure and uncertainty. 'Success' and 'recognition' are always in doubt, undermined by an imperceptible threat of misappropriation, while everything appears to happen in an 'impenetrable' and saturated social environment (Karapostolis, 1985, pp. 52, 86 ff). This means that there is a gap between objective economic success and its subjective perception.

But besides, and next to, the emotional costs of permanent excitation, uncertainty, rivalry and an active-hostile attitude toward things, for an important, perhaps the most important, part of the petit bourgeois strata there was also another cost: the fear caused by the repressive apparatuses of the post-civil war state. This was so because the first wave of the domestic migration had primarily 'political motives and was constituted mainly from EAMite[9] people who could no longer stay in the provinces' (Filias, 1976, p. 62). These were the civil war's defeated – thousands of left-wingers who were morally cancelled, politically marginalized, socially stigmatized and personally exhausted – forced to find refuge in the city. For them, as well as for their immediate descendants, defeat functioned as a 'cultural trauma', as a painful event whose retroactive processing in memory and discourse caused disruptions and reconstructions in their collective identity.[10] Essentially, there was no place for left-wingers in the public sphere, who were treated as second-class citizens. Their political marginalization caused them fear, anger, embarrassment and angst.

Essentially, until the end of the 1950s, the space for any strongly worded discourse challenging the post-civil war establishment was extremely narrow. But since the beginning of the crucial decade of the 1960s that space widened as, on the one hand, the 'Union of the Center' party (Ενωση Κέντρου) challenged the dominance of ERE (the right-wing dominant party) and, on the other, the economic development in the tertiary and manufacturing sector allowed for the massive and very fast accession of the domestic migrants to the labor market. There existed, however, an unbridgeable contradiction: while economic incorporation continues and creates the conditions for social consensus and the gradual de-EAMification of the petit bourgeois masses (Charalambis, 1989, p. 196), the structure of the post-civil war state (palace, army, national-mindedness, etc.) did not allow for the lifting of their political exclusion. The petit bourgeoisified defeated of the civil war, already incorporated in the market and the consumerist way of life, demanded moral recognition and political representation. But they did so in vain, since the mode of political domination placed obstacles in the mode of production (Charalambis 1989, pp. 197–98, 224) leading to the generalized irrationality of the whole system. This blockage, manifesting the crisis of modernization and the prevention of the setting up of a new social contract, radicalized the EAMite petit bourgeois strata, as their fear gradually gave way to resentful indignation. It was precisely because their social opportunity structure had changed and therefore they were able to express the accumulated emotional energy and transform the feeling of indignation to a material-political force: where else could the social rallies for 114, the king's *coup d'etat* and the 'uncompromising (struggle)' be based and in what other way could they be expressed, if not in a mixture of indignation and hope?[11]

But even those rallies were limited. On the one hand, given the neutralization of the left, it was the small-scale property and the vacillating nature of the petit bourgeois masses itself that in the final analysis did not favor the radical changes in the mode of production. This was the first limit. The other was the rigidity of the post-civil war mode of political domination. Under the prospect of losing control in the parliamentary elections scheduled for May 1967, April's *coup d'etat* in effect blocked every outlet for the democratic incorporation of the not nationally minded in the political system and cancelled the mood for further massive protests.

From the perspective of the political sociology of emotions, the seven-year military regime had multiple effects. I will focus on one which I consider to be particularly significant in the context of my analysis: as one would expect, fear and insecurity returned to the left-leaning strata of the population who had staffed and socially supported EAM, Unified Democratic Left (EDA) and Union of the Centre (EK). On top of the cultural trauma of the civil war, there now came the trauma of the imposition of dictatorship. So there was formed a belief in the fatality of political inequality and marginalization and the impossibility of its defeat. The humiliation of the civil war's defeated was not lifted but, on the contrary, accentuated. As a matter of fact, it was passed down to the next generation which immediately after the dictatorship constituted the new educated petit bourgeois strata (lawyers, doctors, engineers, professors in secondary education, etc.) which later supported with fervor Andreas Papandreou's PASOK.

But at the same time, the majority of these strata, despite their increasing political marginalization, started gradually to accept the market economy in which they were becoming an active part, mainly in an extra-institutional way (gray-economy, tax evasion, etc.). Economic robustness did not go hand in hand with political and, in a broader sense, public recognition. For 15 years (1960–1975), that is, even after the end of the dictatorship, 'consciousness remained stuck to the past of political repression, while the specific practical behavior was already operating within the bounds of the market and the objective of economic profit' (Charalambis, 1989, p. 304).

So the petit bourgeois strata found themselves in a societal field overdetermined by two contradictions: on the one hand, there was the contradiction between political consciousness and actual economic behavior in real time, while, on the other, there was the demand for full-fledged citizenship and the impossibility of achieving it. These two contradictions had special repercussions on the affects of these strata, especially during the dictatorship. To begin with, in relation to the first contradiction, increasing economic prosperity (privately owned flat, car, television, country house, etc.) relieved them from poverty and mainly from the fear of returning to their former condition of being a poor domestic migrant or a still poorer farmer. This relief strengthened the sense of security and the optimism as to the prospects of their socio-economic position. But at the same time the trauma of defeat and the humiliation of political marginalization made them look and feel different from what they economically were. The trauma of the civil war and the dictatorship was not a past present, but a present past. In other words, it was alive and produced feelings and attitudes that did not 'correspond' to the real economic condition and the consuming ability of the petit bourgeois subjects. Thus unjustified complaints and self-victimization were not rare in their daily encounters.

The peculiar outcome of the first contradiction supports the effect of the second: the contradiction between the desire for political and moral recognition and the powerlessness to impose it – combined with the chronic and traumatic reliving of endless vindictiveness, hostility, jealousy and indignation – produces *ressentiment*. I believe that Scheler's analysis finds here an exemplary application. Political marginalization and the post-civil war establishment are now perceived to be an inescapable fate. There is not an active and energetic attitude that opposes experienced injustice. Simultaneously, the petit bourgeois strata have undergone a decisive transvaluation: while traditionally it is in their 'nature' to orient themselves to the upper class, precisely because of their *ressentiment*, they now begin to evaluate those that are 'below'. Risking oversimplification, I would say that a significant portion of pre-dictatorial resentment qua moral indignation, during the dictatorship dematerializes and is transformed into *ressentiment*.

I am of the opinion that this psychic mechanism of transvaluation was the soil on which the post-dictatorial populism as ideology, movement and practice flourished. I do not think that 'the people' could be invested with mythical value so fast had it not previously been subjected to resentful transvaluation. Since the radicalized petit bourgeois strata could not become an 'establishment', they elevated 'the people' to the supreme legitimating and moral reference point. In other words, without being the only one, *ressentiment* functioned as a condition of possibility, paving the way for the formation of populism after the political changeover in 1974.

With PASOK's rise to power, the political opportunity structure for the petit bourgeois strata changed. Andreas Papandreou's policies (the recognition of national resistance, a party clientelistic system) as well as his discourse on the advantaged and disadvantaged Greeks put *ressentiment* to the side. The changes in the political personnel and the governing system dragged the petit bourgeois strata out from political invisibility, something that in its turn functioned as a class-support for the power bloc, to use Nicos Poulantzas' concept. To a large degree, passive *ressentiment* gave way to open vindictiveness: party mass clientelism (Lyrintzis, 1984) and the 'green-guards' (PASOK's cadres who dominated in trade unions, the public sector and state mechanisms) were the compensation for the 'stony years' of the political marginalization of the inheritors of the civil war. But yet again, the conflict was not conducted in terms of frontal and organized struggle. Populism was based on, and reproduced, the institutional informality and the anthropomorphism of Greek society. However, the heritage of *ressentiment* during the dictatorship contributed to this: there was a rumination of negative feelings with unclear addressees. This has contributed to the diffuse disaffection of the public against the way democracy functions in Greece as well as to Greeks' widespread dissatisfaction with their overall way of life, documented in various comparative political surveys.

Conclusion

After discussing the relevance of emotions for the understanding of populism, in this Chapter I looked at the Greek case through a political sociology of emotion perspective principally using Max Scheler's phenomenology of *ressentiment*. Deploying Scheler's theory, I tried to isolate and interpret the role of *ressentiment* in clearing the ground for the emergence of populism in post-authoritarian Greece. The rise of the Greek Socialists (PASOK) was buttressed, if not driven, by an array of emotions typical of populations undergoing rapid upward social mobility: repressed vindictiveness and vengeance, spite, envy and *ressentiment*. PASOK was heavily supported by new middle strata created by defeat in the civil war (1946–49). Although they were more or less integrated socially and economically, until the mid-1970s they were politically marginalized and dominated. During the seven-year military dictatorship their political marginalization was experienced as an inexorable destiny leading thereby to an experience of impotence and inferiority. In contradistinction to the 1960s, where the defeated of the civil war articulated public grievances and demands out of resentment qua moral anger, during the dictatorship they developed a deep feeling of *ressentiment*. As soon as PASOK took office in 1981 and the lower middle strata (the 'non-privileged' in Andreas Papandreou's rhetoric) found themselves integrated into the political system, *ressentiment* gave place to vengeance precisely because it could be released and acted out publicly.

All in all, it seems that, over a period of 30 years, the feeling of *ressentiment* grew, withdrew and was replaced by other feelings (fear, vindictiveness, indignation, etc.), which contributed to the forming of collective identities and the consolidation of political institutions and processes. However, my argument cannot but be a simplification, since in real life feelings are in a constant flux and cannot be easily isolated.

Notes

1. As there has been an everlasting debate on the exact meaning of the terms 'emotion', 'feeling', 'sentiment', 'passion', 'affect' in psychology, sociology, anthropology, philosophy and political science, for the sake of brevity I shall treat them as equivalent. Of course, there are differences between them emanating from differences in the semantic fields, the different periods in the paradigmatic development of each single discipline (Shott, 1979; Kemper, 1987; Oatley and Jenkins, 1996). As a working definition, by 'emotion' (or feeling) I refer to the arousal of the human organism that takes place within a definite time context, involves awareness but not necessarily verbalization, and induces readiness for action and evaluations of objects, relations and situations.
2. One can find both uses in the work of a single author; for example, Connolly (1991: 166, 121, 211) who draws heavily from Nietzsche while analysing existential resentment (the emotional response to the question of evil and death), and at the same time uses 'resentment' – not *ressentiment* which appears only three times in his text (*op. cit.* 185, 187, 213) – as a response against injustice in the social distribution of opportunities and resources. In the latter sense, resentment is understood as righteous indignation, a central

concept in Sennett and Cobb's (1972: 117–18, 139, 148) study of the post-World War II American working-class consciousness.

3. The exceptions to this are Barrington Moore's analysis (1978), who does not however use the term 'resentment' but prefers the notions of moral anger and vengeance to describe the emotional investing of injustice, and Zygmunt Bauman's thesis (1982: 179–80) that late capitalist-class realignments and consumption produce a great potential of *ressentiment*.

4. In psychoanalytic terms, Simon Clarke (2004) proposed that *ressentiment* can be thought for the societal level as to what envy is for the individual; that is, as a destructive emotion which damages future generations to the extend that it represents pure negativity. Clarke refers to the Kleinean conception of envy, which is a projection of Thanatos and 'reminiscent of Nietzschean *ressentiment*' (p. 106). Were not transvaluation being central to Nietzsche's, let alone to Scheler's, argumentation I could agree with Clarke's insight. Yet, it seems to me that the nietzschean version of ressentiment cannot be equated with envy; rather, as a negative and complex feeling it contains and somehow submerges envy as long as perpetual powerlessness and relived inferiority block open destructive action or malicious expressions. Transvaluation, then, tames and modulates envy and, in that sense, although *ressentiment* is reactive it is not primarily destructive.

5. Turning upside down Nietzsche's notion, Solomon (1994) claims that trans-valuation *qua* passivity is a strategy of the will to power specific for the weak. Consequently, powerlessness is not seen as a cause of *ressentiment* but as an outer manifestation of the weaks' eagerness to take revenge in their own terms, as an expression of their own will to power. For Solomon *ressentiment* is the ever most clever and life-preserving emotion of the slave in his confrontation with the master.

6. Emphasis should be placed here on 'rightly', on the sense of justice that accompanies the vindictive joy one experiences facing the sufferings of a third person ('he went for it', 'he should have watched his step'). If there were not for the dimension of justice we would be dealing simply with grudging-ness. For a sharp-witted analysis of *Schadenfreude*, see John Portman (2000).

7. Here I do not indent to offer even a working definition of populism, as the discussion about the definition(s) of this concept is really endless.

8. Additionally, I would argue that the nodal point of this assumption is the signifier 'the people'. The use of 'the people' is a necessary (even though not sufficient) condition for the constitution of populist discourse.

9. EAM: the Greek National Liberation Front. It was a left-wing resistance army against the German and Italian occupation (1941–1944).

10. For the concept of 'cultural trauma', see Alexander *et al.* (2004).

11. In July 1964 the king refused to appoint the leader of the majority, George Papandreou, as Prime Minister, a long-term centre-left opposition was emerged as a result.

8
Anger and the Struggle for Justice

Simon Thompson

> *Let anger, then, be desire, accompanied by pain, for revenge for an obvious belittlement of oneself or one of one's dependants, the belittlement being uncalled for*
>
> Aristotle, *Rhetoric*, 1378a

Introduction

It has been argued that the emotion of anger plays a central role in politics. As Peter Lyman says, 'one can define anger as the essential political emotion' (1981, p. 61). The authors who contributed to the 2004 special edition of the *European Journal of Social Theory* on 'Anger in political life' suggest reasons why anger is of such importance. In Mary Holmes' words, anger 'is the essential political emotion because it is a response to perceived injustice' (2004, p. 127). Or, as David Ost suggests, if we adopt a 'conflict theory of politics' – as he thinks we should – then 'emotions and the mobilization of anger become central to politics' (2004, p. 239). We can see two distinct, albeit closely related ideas at work in these remarks which suggest why anger is of such importance. One idea is *mobilization*; here the implication is that anger is the emotion which is capable of motivating people to engage in political action. The other idea is *injustice*; here it is implied that the reason why people mobilize is in order to overcome such perceived injustice. These two ideas in conjunction suggest that close attention to the emotion of anger can help us to understand the political world. From the perspective of political philosophy, politics is a matter of debate about the nature of the just society. From the perspective of political science, politics involves struggles for resources, status and, more generally, power. Anger can play a key role in both these sides of political studies. If it is regarded as the emotion which people feel when they experience injustice, then understanding anger may offer us insights into the nature of justice itself. If it is regarded as the emotion which motivates political action, then it may help us to understand the character of struggles for power. Bringing these two perspectives together, attention to anger may enable us to explain how and why people engage in collective action in order to try to achieve justice together.

In this chapter, I want to examine one particular account of the emotion of anger which gives it an important role both in the determination of social justice and in the explanation of political action. Axel Honneth, one of the most important contemporary representatives of the tradition of German critical theory, argues in his book *Struggle for Recognition* (1995) that a just society would be one in which all individuals are shown due recognition. In such circumstances, he believes, it would be possible for everyone to achieve self-realization. As he defines it in a later article, self-realization is a person's capacity 'to freely determine and realize his own desires and intentions' (2002, p. 516). It is important to understand that, for Honneth, recognition is not a uniform and homogenous substance, but rather takes three distinct forms. Love, the first mode of recognition, is the strong affective attachment between specific family members, lovers and friends. Respect for rational autonomy is a universalist mode of recognition which should be enjoyed by all human beings equally. Esteem is a feeling of solidarity which individuals can have with particular others who share their values. Honneth does not regard his account of a society in which individuals can enjoy all three modes of recognition merely as an exercise in wishful thinking. Instead he wants to show how this ideal is rooted in existing social reality. In order to do so, he argues that 'negative emotional reactions' (1995, p. 135) such as anger provide the motivating force behind struggles for recognition. The experience of anger is evidence of perceived injustice, and thus it gives people the impetus to engage in collective action in order to overcome this injustice. Honneth argues, moreover, that the effect of a series of such struggles is the development of fully fledged relations of recognition. If such relations are in place, then people are able to enjoy the love, respect and esteem from others, which makes their self-realization possible. However, since some parties will resist other parties' attempts to gain recognition, struggle is inevitable, and it is only through a series of such struggles that recognition will be achieved. In short, emotions such as anger mobilize people to achieve recognition.

In the next section, I sketch the fundamental elements of Honneth's account, focusing in particular on the links that he makes between negative emotions, consciousness of injustice, and struggles for recognition themselves. In the section after that, I compare and contrast his account of anger with that of Aristotle. I believe that this comparison will throw very interesting light on Honneth's theory, and especially on the place of emotions within it. In particular, I use this comparison to bring out the way in which Honneth seeks to give a dual role to emotion, both as a source of knowledge and as a source of motivation. In the following section, I use this comparison to establish a framework within which to conduct a critical assessment of Honneth's theory. I evaluate a number of criticisms that can be made of this account, concentrating in particular on the series of links in his argument which I have just mentioned. I focus on two particular areas of concern: the status and justifiability of emotions, and emotions as stimuli for collective action. In the final section of the chapter, I reach a verdict about the cogency of Honneth's account of emotions as the key motivating factor in struggles for recognition. I seek to determine in particular whether this account successfully shows how anger can perform both an epistemic and a mobilizing function in collective action – how, in other words, it can be both a source of knowledge and a source of motivation. My principal argument will be that Honneth is pulled into two very different directions. On the one hand, he wants to argue that emotions can give us privileged insight into our situation; but on the other hand, he accepts that such emotions are necessarily mediated and hence shaped by various social institutions.

Struggles for recognition

The idea of struggle plays a vitally important part in Honneth's account of recognition. He believes that recognition, by its very nature, is only likely to be achieved through what Joel Anderson, his translator, calls a 'conflict-ridden developmental process' (Honneth, 1995, p. xi). This explains the full title of Honneth's book *The Struggle for Recognition: The Moral Grammar of Social Conflicts*. Here we can see the strong connection that he makes between normative theory and social conflict. Looking at it one way, social conflicts can be explained by using the idea of recognition. Such conflicts occur, Honneth believes, when people demand the recognition which they are presently denied. In order to understand the history of the American civil rights movement, for instance, it would be useful to regard this movement as a series of struggles by African-Americans to obtain due recognition.

Looking at it the other way around, Honneth thinks that it is possible to shed light on the idea of recognition by examining social conflicts. Such conflicts tend to move the society towards the realization of undistorted relations of recognition. Thus, by looking in the direction to which these conflicts point, we can understand what full recognition would be like. This hints at a third element to Honneth's account. Since he argues that struggles for recognition move society towards an ideal state characterized by undistorted relations of recognition, he believes the idea of recognition also holds the key to a theory of moral progress. In other words, the moral development of society takes the form of a gradual expansion of relations of recognition. In this way, Honneth combines a normative theory of recognition (which describes the ideal form that a society should take) with a theory of social conflict (which explains why such conflicts occur) and a theory of moral progress (which explains how the ideal society can be achieved through a series of social conflicts). In what follows, I concentrate on the first two stages of this ambitious argument. In the first stage, it is argued that negative emotions such an anger may be understood as evidence of injustice. In the second stage, it is suggested that this awareness of injustice can motivate collective struggles. The final stage of Honneth's argument, in which he argues that recognition struggles have the potential to move society towards a state in which there is a complete realization of the idea of recognition, raises issues way beyond the ambitions of the argument I am developing here.

In the first stage of his argument, Honneth uses what he calls an 'empirically grounded phenomenology' (1995, p. 162) to establish the foundations of his account of recognition. In other words, he examines the domain of ordinary human lives – and, in particular, the quality and texture of affective experience – in order to find evidence of the importance of recognition. It is for this reason that he pays close attention to people's 'hurt feelings' (1995, p. 163) or 'negative emotional reactions' (1995, pp. 135, 136, 138).[1] Consideration of these phrases might suggest that Honneth's account of emotions is entirely descriptive. It looks as if he is simply describing how people feel in particular circumstances. At other points, however, he is clear that these emotions are bound up with normative judgements. Hence he talks about 'moral experiences' (1995, p. 162; 1994, p. 268) and 'moral feelings' (1995, p. 168). This means that negative emotions are infused with normative content: to experience these emotions is also to make a (more or less explicit) normative judgement, a view akin to Martha Nussbaum's (2001) idea of the 'intelligence of the emotions'. If I feel angry, it is because I believe a particular situation to be unjust. Even more strongly, Honneth suggests that feelings like anger constitute an 'affective source of knowledge' (1995, p. 143). As he says, these emotions can give us 'moral insight' into our situation; indeed in certain circumstances injustice can 'cognitively disclose' itself (1995, p. 138). In other words, to experience a negative emotion is not just to make a moral judgement: it is also to find out something about the circumstances in which I find myself. If I attend to the anger I feel, I can gain valuable insight into my situation.

Thus the experience of a negative emotion has both normative and epistemic dimensions. To have such a feeling is both to make a moral judgment and to achieve insight into a situation. Honneth fills in this account by suggesting why we feel as we do in particular circumstances. His hypothesis is that hurt feelings such as anger are triggered among other things by the denial of various forms of recognition. Here he talks about the 'violation of implicit rules of mutual recognition' (1995, p. 160) or the 'violation of deeply rooted expectations regarding recognition' (1995, p. 163). In other words, it is because I anticipate being recognized, but then fail to enjoy such recognition, that I feel as I do.[2] At one point, Honneth suggests that there are in fact three distinctive forms of violation, corresponding to the three forms of recognition themselves (1995, pp. 132–34). If people are maltreated, they will feel humiliated, and their self-confidence will be damaged. He suggests that attacks on the very integrity of the human body – in the form, for instance, of torture – will make humans feel this way. If people are excluded from citizenship, and denied the rights to which they believe themselves entitled, then their self-respect will suffer. It could be argued that, at the start of the civil rights movement, this is exactly how black Americans felt. If the way of life with which people associate themselves is denigrated, then their self-esteem is at risk. British Muslims experiencing various forms of Islamophobia are likely to feel this way (Runnymede Trust, 1997). In this first stage of Honneth's argument, then, he seeks to demonstrate that hurt feelings can be understood as evidence of injustice. Feelings such as anger are triggered by violations of expectations about recognition, and thus these feelings tell people that they are being denied the recognition which is their due.

In the second stage of Honneth's argument, he seeks to show that the sense of injustice generated by emotions such as anger can motivate collective action. As he puts it, 'negative emotional reactions' provide the 'affective motivational basis' (1995, p. 135) for collective protest and resistance. To be specific, people who experience a lack of recognition will struggle to achieve such recognition. Thus the experience of 'disrespect' – which Honneth uses as a general term for the lack of recognition – can provide 'the motivational impetus for social resistance' (1995, p. 132). Or, as he says a little later on, 'the violation of implicit rules of mutual recognition' leads to 'social conflicts' (1995, p. 160). In order to show how a sense of injustice can lead to collective action, Honneth argues that individuals can come to realize that the private injuries from which they suffer are the result of public injustices. Rather than each individual thinking that their anger is an entirely subjective and wholly irrational feeling, they can instead come to see it as evidence that an injustice is being done not just to them but to all people who are located in a relevantly similar position. In order for this to happen, Honneth argues, there must be a 'semantic bridge' between 'private experiences of injury' and the 'impersonal aspirations of a social movement'. This bridge is provided by an 'intersubjective framework of interpretation' (1995, p. 163) which can help individuals to see that their hurt feelings are the result of social processes to which a whole set of people are subject. One important type of framework is that constructed from 'moral doctrines or ideas' (1995, p. 164). Such a doctrine provides a language in which it becomes possible to understand that a set of apparent discrete private injuries are in fact the result of a systematic public injustice. Here Honneth's account closely resembles David Snow and Robert Benford's work on 'frame alignment' (1988, 2000). In particular, by placing the idea of 'motivational framing' alongside 'diagnostic framing' ('what's the problem?') and 'prognostic framing' ('who is to blame?'), they open up a space in which to understand the role of the emotions in social mobilization.

One useful example of a framework of interpretation is that of second-wave feminism. It has been suggested that, before the emergence of this form of thinking, women in western societies who experienced anxiety and depression tended to believe (or at least were told) that their problems were caused by personal psychological maladjustment. However, looking through the lens of second-wave feminism enabled these women to see that in reality their problems resulted from an imbalance of power which led *inter alia* to their exclusion from the labour market and their confinement to the domestic sphere. This realization enabled women to feel angry about the situation in which they found themselves, where this emotion had been previously repressed or simply did not exist. In the late 1960 and 1970s, 'consciousness raising groups' specifically served this purpose of enabling a transformation from something primarily affective and individualized to something shared in common and more fully understood. Thus a new collective identity – the women's movement – emerged in order to draw on the energy of this anger in the struggle against these unjust conditions. In this example, we can see how the use of a particular interpretive framework made it possible to convert particular subjective feelings into awareness of objective oppression. Each woman's awareness that her feelings of anger resulted from the unjust conditions in which not just she but many others found themselves gave her reason to join with these others in order to fight it. In other words, it was women's realization that they were suffering a collective injustice that motivated their collective struggle against that injustice. To sum up, negative emotions such as anger perform two closely related functions in Honneth's argument. First, they provide cognitive insight into the situation of the people experiencing these emotions; second, they provide motivational impetus for those people to try to break out of that situation. Thus anger performs both a cognitive and a mobilizing role in Honneth's politics of recognition.

Aristotle and Honneth

As we saw in the epigraph to this chapter, Aristotle holds that anger is the emotion we feel when we have been unfairly insulted; he believes that the pain this causes leads us to contemplate revenge. His analysis of the emotion of anger can be divided into three distinct parts. First, the *subject* must be in a particular psychological state which means that he will become angry in certain circumstances.[3] To put it in the words of one of his editors, Aristotle presumes that the subject must have aspirations or needs which can be 'blocked or frustrated, the blocking or frustrating of which being the key factor in the development of the anger' (Lawson-Tancred 1991, p. 23). Second, there must be an appropriate sort of *stimulus* in order to provoke anger in the subject. In the specific case of anger, the stimulus is a perceived insult. In fact, Aristotle says that there are three types of insult. In the case of contempt, something valued by the subject is judged to be worthless. Spite occurs when the subject's wishes are blocked merely to disadvantage him. Insult is a matter of shaming the subject for the sake of it (*Rhetoric*, 1378b). Aristotle gives a detailed list of possible forms of belittlement. Here are a few specific examples. Men are angry with: 'Those that laugh at them and scoff at them'; 'Those who speak ill of or despise the things about which they are especially serious' (1379a); 'Those who are accustomed to respect them and show them consideration, if they do not on another occasion so address them'; and 'Those in opposition to them, if they are inferior' (1379b). Finally, there must be an *object* who can be held responsible for the stimulus and towards whom the subject can direct his anger. In this specific case, the object is the person who belittles the subject. According to Aristotle, this object must be of a certain kind. To begin with, he says that the angry man is always angry with a *particular person* rather than 'mankind' as a whole (1378a). Nor is it possible for him to be angry with someone more powerful than himself, since here the appropriate emotion is fear, and it 'is impossible, after all, to be angry and afraid at the same time' (1380a). Nor finally is it possible for the subject to remain angry with those weaker than himself, if they show genuine contrition for their action. To bring these three elements together, if the subject is insulted by the object, then, so long as the various conditions specified above hold, he will become angry with him. According to Aristotle, this will mean that the subject is in pain, in the sense that he is aiming at something he does not have (1379a). As a result, he contemplates revenge on the person whom he holds responsible for causing that pain. This contemplation then gives him a certain amount of pleasure as he imagines achieving the revenge which he seeks (1378b).[4]

In the present context, several elements of Aristotle's analysis are worth drawing out a little further. First, it is a *cognitive account*. It could be argued that, according to Aristotle, experiencing an emotion is not opposed to thinking rationally. Feeling angry does not mean that one's critical faculties are suspended. In fact, quite the opposite is the case: in particular circumstances, it is entirely rational to be angry. As we shall see, this does not mean that anger is always justified – only that it is *capable* of being justified. Second, and closely related to the first point, Aristotle believes that anger can be assessed according to particular *criteria of justification*. While, in the circumstances outlined above, anger is the appropriate response, in other circumstances, it may not be appropriate. For instance, the subject's actions may be such as to justify the suffering inflicted on him. In these circumstances, he will not become angry. As Aristotle says, 'anger does not arise against justice' (1380b). Perhaps more importantly, it is possible for a person to feel insufficient or excessive anger. In D. S. Hutchinson's words, if an emotion is 'incorrectly adjusted', then it 'is felt either too much or too little' (1995, p. 215).[5] In the present case, bad-tempered men feel too much anger, while stupid and slavish men feel too little (Aristotle, *Ethics*, 1125b–1126b). Third, one implication of Aristotle's account is that emotions may be an important element in the *explanation of action*.

Each emotion is associated with an experience of pleasure and/or pain which goads people into action. In the present case, being belittled causes the angry man to feel pain; at the same time, he experiences pleasure in the anticipation of revenge. Hence it could be argued that his act of revenge can be explained by reference to his experience of anger. Fourth, if Aristotle's various remarks about expectations of respect and deference are brought together, it could be said that there is an *ethics of recognition* at work in his account.[6] In particular, he assumes that individuals expect to be treated in a way appropriate to their situation and status, and that they will feel angry if they are not so treated. To be specific, they expect to be respected and will be angry when they are insulted instead. Fifth, one key assumption lying behind Aristotle's analysis is of the *appropriateness of hierarchy*. He assumes a hierarchical society in which inferiors should show their superiors respect, and in which the superiors rightly expect deference from them: 'men think it right that they should be revered by those inferior to them by birth, by power and by virtue and in general by whatever it is in which they much excel' (Aristotle, *Rhetoric*, 1378b–1379a). In short, relative status has a strong influence on the appropriateness of emotions.

This is a fascinating and perspicacious account of anger, and certainly not one that is of merely historical interest. Indeed the debt that many contemporary accounts of anger owe to Aristotle is clear. It can be seen, for instance, in Theodore Kemper's suggestion that '[d]isappointment and anger result when the actor deems the other the agent – the willing, knowing actor who failed to accord sufficient status' (2001, p. 64; cf. Holmes 2004, p. 126). In other words, anger is the emotion people feel when they are not given the respect or recognition which they expect from another. By contrast, Honneth – at least to the best of my knowledge – makes no reference to Aristotle in the exposition of his own account of emotions. Nevertheless I believe that it will be instructive to compare and contrast these two accounts. To begin with, let us consider the three principal elements of Aristotle's analysis. First, both thinkers make certain assumptions about the nature of the *subject*. For Aristotle, it is the fact that humans can have their aims frustrated by others that is of crucial importance in explaining their potential for anger. It could be argued that Honneth offers a specific version of this general argument, suggesting that it is their capacity for self-realization which may be frustrated by the circumstances in which humans find themselves. Second, there are also similarities to be found in the two thinkers' accounts of the *stimulus* which causes the subject to feel angry. Aristotle regards belittlement as the (necessary and/or sufficient?) cause of anger.

As I have suggested above, his list of examples of belittlement includes a number of references to respect, and in general to the subject's expectations about how he should be treated by others. For his part, Honneth is clear that it is the violation of expectations about recognition that leads to hurt feelings such as anger. Third, it is with regard to their analysis of the *object* that the difference between these two thinkers' positions is most clearly marked. While Aristotle argues that an insult which causes anger can only come from a specific individual, Honneth implies that anger can also be rightly directed towards impersonal social systems. For him, systems of rights which fail to respect, and horizons of value which provide no opportunity to win esteem, can be the direct objects of anger.

Now let us turn our attention to the specific features of Aristotle's account which I have already highlighted. Here a number of other similarities and differences come into view. First, I have argued that Aristotle endorses a *cognitive account* of the emotions. He does not oppose reason and emotion, suggesting instead that there are circumstances in which it is entirely rational to be angry. It seems as if Honneth does not oppose reason and emotion either. He assumes rather that emotions, by giving us information about our situation, can give us good reasons to act. In fact, this may be a stronger position than Aristotle's, since Honneth says more boldly that it is possible to have an intuitive (felt) sense of how things really are. Second, with regard to the closely related issue of the *criteria of justifiability*, Aristotle believes that in some circumstances anger can be justified, whilst in others it cannot. For instance, if I have acted badly, I would not be justified in being angry with anyone who criticizes my action. Honneth, by contrast, does not seem to be aware of the fact that emotions can be more or less justifiable. Indeed, he is sometimes tempted to treat them as pristine sources of knowledge about my situation. I shall pick up this point in the next section. Third, both thinkers imply, more or less explicitly, that emotions can have a role to play in the *explanation of action*. Aristotle suggests that, since they are always accompanied by pain or pleasure, emotions are able to explain why we act as we do. Honneth is in full agreement with Aristotle. The principal aim of his account of emotions is to show how feelings can motivate people to act, and specifically to struggle for recognition. I shall also pick up this point in the next section. Fourth, both Aristotle and Honneth endorse what I have called an *ethics of recognition*. In other words, recognition plays a central part in a set of rules which are located in a specific value-horizon. While Aristotle suggests that we become angry when we are not given the respect we expect, Honneth argues that our negative emotions arise from the violation of our expectations of recognition. Fifth, both thinkers make certain assumptions about the status order which forms the context for their accounts of emotions. It is here that another fundamental difference between them emerges. Aristotle assumes the *appropriateness of hierarchy*. The fact of hierarchy then shapes the sort of emotions which occur in this society. Thus *ceteris paribus* one is more angry if insulted by an inferior than by an equal. In sharp contrast, Honneth marks a distinction between pre-modern societies in which recognition was distributed hierarchically, and modern societies in which it is distributed according to strongly egalitarian principles. For him, the transition from pre-modern to modern society is without question a matter of moral progress.

Criticisms of Honneth

Aristotle's and Honneth's views diverge at several important points. While the former believes that it is only possible to be angry with a particular individual, the latter assumes that it is also possible to be angry with impersonal social systems; and while the former defends a hierarchy of status, the latter is strongly egalitarian. Despite these important differences, there are also a number of striking resemblances between these accounts. In particular, both argue that the experience of anger is associated with the frustration of a capacity; that people feel angry if they are not appropriately recognized; and that this anger goads them into action in order to put this injustice right. In the light of this degree of similarity, I would argue that Honneth endorses what can be called an Aristotelian account of anger. In this section, I want to draw on this comparison and contrast between Aristotle and Honneth in order to frame a critique of the latter's account of the emotions. I focus in particular on two areas of concern. First, I consider further Honneth's views about the status and justifiability of emotions. Does he successfully show that they have a cognitive status? And does he pay sufficient attention to Aristotle's insight that emotions can be inappropriate and disproportionate? Second, I consider in more detail the idea that negative emotions can act as stimuli for collective action. Does Honneth offer a sufficiently nuanced account of the role that such feelings can have in explaining struggles for recognition?

A cognitive account

I have suggested that Aristotle enables us to see that emotion is not normally opposed to reason. If certain conditions are in place, then anger may be the appropriate and rational response to a particular situation. I have also suggested that Honneth is in agreement with Aristotle on this point. He believes that emotional experience is closely bound up both with moral judgements and cognitive insights. In this sense, both thinkers can be said to endorse a cognitive account of the emotions. As Robert Solomon defines it, 'An emotion, on this cognitive account, consists of a certain way of conceiving of and responding to the world, accompanied, perhaps, by certain feelings, expressed in certain types of behaviour and further explained by certain neurophysiological discoveries' (1998). Here 'conceiving of' and 'responding to' correspond to the epistemic and moral sides of Honneth's account respectively. In other words, to feel anger is to understand and react to the world in a particular way. It is clear that to defend a cognitive account of the emotions is to make a very bold claim about their status and justifiability. In this sub-section, I want to consider whether Honneth is able – and, in some instances, prepared – to support this claim.

I begin by considering a couple of preliminary questions. The first is this: does Honneth believe that his analysis applies to all emotions of all kinds? Or does it just apply to 'negative' emotions? Or just to some sub-set of these? For example, would it apply to what James Jasper calls 'moods' such as 'sadness and joy' (p. 26)? Such moods lack a definite object in the sense that they are not *about* some specific thing. In this case, since there is no state of affairs into which the emotion could give cognitive insight or on which moral judgement could be passed, it is difficult to see how they could be covered by Honneth's analysis.[7] To take another example, could Honneth's analysis apply to what Jasper calls *'reflex emotions'* which are 'quick to appear and to subside' (p. 16)? It seems unlikely, for instance, that disgust could be said to embody complex moral and epistemic evaluations.[8] The second preliminary question I want to consider is this: do the emotions to which Honneth thinks his analysis applies necessarily involve moral judgement and cognitive insight? For instance, are all forms and instances of anger amenable to his analysis? While the anger of the politically marginalized does fit, it seems unlikely that the same could be said of those experiencing road-rage. To take another case, is shame always a reaction to the violation of expectations about recognition? In some cases, shame is felt by individuals who fall short of their own self-imposed ethical ideals. Here the connection to an ethics of recognition seems tenuous to say the least.

Let us put these questions aside, and assume that we have identified a sub-set of emotions, and a sub-set of circumstances, in which Honneth's analysis does apply. We can then approach what to me appears to be the central issue: Do these emotions always function in the way that Honneth imagines? That is to say, do they always provide reliable insights into our situation and justifiable evaluations of that situation? As I have already suggested, Aristotle identifies a number of circumstances in which it would be inappropriate and irrational to feel anger, and other circumstances in which this emotion may be felt to a disproportionate degree. If Aristotle's argument is accepted, then it is necessary to ask whether anger is justifiable in each specific case. His own answer depends on his particular account of ethics, and in particular of the moral virtues. He argues that, if these virtues have been correctly inculcated in us, then our emotional reactions in particular situations will be appropriate. However, since this account depends on a strong ethical vision of human excellence, Honneth cannot follow it himself. Since he accepts that the citizens of contemporary societies endorse a plurality of reasonable values, he concludes that it would be unfair to impose one particular set of values on all of them. In this case, it is necessary to consider how he might deal with this challenge. To bring matters into focus, I want to review two sets of criticisms, and to consider how Honneth might respond to them.

According to one sort of criticism of the link between 'negative emotional reactions' (1995, p. 135) and judgements of injustice, hurt feelings such as anger may not always be reliable evidence of injustice. Negative emotional reactions may sometimes be unjustified: people may feel that they are being mistreated, when in fact they are not. There are two possibilities to be considered. First, there may be a problem of *false comparison*. People may feel unfairly treated when they compare themselves to others such as immigrants. If they believe that these others are doing much better than they are, they may feel anger and demand recompense. However, these feelings may result from a misleading or false comparison, and thus the case for compensation may not be justified. The implication is that, although people may feel anger towards another group with whom they compare themselves, this feeling may not be justified.[9] To generalize, even if people feel hurt, this does not always mean that they do so with good reason. Another reason for thinking that hurt feelings may not be proof of injustice is that people can feel hurt and think they are treated unjustly as the result of a *distorting interpretive framework*. That is to say, they may have a way of looking at the world which causes them to feel angry. A nationalist framework of interpretation, for instance, may tell a group of people that they have been humiliated by their rival nations, that their culture is under grave threat or that their resources are being drained away by a shadowy group of international bankers. Yet this nationalist framework may be generating a feeling of anger and a sense of injustice which are in fact the products of paranoid fantasy (Zizek, 1989).

In both of these cases, people may feel angry, see this as evidence of injustice and thus struggle against this injustice. If, however, this feeling of anger is shaped by a false comparison or a distorting interpretive framework, then it may not accurately indicate the presence of injustice.[10] In neither of these cases does the feeling of anger necessarily provide reliable evidence of maltreatment. People may feel hurt without good reason; to put the point at its crudest, sometimes people just whinge.[11] These possibilities threaten to sever the link that Honneth makes between hurt feelings and judgements of injustice. I would suggest that, in response to this type of criticism, Honneth has two possible lines of defence. First, he could try to argue that emotions are always a reliable source of knowledge about the situations to which they are a response. This assumption can be seen at work in his claim that emotions are 'pretheoretical facts' (1994, p. 263). They are, in other words, the raw and pristine data on the basis of which accounts of social justice and moral progress can be built. Second, Honneth could admit that the right sort of framework of interpretation is vital in order to determine when negative emotions are reliable indicators of injustice. I shall argue in a moment, however, that neither of these options comes without cost.

A second criticism that can be made of this part of Honneth's argument effectively makes the opposite point to the first: rather than suggesting that hurt feelings may not reliably indicate injustice, it suggests instead that injustice may not be accompanied by hurt feelings. The objective fact that someone is being mistreated may not be accompanied by subjective awareness of this mistreatment. In other words, being unjustly treated does not necessarily lead to feelings of anger. Again, I shall consider two distinct possibilities. The first of these suggests that what, for the sake of this argument, I shall call *ideology* can block the conversion of the experience of private injury into the consciousness of public injustice. Roger Foster makes an argument of this kind. He begins by suggesting that 'particular structural arrangements' may 'incapacitate cultural resistance' (1999, p. 7). In this case, in order to determine whether a struggle for recognition is likely to occur, it is necessary to look at the structural arrangements in which the people affected find themselves. With the wrong conditions in place, consciousness of injustice may not occur. A second possibility is that awareness of maltreatment can be blocked by what I shall refer to as *trauma*. Here attention is shifted away from the ideological and towards the social psychological dimension of struggle. Elliot Jurist makes an argument of kind, suggesting that Honneth fails 'to contend with the painful truth that victims of aggression are often too traumatized to struggle in response' (1994, p. 176). In this case, the reason why hurt feelings fail to create a sense of injustice capable of motivating social protest is that the victims of that injustice suffer a form of psychological damage that renders them unable to clearly understand their condition and thus unable to struggle against it. Victims of rape and concentration camp survivors who blame themselves would be examples of this phenomenon in practice. The cruel irony is that, in these circumstances, people are too traumatized precisely by the injustice itself to be able to resist it.

These two possibilities present important challenges to Honneth's optimistic account. If ideology or trauma severs the link between unjust circumstances and a sense of anger, then people who are being treated badly may not be aware of this treatment, and they will thus lack an effective motive to struggle for recognition. It would also follow that the absence of hurt feelings does not necessarily prove absence of mistreatment. To put this more strongly, just because people do not feel an emotion such as anger in particular circumstances, it does not mean that they *should not* feel anger. Once again, Honneth could offer two distinct lines of defence against this sort of criticism. First, he could turn to what some of his critics see as his anthropological assumption that human beings have an innate drive for self-realization. As Jeffrey Alexander and María Pía Lara put it, he has a 'submerged developmental commitment to an anthropological imperative' (1996, p. 134; cf. Zurn, 2000). In this case, Honneth could argue that this imperative is strong enough to be able to overcome ideology or trauma, so that anyone who is frustrated in their attempts at self-realization by being denied recognition could not fail consciously to experience the hurt feelings accompanying such a denial. Here it may be useful to recall Aristotle's assumption that the subject of anger is a person who can be frustrated in the exercise of his capacities. Second, Honneth could repeat the same line of defence which I suggested he could make to the first type of criticism, and acknowledge the role that social institutions and the ideas associated with them can play in filtering and interpreting emotional experience. In this case, he could argue that, in a public sphere constituted in the right way,[12] hurt feelings would lead to an appropriate sense of injustice.

What are we to make of the various responses that Honneth could make to his critics? In the first place, it could be argued that in both cases the two suggested lines of defence work against each other. On the one hand, if the first line works, the second is redundant. If it can be shown that emotions are reliable sources of knowledge, or that humans possess an indefeasible imperative to achieve self-realization, then there is no need for the right sort of interpretive framework. On the other hand, if the second line of argument is necessary, the first must have failed. That is to say, if it is conceded that the framework of interpretation plays an active role in shaping emotions, then it follows that they cannot be a reliable source of knowledge about justice in themselves, or that the anthropological imperative can sometimes fail. In addition, each line of defence faces its own problems. The idea that emotions can be 'pre-theoretical facts' is highly implausible. In general, facts only exist within the framework of a particular theory. In this particular case, emotions are always mediated by a particular set of social understandings. The idea of an anthropological imperative can only be redeemed by a highly ambitious account of human nature which would certainly not escape criticism. The idea that mediation always plays a role in our emotional life is plausible. But acceptance of this idea places all the weight on the mediating institutions, rather than on the emotions themselves. I shall develop each of these points further in what follows.

Explanation of action

A second set of criticisms that can be made of Honneth's account focuses on his assumption that the feeling of anger can provide sufficient motivation for people to struggle for recognition. These criticisms raise doubts about whether Honneth can explain why struggles of recognition occur simply by referring to people's negative emotions. In other words, they challenge his assumption that hurt feelings are either a necessary or a sufficient condition of such struggles. There are two distinct issues which need to be considered.

One issue arises from the likelihood that in modern societies there will be a variety of frameworks of interpretation. It seems reasonable to assume that these frameworks will interpret the same emotional experience in very different ways, and will thus reach very different normative conclusions. Honneth appears to assume that, at least under all normal conditions, his framework of interpretation will win out over others. He needs to make this assumption in order to demonstrate that, as a result of struggles for recognition, relations of recognition will expand rather than remain static, get distorted or even contract. But how can he justify this assumption? To bring this problem into focus, let us consider the status of what for the sake of this argument I shall call the neo-Nazi interpretive framework. This is grounded on the same emotions of anger and humiliation that catch Honneth's attention. However, in contrast to Honneth's account, the neo-Nazi world-view assumes that the protection of its members' collective self-esteem necessitates despising all of those outside its own narrow community of value. As Alexander and Pía Lara put it, 'esteem is, in fact, often provided within the particularistic, self-affirming boundaries of segmented communities which experience themselves as downwardly mobile'. 'Based on deep resentments', they suggest, the demands for recognition made by such groups 'can easily become demands for domination' (1996, p. 134). Focusing on the emotion of shame, they conclude that 'as the history of reactionary social movements that have marked the twentieth century indicates, grasping a moral content in response to feeling publicly and privately shamed is not particularly likely in an empirical sense' (1996, p. 135). Indeed, it is more likely that the experience of shame will lead a group to adopt values which, for instance, extol its virtue and purity whilst condemning the viciousness and dirtiness of all outsiders. In short, this criticism suggests that there is no certainty that emotional experience will be interpreted in the way that is necessary if relations of recognition are to develop in the way that Honneth hopes.

At one point, Honneth discusses the neo-Nazi case himself. In an article written at about the same time as *Struggle for Recognition*, he acknowledges the danger that Alexander and Pía Lara describe: 'the experience of social disrespect' can lead to a search for 'social esteem … in small militaristic groups, whose code of honor is dominated by the practice of violence' (1994, p. 268). For him, this presents 'the question of how a moral culture could be so constituted as to give those affected, disrespected and ostracized, the individual strength to articulate their experiences in the democratic public sphere, rather than living them out in the countercultures of violence' (1994, p. 269). The implication of this remark is that if a 'democratic public sphere' were in place, then those who might otherwise become neo-Nazis would have the chance to voice their disquiet in the public sphere. Honneth's assumption appears to be that, since they will feel included in public debate, it is less likely that these alienated citizens will become neo-Nazis in the first place. Here he endorses the idea that the structure of the public sphere can have a crucial influence on the interpretation of particular negative emotional reactions, and therefore on the motives that are generated by this interpretation. To put this in the terms he deploys in *Struggle for*

Recognition, it follows that the sort of 'moral-political conviction' generated depends on the 'cultural-political environment' in question (1995, pp. 138–39). It is possible, in other words, deliberately to create the conditions in which hurt feelings will move a group in one direction rather than another. Since each particular environment is more likely to produce certain convictions rather than others, frameworks of interpretation are not neutral: different frameworks will push a particular group in different directions. Hence it is possible to create an environment in which the reaction to shame is to adopt the 'right' rather than the 'wrong' ethical values. It should be noted, once more, that this acknowledgement of the role of mediating institutions is in tension with Honneth's claim that emotions can be regarded as 'pretheoretical facts'.

As we have seen, Honneth concedes that an interpretive framework is necessary to convert private feelings into public judgements of injustice. He assumes that such judgements are then capable of providing sufficient motivation for people to engage in collective resistance against the unjust conditions which cause those feelings. I feel hurt, realize that I am not the only one who feels hurt and hence join with those others collectively to struggle against the conditions that are causing this hurt. However, according to a second criticism of this stage of Honneth's argument, this is a very narrow and partial account of the factors which are likely to determine the likelihood of social resistance. It is an account which relies exclusively on the idea that such resistance will be triggered by an interpretation of negative emotions. It is because people feel as they do, and give their feelings a particular ethical interpretation, that they will struggle to escape their situation. It could be argued that this account overlooks a wide range of other factors which determine whether or not struggle will occur (and whether that struggle is likely to be successful). The extensive body of empirical research on social movements identifies a number of other factors which will be important in determining whether struggles take place. Let me mention five distinct – although clearly interrelated – categories: available resources, rational incentives, strategic choices, cultural factors and the prevailing political opportunity structure. First, what money and other resources does a group have at its disposal? Poor social movements may face particular difficulties in struggling against the injustice they suffer (Piven and Cloward, 1988). Second, are there reasons of rational self-interest for this group to engage in struggle? That is, can it calculate that certain advantages will be gained by such struggle (Chong, 1991)? Third, what strategic options does the group have available to it? For example, has the group adopted particular forms of political action over time? And what sort of established repertoire of action can it draw on? Fourth, does the dominant culture or the group's own subaltern culture provide motivation for resistance? Fifth, is the structure of the state conducive to struggle or not (Tarrow, 1989)?

All these questions will need to be answered in order to determine whether a struggle for recognition will break out in particular circumstances. Turning back to Honneth, I would argue that it is not enough simply to think that the collective interpretation of emotional experiences will necessarily trigger collective action. Absent resources, incentives, opportunities and so on, negative emotional reactions may very well not be converted into positive struggle. If the state is too repressive, or the group too poor, or the likelihood of success low, then feelings of rage and anger, and the sense of injustice which they fuel, may not lead to active struggle against such injustice. Here is it interesting to recall Aristotle's remark that one feels fear rather than anger before those more powerful than oneself. It could be argued, furthermore, that these various factors will also need to be taken into account in order to determine the chances of a struggle being successful. When will a struggle achieve its aims and when will it simply be crushed? To answer this question, it will be necessary to look beyond hurt feelings and moral experience to consider resources, strategy, culture and so on. I do not think there is any way that Honneth could deny this. At best, he could argue that, while his account of recognition struggles does not provide an exhaustive analysis of all the factors involved in such struggles, it does help to rectify the existing balance by giving due consideration to the hitherto neglected role of emotions.

Conclusions

In this chapter, I have conducted a critical examination of Honneth's account of the role of emotions such as anger in struggles for recognition. In giving both a cognitive and a mobilizing role to emotions in the explanation of political action, I have suggested that Honneth's theory bears a remarkable resemblance to that of Aristotle. His highly ambitious thesis is that it is possible to connect an account of 'everyday suffering', a theory of justice, and a theory of collective action. He attempts to combine an empirical analysis which aims to explain the character of social conflicts with a normative theory which aims to describe and justify an ideal society. It is no surprise to find that Honneth's highly ambitious account has attracted its critics. Focusing on the link that he makes between the experience of hurt feelings and a sense of injustice, I considered various ways in which this link could fail. In particular, I suggested that there could be hurt feelings without injustice, and injustice without hurt feelings. Moving onto the relationship which he believes exists between a sense of injustice and the outbreak of struggle, I highlighted the vital role that frameworks of interpretation play in mediating that relationship, and I suggested that a range of other factors may also intervene. I also suggested that Honneth, in his response to these criticisms, finds himself pulled in two different directions. At some points, he aligns himself with those philosophers who defend a strongly cognitive account of the emotions. Either he asserts that emotions constitute a source of knowledge about social conditions which is in a sense uncorrupted by those conditions, or he relies on the anthropological assumption that an innate urge to achieve self-realization will produce certain specific forms of political life. At other points, Honneth tries to allow that various mediating institutions and the ideas with which they are associated can play a key role in determining the significance of the emotions. We see this in his references to the role of 'moral doctrines or ideas' and 'moral culture', and in his insistence on the importance of an appropriately constituted 'democratic public sphere' within which emotions can be adequately expressed.

The problem is that these two impulses are in tension with each other. On the one hand, in order to show that hurt feelings can be used as the basis of a normative critique of society, or that it is possible to deduce certain conclusions about political life directly from assertions of features about human nature, Honneth must play down the role of mediation. In doing so, he overlooks the role of symbolic institutions in mediating between human beings and politics. To be specific, he neglects the role of culture – or, better, cultural institutions – in mediating emotions. Without taking mediation properly into account, however, he is vulnerable to the criticism that his theory depends on an anthropological or social psychological foundationalism (Fraser, 2003). On the other hand, if Honneth did take on board the importance of the 'cultural-political environment', then his account of the link between a sense of injustice generated by feelings of anger and the motivation to engage in struggles for self-realization would be much more nuanced. He would be much better able to specify the role of mediating institutions in this relationship. This in turn would mean that he would also be better able to determine the likely chances of success of his framework of interpretation over its rivals. However, by placing more weight on the role of mediation, Honneth would diminish the power of his original insight about the vital role of emotions like anger in the explanation and justification of collective action. I can see no easy way in which he could square this circle.

Notes

1. In this chapter, my principal interest is in Honneth's analysis of anger. However, it should be noted that for him this is only one of a number of negative emotions of relevance to his analysis. In addition to the emotions of anger, rage and indignation (1995, p. 136; 1994, p. 263), he also refers, for instance, to shame (1995, pp. 119–20, 135, 137–38, 164; 1994, p. 263), humiliation and degradation (1995, p. 164).
2. Compare Judith Shklar's suggestion that our sense of injustice arises 'when we do not get what we believe to be our due' (1990, p. 83).
3. Since Aristotle's audience was exclusively male, and he believed that he was talking exclusively about men, I shall follow his use of the male gender when explicating his views.
4. It is important to understand that this is not the sort of imaginary revenge involved in what Nietzsche calls *ressentiment*. In that case, one imagines an act of revenge that can never be carried out. By contrast, Aristotle thinks that the angry man contemplates revenge as an entirely realistic course of action. For further discussion of *ressentiment*, see Simon Clarke's and Nicolas Demertzis' chapters in this book.
5. Hutchinson explains that 'moral virtues' are 'dispositions of our emotions which enable us to respond correctly to practical situations' (1995, p. 206). Absent the appropriate virtues, our emotional responses may go awry.
6. The reason why this is an ethics rather than a morality will become clear after consideration of the next point.
7. Paul Hoggett disagrees with this point, suggesting that just because we are not aware of what our mood may be about, it does not follow that it has no meaning.
8. Nussbaum would disagree with this claim since she gives disgust central importance, seeing it as a threat 'to the idea of equal worth and dignity of persons' (2001, p. 221).
9. On this subject, see Simon Clarke's chapter on envy in this book.
10. It should be noted that this line of reasoning does not require a commitment to a highly unfashionable concept such as 'false consciousness', but merely to the idea that ways of understanding may sometimes lead people to make cognitive errors.
11. Another possibility is worth mentioning. In some circumstances, people may argue that they are victims of some injustice in order to claim compensation. They may, for instance, claim that their cultural identity has been unduly neglected in order to try to obtain certain resources. In some cases, of course, this claim may be quite genuine. But it is also possible that there may be a strategic choice deliberately to exaggerate or deceive in order to gain particular advantages. I do not consider this possibility in the main body of my argument since, strictly speaking, it is not a case of hurt

feelings without just cause, but rather a case of *falsely asserting* that one's feelings are hurt.

12. It is not easy to say how this phrase might be unpacked. One possibility would be to say that a public sphere is constituted in the right way if it facilitates the development of the relations of recognition which are the necessary condition of individual self-realization.

9
Pity, Compassion, Solidarity

Paul Hoggett

Introduction

Compassion plays a key role in politics. It is a key, perhaps *the* key, moral sentiment and perhaps along with anger at injustice (the focus of the previous chapter by Simon Thompson) it is central to what we might think of as "progressive" political struggles and campaigns. For example, Blair's recent attempt to kick-start a concerted international strategy for ending poverty in Africa seems predicated upon the politics of compassion. And yet, as this example might indicate, compassion seems to be an emotion capable of taking on many hues. As Lauren Berlant (2004), for example, notes, it can also provide the motif for the state's disengagement with its own poor. "Compassionate Conservatism" shows its solidarity with the suffering of the poor in American society by freeing them from their dependency upon the so-called "infantilising government aid programmes". And in Britain too, "tough love" has become the inspiration behind a Blairite social policy which promises "hand ups not hand outs". It seems that no one has a monopoly on compassion. Indeed Sara Ahmed (2004) argues persuasively that love and compassion are also central to the way in which fascist groups in Britain and the USA see themselves in their struggle to protect the vulnerable body of the white race. So compassion may be a more slippery emotion than one might at first think, one easily deployed by a wide range of normative discourses.

In what follows I will consider the work of Martha Nussbaum in this light. First I will argue that her liberal discourse is in fact insufficiently liberal as it depends upon a concept of personhood which is without agency and autonomy – the object of Nussbaum's compassion is essentially passive. Then I will offer a more socialistic discourse of compassion.

Central to my argument is the need to move away from a concept of compassion which is infused with the sentimentality of pity towards a concept which is more akin to solidarity. In other words, I argue for the fusion of compassion towards social suffering with anger at the injustices which underlie that suffering. Moreover I will argue, perhaps counter-intuitively, that whereas idealisation of the suffering other appears to be crucial to liberal perspectives a solidaristic notion of compassion is one directed towards a flawed human subject, both a victim of circumstance and, always to some extent, an agent of both their own misfortune and salvation.

The intelligence of compassion?

Martha Nussbaum, in her book *Upheavals of Thought* (2001), provides an extended analysis of the nature of compassion drawing upon philosophical sources, particularly the Stoics, and upon the psychoanalysis of Klein and Winnicott. Eschewing the idea that reason and emotion are antithetical to each other, Nussbaum seeks to demonstrate the intelligence of compassion by delineating three cognitive elements of judgement which are inherent in the emotion's make-up. First, there is the judgement of size – I feel compassion if the misfortune of another is serious rather than trivial. Second, there is the judgement of non-desert – the person did not bring the misfortune upon herself or himself. Third, there is what she calls the "eudaimonistic judgement", that "this person, or creature, is a significant element in my scheme of goals or projects, an end whose good is to be promoted" (2001, p. 321). Regarding the latter element, Nussbaum adds that it will often "make me more likely to see … *the other's* … prospects as similar to my own, and of concern in part for that reason" (p. 331), something she elsewhere describes as "the judgement of similar possibilities" (p. 351). In other words, when observing the suffering of another, one is more likely to feel compassion if one has the thought "there but for the grace of god go I"; but, she emphasises, this is not an absolutely necessary condition.

Whilst Nussbaum's project, to offer an analysis of emotion that gives emphasis to its rationality, is to be welcomed, I fear she nevertheless pursues this project within a narrowly rationalist framework. This is one which underestimates the affective and bodily dimensions of compassion and assumes a unitary view of the human subject which cannot properly grasp how it is possible to hold contradictory feelings, nor how one can be both object and agent at the same time.

First, let us consider "the judgement of similar possibilities". My feeling is that Nussbaum resorts to a cognitive framework to analyse the nature of similarity between self and other because she is unable to understand the concept of identification. Identification occurs where there is a blurring of the boundary between self and other. It is crucial to human development, for example to the developing bond between mother and infant. But it can also be a crucial obstacle to this development, as the blurring of self and other also prevents the realisation of the other's difference and separateness. Despite Nussbaum's sincere efforts to draw upon psychoanalytic theory I am struck by the fact that there is no reference to identification or projective identification in the index to *Upheavals of Thought*. One of the distinctive contributions of psychoanalysis to our thinking about the human subject is its development of a range of concepts to refer to processes – identification, projection, projective identification, splitting, condensation, displacement, denial, and so on – which form the elements of "psycho-logic" or, if you like, "psycho-rationality". To reduce these processes to "mechanisms of defence" would be mistaken. They are not just a source of pathology in mental life, they also constitute part of the foundation for our reasoning, decision-making and creative capacities as we will see later in the case of identification and dis-identification. Nussbaum's rationalist schema is unable to incorporate this and yet these processes are crucial to the mediation between affect and cognition. Let us examine her analysis of empathy in this light.

Empathy

In relation to compassion Nussbaum construes empathy as the "imaginative reconstruction of the experience of the sufferer" (p. 327). In a footnote she then reflects upon Schopenhauer's linkage of compassion with identification and cites two extracts from his *Preisschrift über das Fundament der Moral*, in the first of which he stresses the creative role of identification and in the second its "pathological" role. She concludes, "thus the type of fusion he has in mind remains somewhat unclear" (ibid.). It is as if the role of identification has to be either constructive or pathological; it is the possibility that it might be both that she seems to find confusing. When I spoke earlier of identification, splitting and so on as aspects of "psycho-rationality", it might be objected (indeed I think Nussbaum would object) that such mechanisms cannot be "rational" in any shape or form because as mechanisms of defence they are the foundation of psychopathology and therefore lie at the root of our inability to be realistic. But this is not how psychoanalysis thinks. Although identification is central to narcissistic pathologies in which self and loved object become hopelessly confused (as in nationalism for example) Freud was absolutely clear that identification was also crucial to the development of the healthy personality, to effective followership and to the development of solidaristic bonds between people. Similarly Kleinian and post-Kleinian developments have demonstrated how projective identification provides the basis for non-verbal communication, how splitting is essential for action in situations of moral uncertainty, and so on. All of these psychical mechanisms are therefore "Janus headed"; they can help us face and deal with reality and they can provide the basis for avoiding reality.

Paradoxically, the limitations inherent to Nussbaum's way of thinking are indicated when she makes the perceptive link between empathy and Method Acting, "empathy is like the mental preparation of a skilled (method) actor; it involves a participatory enactment of the situation of the sufferer, but is always combined with the awareness that one is not oneself the sufferer". She adds, "if one really had the experience of feeling the pain in one's own body, then one would precisely have failed to comprehend the pain of another *as other*" (her emphasis) (pp. 327–8). What Nussbaum cannot quite grasp is that in fact, when empathising, one feels the pain of the other *and* one does not. Infancy research describes this process as "affect-mirroring" (Fonagy *et al.* 2002). The mother demonstrates her empathy with her infant's distress by an exaggerated mirroring. Typically, in a carefully modulated way, she acts as if she is herself distressed, sometimes for example by "oooing" and "ahhing" in a sympathetic way which symbolises the infant's own distress through a gentle playfulness. Jessica Benjamin describes this as "differentiation with empathy" (2004, p. 25), as the mother both identifies and dis-identifies with the infant. But we cannot understand this process properly if we adhere to a unitary conception of the self. Part of the mother (the infant in the mother) identifies with the infant, feels the distress as her own *and is affected by it*. But another part of her (the adult in the mother) remains separate, distinguishing the infant's distress from her own and is therefore able to retain perspective and the capacity for thought and judgement. If the mother is not affected, "if there is no identificatory oneness of feeling the child's urgency and relief" (Benjamin, ibid), then the mother can only respond out of duty, not with passion.

My suspicion that Nussbaum adopts a view of compassion which is too cognitive is confirmed in her discussion of Aristotle's view that compassion is a particular type of pain. Nussbaum admits that compassion does refer to a psychical disturbance, "a tug at the heart strings" (Nussbaum, p. 325), but she insists that the pain is caused by the thought and does not have much if any "causal independence" (p. 326). But we are back to familiar territory here, namely the difficulty political theory and political science have in grasping the independence of affect and the possibility that it is not always bound to thought. Anxiety is a classic example. Indeed one of the distinctive characteristics of anxiety is that it is "free floating", attaching itself to all sorts of objects and ideas none of which can give it satisfactory representation. Freud was absolutely adamant about this, insisting that the object of the affect was always its most contingent component. We might say that Freud went too far in the other direction, seeing the conscious mind almost as an epiphenomenon, pushed hither and thither by powerful unconscious drives, but in some ways this insistence of his may prove salutary, particularly when we begin to think of the powerful hold of the emotions upon the group, rather than of the emotions as always being a property of the individual.

On being affected

To return to my discussion, the "tug at the heart", the "throbbing" and "aching", are, from the perspective I am advancing, essential elements of the feeling of compassion because if we are not affected by the suffering of the other, our response becomes primarily an expression of duty, compliance or social conformity. Nussbaum has offered us three cognitive elements of compassion. We are now in a position to suggest one affective component: that a condition for compassion is that self is affected by other's suffering in some way – touched by it, moved by it, pained by it, perhaps even shocked by it. In other words, as Sara Ahmed (2004, p. 8) puts it, the suffering leaves "an impression". Each of these impressions has something in common – to touch, to move, to feel pain or shock reminds us of the physical and corporeal dimension of what it is to be affected. But, and here's the rub, I think that what I am describing is, strictly speaking, not empathy.

When empathising, I project myself imaginatively into the position of the other. Here all the mental activity is with me, the other is the recipient. It is for this reason that empathy can so often prove to be an unreliable guide. Nussbaum is well aware of this but it does not lead her to question whether empathy is the only transaction which occurs when a relation of compassion connects self and other. Indeed, psychoanalysts influenced by Klein and Winnicott do not refer much to empathy. Instead, since the early 1950s, one of the dominant ideas within these traditions refers to the centrality of the counter-transference in relations between analyst and patient. Now the idea of the counter-transference refers to a quite different process to empathy, for it refers to self's capacity to be receptive to the affective communication of other. Bion (1962) captured this idea through the concept of "containment" – the capacity of self to contain the unprocessed mental material of the other. This might be the other's grief, hatred or suffering. Now here the issue at point is not so much self's capacity to actively and imaginatively project onto the other but, rather, self's capacity to be disturbed by the other, to be affected by the other. Here the other's suffering actively seeks to get through to self, the other is active and the disposition needed in self is one of a kind of passivity that Benjamin (2004) terms "surrender". Lacking this capacity, other can never leave their imprint or impression upon self.

Empathy, as it is classically understood in philosophy, assumes a kind of asymmetry between self and other; there is the one who suffers and there is the one who empathises. As Iris Marion Young (1997) has noted, it is this very asymmetry which often means that in relations between different others – black/white, male/female, European/African – empathy can itself be imperialistic, a form of "falsifying projection" in which self projects its own assumptions and values onto what it believes to be the experience of other. However, this non-empathic compassion takes us in a different direction; it poses questions about the frontiers and barriers that self constructs in order not to be disturbed by the suffering of others; it questions self's assumption that compassion is something one can choose rather than be forced into by other. It also poses interesting questions about government.

Using Winnicott's notion of the "facilitating environment", Nussbaum (2001, pp. 224–229) reflects on the contribution of psychoanalysis to ask what kinds of institutional frameworks are most likely to facilitate human flourishing? Her answers are thoughtful; they include the idea that institutions are needed which support reparation but do not reinforce shame and that contribute to the formation of personalities which are more likely to be intensely concerned with the needs of others. But one can see here how Nussbaum endorses what some more radical critics have termed a "traditional liberal affectivity" (Berlant, 2004) for there is an elitist and non-egalitarian strain running through her thought. If we consider non-empathic compassion then the implications for the institutions of government become clear. We can begin to see how part of the function of the liberal state is to protect us from the sufferings of others, to create an impermeable membrane which is resistant to disturbance, to be both "thick skinned" and unresponsive to the suffering of some of its citizens (particularly those regarded as "undeserving") whilst trying to appear responsive to the demands of the deserving (those it increasingly likes to think of as its "customers"). In particular we can see how the "dull maximum" of liberal democracy must limit the impact of "voice" in all its forms for it is this very limitation which is necessary to stop social suffering, the suffering of our own poor, from getting through to us. From this perspective, the flourishing of citizens would require an altogether different kind of state, one which would welcome disturbance and the upheavals that impassioned voices would bring. This is something we have described elsewhere as "a democracy of the emotions" (Hoggett and Thompson, 2002).

The problem of desert

I now want to turn to Nussbaum's second cognitive element of compassion, the judgement of non-desert. According to this judgement I am likely to feel compassion where I consider that the suffering of the other is due to no fault of their own. Their suffering is brought about by circumstances which are beyond their control. One thinks of the Tsunami victims, pictures of African children dying from AIDS or the innocent victims of a terrorist outrage like the children of Beslan. Many such occurrences bring forth outpourings of compassion: millions of dollars are raised in collections by charities whose work often spurs governments towards some kind of action. Nussbaum also allows for the possibility that compassion may be felt even where there is an element of responsibility as, for example, when an adolescent is arrested for drunk driving, for we may still make the judgement that this is an expression of "the predicament of adolescence" (Nussbaum, 2001, p. 314). But such qualifications do not undermine her perspective which views the objects of compassion as undeserving of their suffering, basically good people to whom bad things have happened.

To base compassion upon a judgement of non-desert is to offer little or no protection to those who are increasingly termed "the undeserving poor". The capacity of western citizens to suffer alongside others increasingly occupies a continuum. At one end we can place the children of Beslan, the victims of Chechen terrorists, the epitome of inno-cent victimhood. More equivocally, even for a liberal audience, the Kosovan refugees – objects of pity when subject to Serbian aggression, less so when approaching your car with a "squeejy mop" as you sit in a traffic jam on a London street. But who is situated at the opposite end of this continuum to the innocents? Whose suffering no longer meets with our compassion? Perhaps our own poor. Perhaps the kids running wild who in the UK are increasingly subject to Anti-Social Behaviour Orders (ASBOs), the "slobs" and "trailer trash" who eat junk, smoke, watch TV all day and take no exercise, the uncivil neighbours, the unshaven fathers who spend all day in the pub or bar, the mothers who seem unable to speak to their children except by shouting and so on. In a strange sort of way, the sufferings of our own poor seem more out of sight than the suffering of the poor in Dafur, or the innocent victims of the latest bomb outrage in Baghdad. If only our own poor could present themselves as innocents, essentially virtuous but the victims of forces beyond their control, then they could receive our fellow feeling. But, increasingly, they do not. Like the survivors of Hurricane Katrina in New Orleans they are often angry, troublesome, ungrateful, sometimes their own worst enemies and so on.

There is something far too neat about Nussbaum's analysis. As Maureen Whitebrook (2002) has noticed, good and bad, innocence and responsibility are too conveniently separated. In real life (and Whitebrook uses characters out of Toni Morrison's novel *Beloved*) things are more complicated. Following Whitebrook, I will later make the case that compassion should be and often is extended to those who are not innocent victims, indeed that this form of compassion is more compatible with a model of developed human ethical capacities than Nussbaum's more restricted version. But first I want to argue that certain changes in modern capitalist societies are undermining even this more restricted form of compassion, that is that which is shown to victims of circumstance.

Structural inequalities and compassion fatigue

When we consider individuals or groups who are largely victims of fate, chance and circumstance, we consider them in terms of what Timpanaro (1975) called the "passive aspect" of relations between humanity and nature. Injury, illness, old age, incapacity, disability, mental turmoil remind us that we are nature's objects and, whilst we might use our own sense of agency to surmount some of the obstacles presented, such conditions put us back in touch with our dependency on others. Unlike in the many so-called "less civilised" societies, western democracies betray a profound ambivalence towards such dependency. A culture has emerged which is profoundly discomforted by the idea of any limits or constraints to human possibilities, including the constraint of mortality. It is a culture so enraptured by an "active voice" which fetishises change and newness that the "passive voice" is almost treated with suspicion. I have argued elsewhere (Hoggett, 2000) that in western democracies, particularly those which have dismantled aspects of what they term "welfarism", there is in fact a hatred of dependency (and therefore of interdependency also). This is a hatred for the suffering of others, including the "other" that constitutes that suffering part of oneself. It is this hatred which has undermined the solidaristic ties upon which the idea of common welfare rests. In its place we find a "market for care" emerging which colludes with those omniscient feelings of invulnerability – the allure of a phantasised "security" which I can buy for me and my family.

In the field of British social policy, Roger (2003) has recently argued that solidarity towards the stranger, the foundation of the welfare state according to Richard Titmuss (1968, 1971), is being eclipsed by "amoral familialism". This is an increasingly selective form of mutuality towards my group, indeed my family group. The US model of mutual insurance captures this. I put in so that I might take out or, "from my ability to put in springs my capacity to take out", an entirely different principle to "from each according to her ability, to each according to her need". Paradoxically, both the Republicans in the US and the Labour in the UK preach "community" but all the signals and incentives encourage citizens to put their families first. Drawing upon an extensive body of European research on public attitudes towards the welfare state, Roger notes a general trend towards an undermining of what he calls the "affective basis" of solidarity. He sees the emergence of a more "pragmatic and calculating approach to social welfare issues rather than a passionate commitment to and empathy for fellow citizens" (Roger, 2003, p. 416).

Here we can begin to see the way in which social change impacts upon structures of feeling (Williams, 1977). The neo-Liberal trajectory of Britain and the USA in the context of globalisation has led both societies towards increased structural inequality (the emergence of "dual labour markets" and the "underclass") and the erosion of affective solidarities between social groups and classes. We often think of "compassion fatigue" in terms of the response of western citizens to calamities around the world but this takes our attention away from what is happening within our own societies. Even Nussbaum's more restricted notion of compassion, that which we show to the sufferings of others produced through no fault of their own, is becoming undermined.

And it is becoming undermined precisely because conventional liberal notions of compassion are defenceless against new-right ideologies which stress the culpability of the disadvantaged, the idea that in some sort of way the poor, the unemployed, the single parents and even the aged and infirm are responsible for their own plight (in the latter case one hears increasingly of individuals' "failure" to make provision for their own retirement). The moment has therefore come to problematise conventional liberal conceptions of compassion which stress the judgement of non-desert.

The restricted nature of liberal compassion

Helen Bamber (founder of the Medical Foundation for the Care of Victims of Torture) was one of the first "aid workers" to go into Belsen at the end of the Second World War. She notes that many of the inmates remained behind barbed wire for several years whilst the "allies" struggled to come up with a solution to the "survivor problem". Emotional reactions of those in contact with them quickly shifted from shock and pity to a more institutionalised coldness (as Helen put it, the care, and not just the sheets, got "starchier") and eventually to irritation and hostility (the abandonment of Jewish survivors by the Allied powers is extensively documented in Kolinsky's (2004) research). The survivors became increasingly troublesome. Widespread protests, for example, were organised throughout Germany when several thousand illegal Jewish immigrants were turned back by the British authorities at the port of Haifa in 1947. Eventually many Jews started to organise their own solution. Through networks linked to Irgun many "escaped" from what effectively had become internment and became ardent Zionists in the new Israel.

The story tells us a lot about compassion. Pity requires an object whereas compassion requires a subject. The object of pity is innocent, a "pure" victim, without subjectivity. Compassion, in contrast, does not require innocence. The object of pity exists primarily within the realm of the imaginary; it is an impossible condition – a pure, helpless, innocent being. The closest we come to it is the suffering animal. Hence no doubt the peculiarly British capacity to feel so much towards mistreated animals as opposed to our own street sleepers and drug users. In contrast, compassion remains steady even when the "object of pity" becomes difficult, starts to complain, becomes unmanageable, does things which seem to put him or her in a bad light, lacking in virtue. Perhaps, then, compassion can even be felt towards the suicide bomber.

Helen Bamber tells another story. Japanese prisoners of war returning to the UK after the Second World War found that no one was able or willing to listen many of the harrowing experiences that had happened to them. After many years they created what was, in a sense, their own "survivors network", some members of whom eventually contacted the Medical Campaign in the late 1980s. For many years Helen worked with a group of them, travelling to meetings with them in the north-east of England where she listened to their stories, offering them something that they had not experienced for 30 years since the war – recognition and acceptance, the sense of finally "being understood". She had (and still has) enormous compassion for this group of grumpy old men. One of them has told his story in book form (Lomax, 1996). It is a very powerful and moving book about the difficulties of reconciliation. But speaking to her I was surprised to hear what a difficult man Lomax was. Helen said that he was fairly typical of that group.

These examples suggest the value of following a distinction made by both Whitebrook (2002) and Roger (2003), between pity and compassion. Is our feeling towards the suffering of the other withdrawn once the object of this feeling loses its innocence and reclaims its subjectivity? This takes us back to what Nussbaum refers to as the "ambivalence crisis" (the crisis of the "depressive position" in Kleinian terms). For Klein the achievement of the depressive position is the capacity of the child to love the other despite the ways in which it has been and is continuously failed by this other. And this is possible because the child has come to recognise that the very things it hates in the other it can begin to identify in itself. Here we can include the other's "callous" need for her own life and the very many reasons she has for hating this baby that she also loves (see Winnicott's (1947) marvellous list of 18 reasons why the mother hates her baby). From this position the world is no longer neatly separated into good and bad, innocence and culpability. It enables us to see that many people, like the characters in Toni Morrison's novels, who are victims of circumstance also often adopt psychic survival strategies which make things worse for themselves and for others. In life there are many victims of circumstance but very few who can claim total innocence. The point about the depressive state of mind is that self continues to love and show compassion despite the flawed nature of the other, despite this other being a complex mix of good and bad. The idealisation of innocence is no longer necessary because self is no longer innocent about himself or herself.

A different kind of identification seems to occur in pity compared to compassion. When we feel pity, because of the nature of the other required for pity to find realisation, we load upon the other an impossible identity, something they cannot live up to, since no one can be that virtuous. This is what the Kleinians would call a form of projective identification in which a part of self becomes located in the other (Iris Marion Young's "fasifying projection"). The other becomes idealised, it comes to represent an idealised but split-off part of ourselves (innocent, virtuous). As a momentary expression of feeling, there is nothing wrong with the outpouring of pity which can occur at Beslan and elsewhere. But the point is that it cannot be sustained, and the struggle is to replace it with compassion rather than indifference or irritation.

In compassion the nature of our identification seems different. The other is tolerated in his or her otherness – someone with flaws, lacking in some or many virtues, wilful but also still suffering, still to some extent a victim of fate or injustice. This other is therefore many sided, and includes the space for culpability, ungratefulness, ugliness and bloody-mindedness. To be compassionate therefore requires patience, tolerance of frustration, the capacity to withstand disillusionment. One thinks of caring for difficult elderly relatives or troubled children, of working with drug abusers and so on. Compassion requires the ability to identify with the point of suffering in the other and with the frightened and destructive forces that this suffering unleashes. To repeat, if one cannot accept the destructive parts of oneself, one has no basis for anything other than an intellectual acknowledgement of these aspects in the other.

So, whereas pity is subject to rapid fatigue, compassion is more enduring (indeed still endures or can be revived after conflict with the other). To say that it endures is not to say that it is a constant – patience snaps, sympathy curdles – but it is to say that it does not die simply because the generous impulse behind it meets with rebuff. It follows that, whereas pity is made manifest in the spontaneous gesture (the donation, the teddy bear through the post, the commemorative flowers), compassion, because it endures, is manifest in action.

Commitment and solidarity

Roger (2003) basis his distinction between pity and compassion on the concept of "post-emotionalism" which he derives from Mestrovic. According to Mestrovic (1997, p. 64) "everyone knows that emotions today carry no burden, no responsibility to act". In the post-emotional society the emotions themselves have become subject to modernisation "bite sized, pre-packaged, rationally manufactured" (p. xi). In particular, and here he draws on Baudrillard, post-emotions are simulations which do not lead to anything. We appear to become more and more civilised, our emotional range now seems so great but, for Mestrovic (pp. 49–52), this vast array of post-emotions are superficial, easy to slip on and off. They become part of the emotion management necessary to get on in an other-directed society. Today, in the West, emotions should not get in the way; they should not be troublesome, disturb the sleep, provoke strange dreams, cause outbreaks of bodily pains, distraction or irritability because these get in the way of managing the project called "my life". Not surprisingly, therefore, Mestrovic argues that we no longer feel compassion but pity and we no longer feel anger but indignation. These post-emotions such as pity, indignation and so on are as noisy and clamorous as they are shallow and ephemeral, turned on and off by journalists, politicians and others. Crucially, Mestrovic argues, the link between feeling and action has been broken, the feeling no longer brings with it any real commitment. In contrast to the restricted concept of compassion, more akin to pity, that Nussbaum and others have used, I am arguing for something more durable, less conditional, more committed. This may seem like an impossibly taxing demand but my own research on the lives of professionals working within the British welfare state suggests that it is precisely this kind of commitment which continues to provide the foundation for an ethic of public service. In what follows I will use material drawn from a series of extended interviews with youth workers operating in some very socially disadvantaged areas of the UK.

Despite being subject to physical attack on several occasions, having his staff abused, seeing kids he knows becoming addicts or prostitutes and so on, Si retains a stubborn capacity to see some good in even the most desperate and ugly kids – even one who attacked him and ended up in jail. He speaks eloquently about this when describing his feelings upon seeing the pictures of several youths, some of whom he knew well, who had been subject to ASBOs for their violent and disorderly behaviour on the housing estate where they lived.

> Last week I saw all the shops around here have mug shots of the 10 most difficult young people and I was at a meeting of the shopkeepers and I saw these, sort of, rows of photographs and they're a very desperate bunch. I mean, I was probably the only person in the room who knew all the people and it's just very sad to see this. I know they're dangerous. . . . but there is just a feeling of, is this the right way, but I can't think of another way. You know, I can't think of another way of getting these people out of their desperation. I mean,

what struck me most about them is that they are a very unloved group, but all we can offer them is disciplinary, um, sort of, measures against them. We can't actually offer them love. It would be asking too much of us. . . . . My main feeling is, yes, they just have absolutely no love in their lives at all and all we're doing is punishing them more and more. It feels, kind of, wrong.

Si feels totally conflicted about this, not only recognising that they are a "bad bunch" but also feeling genuine compassion for them, accepting that they are dangerous, seeing the vulnerability in their violence, wanting to do something but not knowing what and yet also being aware that he is colluding with their suppression. Some youth workers would steadfastly refuse to see such youths as bad, they would blame the youths' circumstances thereby keeping them "innocent" and sustaining their good feelings towards them. Si is not like this. He accepts that these youths can be nasty and something needs to be done. But he does not see them as irredeemable and it is because he still has this hope that he finds the mug shots so painful. He just about manages to retain some kind of hopefulness because he can still see the good within the bad. He does not oppose ASBOs on principle like some might, yet he also feels that they are not the solution, but he does not know what the solution is (and probably believes that there is not one). The ability to hold such contradictory views and feelings in mind without rushing to resolve them one way or the other exemplifies the ethical capacity of the depressive or tragic position. Think of it this way. If we imagine a film director doing a film about this situation, my guess is that whereas someone like Ken Loach would make an angry film which drew attention to the injustice of the young people's situation, someone like Mike Leigh might paint a more tragic picture which, whilst not denying the impact of the environment, also showed how these youths were, in some way, often their own worst enemies.

The point is that Si sees the suffering behind the badness, he sees how the pain manifests itself in the youth's violence and hatred, he can see how they are both innocent and responsible. Accepting the badness of the youths' behaviour does not in anyway undermine his sense of the injustice of it all, if anything it strengthens this. For he can see how, in subtle ways, people get destroyed inside by the world in which they live, and this makes him all the more angry. But he also knows that these young people could have acted differently for he knows many of their mates, and not all of them have taken the same path. He can therefore feel angry for them and angry at them. This is not a question of either/or but one of both/and.

Nussbaum's tidy distinctions – between innocence and culpability, non-desert and desert – break down here on the housing estates of Britain's poor. Professionals like Si (who has worked on the same estate for over twenty years despite many opportunities he could have taken to leave) work in this grey zone of conflicting obligations, values and feelings with a commitment which is salutary for those, like myself, with a more comfortable life. Because he has worked there so long although he is an "outsider" he knows more about the young people and their lives than most "insiders". And because of this knowledge he is able to empathise with them accurately. But it is the non-empathic aspects of compassion that affect him most deeply. He may choose when to empathise but he cannot choose the moments when something, like the mug shots, suddenly gets through to him.

Fitz, another youth worker in our research, although younger has gone through similar things. Fitz's experience indicates the complex movement of identification and dis-identification, openness and closedness which is necessary if a compassionate commitment is to be sustained. In this sense compassion inevitably involves transgression. At times it seems to necessarily entail an element of over-involvement in which reserve and professional distance are sacrificed. Fitz told us that life was easier now that youth work had become more managerialised; he found the more structured environment provided him with greater security, he was more able to sustain an effective work/family balance and so on. But he also felt something crucial was missing and this "something" seemed to be a real feeling of emotional contact with young people. The story he told was of qualifying as a youth worker, being given the keys to the youth club where he still works and being told to get on with it without any support only to find that the club was effectively in the hands of a group of young men who bullied and terrorised, and with whom he engaged in a prolonged war of attrition for about five years until he'd regained control of the club. As Fitz put it, "it just felt that I was working on raw emotion at that time for, for a good few years . . . having no power over young people other than negotiating with them". But interestingly he then immediately added, "but it's strange that my relationship with those young people is so much stronger". In contrast, his experience of the young people he works with today is "slightly colder and slightly more professional". Several of the young men he originally "fought" with he now regards as close friends, several are now fathers in their own right. In the newly managerialised culture of the British welfare state, workers like Fitz are no longer affected by those they work with in quite the way they were in the past. He can still empathise with these young people; like Si he knows enough about them to be able to imaginatively and accurately reconstruct their world. It is his non-empathic immersion in their suffering that he is now increasingly shielded from. It is as if the managerialisation of welfare is partly designed to weaken emotional contact between "the suffering" and the state.

Felt thoughtfulness

I think the idea of "social suffering" popularised by Bourdieu (1999) enables us to think about how we might move beyond both conservative/ blame the victim, and liberal/pity the victim notions of compassion. For the idea of social suffering puts us in mind of the group rather than the individual in the same way that when we read *Beloved* we see beyond the individual agony of Seth and others to the class of black slaves to which they belong. Reading texts such as this, or doing welfare work in the way in which I have just described, puts the observer in touch not just with the pain of others but also with the anger from which intimations of injustice are derived. We are now used to contrasting the ethic of care, introduced into the modern vocabulary by those such as Gilligan, with the ethic of justice, as if the former emphasises the passionate, relational and context bound whereas the latter emphasises the more distanced, universal and dispassionate. But (as the previous chapter indicated) in the politics of social movements and actual political struggle, passion, and specifically anger, is also integral to considerations of justice and injustice.

Several contributors to Lauren Berlant's (2004) book on compassion warn us against a sentimentalisation of compassion. Woodward (2004) for example stresses "the importance of not just feeling pain but of understanding the experience of suffering" (2004, p. 68). Indeed, as Nelson (2004) notes, for someone like Arendt the power of suffering is such that it threatens to overwhelm and destroy public politics. She cites (p. 226) a passage from Arendt's *On Revolution* which I found illuminating. Speaking of Robespierre's sympathy for the destitute masses of Paris, Arendt notes, "he lost the capacity to establish and hold fast to rapport with persons in their singularity; the ocean of suffering around him and the turbulent sea of emotion within him, the latter geared to receive and respond to the former, drown all specific considerations, the considerations of friendship no less than considerations of statecraft and principle" (Arendt, 1990, p. 90). For Arendt it is the overwhelming character of human suffering that potentially destroys our capacity to think. We must find ways of distancing ourselves from it, of not becoming too identified with it, if we are to retain the capacity to face reality. But the balance is a delicate one and I wonder if Arendt and, in a different way, Nussbaum lack the capacity to fully face emotional reality. Not feeling against thought (the sentimentality of pity), nor thought against feeling (the alleged "heartlessness" of Arendt's *Eichmann in Jerusalem*) but, as Raymond Williams (1977) put it, "thought as felt and feeling as thought" (p. 132) – it is this felt thoughtfulness which I believe characterises the reflections of Si and Fitz, something neither sentimental nor intellectualising.

Paradoxically the kind of compassion that I am exploring here requires callousness. To feel as well as think requires a simultaneous identification and dis-identification with the suffering of the other. As I argued earlier, the latter is achieved by a summoning of another part of the self, an observing thoughtful part, alongside that part which empathically or non-empathically identifies. From a rationalist perspective, this is impossible – one is either immersed in the other's suffering or one adopts Arendt's moral hardness. But once we can get beyond a unitary view of the self it becomes possible to see how we might think and feel, or feel different things, at the same time. In summoning this observing self part of our cathexis towards the suffering of the other is inevitably withdrawn. Indeed the other may sense this and may seek to seduce us back into a collusive fellow-feeling, perhaps based upon a mutual idealisation, from which our critical thinking capacities have been banished. This struggle to preserve independence of mind can be felt as a betrayal by other, and in a sense it is. Sometimes to keep on thinking requires an aggressive distancing from other, a kind of coldness. Sometimes we need to be cruel to be kind.

But this callousness that I am speaking of is different to that which Berlant (2004, pp. 9–10) notices. For me, cruelty lies at the heart of compassion as a form of felt thoughtfulness in the face of social suffering; it is neither sentimental nor intellectualising. In contrast, the "witholding" that Berlant notes describes the different ways in which actors avoid fully facing suffering in the first place. Both deployments of cruelty are necessary to compassion for there is indeed something overwhelming about suffering which would otherwise threaten to devour us. But what I am trying to demonstrate is that cruelty is also inherent in a developed capacity for compassion, that is for an intelligent compassion. And it is only an intelligent compassion which can feel the pain *and* think critically about the injustice, thereby fusing an ethic of care to an ethic of justice.

10
Moving Forward in the Study of Emotions: Some Conclusions

Simon Clarke, Paul Hoggett and Simon Thompson

An embryonic field of inquiry

None of the contributors to this book subscribe to the idea that the emotions are inconsequential or stand opposed to reason and rationality. In different ways the previous chapters have demonstrated that the emotions make a substantive contribution to political and social life, that they are not simply the consequence of thought or action but are also a crucial determinant. The contributors go further: whilst they demonstrate how the emotions can contribute to unreason (Alford shows, for example, how hatred can attack the very foundation of thinking itself) they also show how the emotions contribute to struggles against injustice and thoughtful ethical action. Moreover they demonstrate how an understanding of the emotions can provide a richer and fuller understanding of rationality. But there are still some unresolved issues here. In particular there is the vexed question of the precise relationship between thinking and feeling. Can feelings exist which lack a thinker to think them? Are feelings necessarily attached to an individual thinker or can they be the possession of a group? In other words, if the possibility of the existence of collective feelings is acknowledged, in what way are they collective? Do experiences such as social suffering, ressentiment or a shared sense of outrage or shame exist in a kind of social ether or is this to fall into a kind of reification of emotion, one in which emotion becomes some kind of phantasmic force operating above and beyond individual actors? Just how do shared emotions make themselves present, what form do they take?

Or take another set of unresolved questions. Whilst it is clear that the emotions can often be the source of irrationality is it necessarily always the negative emotions such as hatred or envy which prompt irrationality?

What about positive emotions such as love or compassion, can they not also undermine thoughtful political action? But do not these very questions betray a deeper assumption that needs questioning? Why is it always emotion which seems to fuel irrationality, what about thought itself? All these men, from the ancient Greeks onwards, who have given so much thought to emotion and the human sentiments, should we not be suspicious that a very gendered discourse of reason may have emerged over the last two thousand years? Why should thinking seem so innocent? Why do we always tend to think of irrationality in terms of the way in which feeling destroys thought; what about the converse, the way in which thought can destroy feeling?

When it comes to thinking about the emotions as a social and political as opposed to a purely psychological phenomenon the contributors to this book have stressed that we are still at an early stage in the development of analysis. To use an analogy, it is as if we are still stumbling about in the foothills without any clear perspective or understanding of the overall terrain. To pursue the analogy a little further, the chapters in the first section of this book sought to offer some thoughts about the geology of emotions – what is it that constitutes the base material of the terrain that we seek to examine? The introductory chapter offered a way of thinking about the social organisation of emotions which was analogous to geological strata. At the deepest level, part of the base material of society, some emotions can be thought of as part of the human condition. At another level, but still operating largely beneath the surface, "structures of feeling" refer to the particular emotional tone of a historical period or epoch such as the pervasiveness of anxiety in late modernity. "Abiding affects" are still enduring and organised forms of emotion but linked more to conjunctural economic and political processes – ressentiment in Greece after the Second World War, for example. Finally, operating closer to the surface and therefore more visible and noisy, political actors are able to give strategic shape to deeper lying sentiments and, as such, emotions such as compassion and grief can become resources for political action. Moreover, in a media-dominated society, more fleeting but clamorous eruptions of emotion find expression particularly in the shape of moral panics.

Keeping with our analogy just as there are geological strata so there are also different kinds of rock – igneous and sedimentary, for example – and in a similar vein we can distinguish between different kinds of emotion. In Chapter 2 James Jasper makes some useful distinctions here between urges, reflex emotions, affects, moods and moral emotions. He then offers an analysis of the way in which these different types of emotion can influence both the nature of the purposes and goals of political action and the strategies and tactics adopted in pursuit of these goals. Finally, in Chapter 3 Jack Barbalet offers a particular way of thinking about the universality of emotions, one which grounds this in the formal properties of social relationships such as hierarchy and solidarity, rather than in biology or developmental psychology. He then develops an analysis of the interplay between the universal and relational aspect of emotions such as shame or fear and their specifically cultural and historical dimensions (which he terms "iterated"). He also offers an account of the way in which emotions both give shape to political action and are shaped by political actors: in this sense an emotion such as anger provides a resource for groups engaged in political struggle which can be shaped by activists. Thus he offers a further perspective on the strategic deployment of emotion which was outlined in Chapter 1.

The more applied chapters in the second part of this book link back to these foundations in a number of ways. Whereas the chapters by Clarke, Alford and Demertzis consider what Jasper terms "the affects" (ie. of envy, hatred and ressentiment respectively) the final two chapters, by Thompson and Hoggett, explore what Jasper refers to as "moral emotions" – ie. anger and compassion. Each of these chapters also seeks to make the link between a particular emotion and a particular aspect of political life – envy is linked to racism, hatred to genocide, ressentiment to populism, anger to struggles for social justice and compassion to the politics of welfarism.

We hope that each of these chapters will offer readers new insights, indeed will be counter-intuitive in some ways. For example, Alford investigates the way in which hatred can be used not so much to attack another but to attack the capacity for thinking itself. Clarke sees envy as an emotion which, paradoxically, seeks to destroy the object of love and desire. Demertzis portrays ressentiment as a festering cocktail of grievance, complaint and spite which, in and of itself, leads nowhere politically because it is the emotional response of the weak and powerless to perceived injustice. In this sense he contrasts the Nietzschean concept of ressentiment to the more familiar idea of resentment, an emotion which often *does* lead to political action. Finally whereas Thompson indicates how anger can be thought of as a constructive emotion, Hoggett argues that a durable form of compassion requires an element of cruelty. Each of these examples defies simplistic attempts to distinguish between the so-called "positive" and "negative" emotions, and each also reveals the often complex and mediated relation between feeling, thought and action. In what follows we offer some reflections on some of the key themes and conundrums to have emerged in the course of completing this book. We also touch upon some of the issues that this book has not addressed in posing some research questions for the future.

On irrationality

Rationality and irrationality are not distinct concepts covering separate types of behaviour nor even are they are to be understood as points at the opposite ends of a continuum; rather they seem to be inextricably mixed up with each other – rationality is always a matter of "more or less" rather than either/or. As Jasper notes, in politics the separation between ends and means also enables us to grasp the paradoxes and contradictions of rationality. To give an example, the extermination of the Jews and others by the Nazis during the Second World War was made possible by the application of a concerted rationality which drew upon the full range of techniques available under conditions of advanced modernity (Bauman, 1989), but of course the purpose to which these means were applied was completely mad. However we might understand anti-semitism – as a virulent attempt to expunge a phantasised contaminant from the purified body of the Aryan race; as the mobilisation of we-group violence against a projected out-group; or as an attack upon an envied other, the possessor of a strength and enjoyment which had been stolen from "us". What cannot be ignored is the intensity of two emotions, the hatred of the Jewish other and the love for one's fellow German. But equally crucial is the way in which these emotions were linked to powerful products of the collective imagination – the idealised body of the motherland and the denigrated and excoriated figure of the Jewish virus. Now these "collective imaginings" were neither unconscious phantasies (the imagery of the Jew and the motherland were consciously and extensively articulated in propaganda) but nor were they the product of elaborated and sophisticated systems of thought (although they drew upon a huge variety of quasi-scientific and philosophical systems). In other words, the irrationality of anti-semitism seems attributable not just to the presence of powerful feelings but also to the quality and character of the thoughts that constituted this belief system.

The issue is important because of the way, in political science in particular, irrationality has so often been equated with the emotional, as if thought stands on the side of reason whereas passion stands on the side of unreason. In this book all of the contributions have questioned this assumption. Powerful passions have been shown to fuel struggles for social justice. The so-called "negative" emotions such as anger and cruelty have been shown to work in constructive ways. The emotions have been shown to give direction and orientation to individual and collective action (see Barbalet's chapter in this book on "programmatic emotion"); they provide a filter through which reality is apprehended and writers such as Honneth and Nussbaum have argued that some emotions express a more or less explicit moral judgement.

Feeling, thought and action

Advances in neuro-science have indicated that the human organism first registers signals from the environment at an emotional level, through what is called the limbic system and specifically the amygdala. To use a by now well-known example, I am walking down a street, a car careers towards me out of control, before I have begun to formulate the danger in terms of a conscious thought I have registered the threat at a psycho-somatic level, and I am beginning to react before the conscious awareness of my circumstance. In everyday language we talk about "sensing" something. We feel something is not quite right but we may not know what, we may even go so far as to say that at an intuitive level we "know" something even though we cannot articulate what it is that we know. This is what Thompson (in this book) refers to as the epistemic dimension of our emotional lives. It suggests the existence of emotional experience which is pre-discursive. In different ways psychoanalysis and critical theory have stressed the same point. Psychoanalysis insists that the earliest experiences of infancy are both formative and pre-discursive ("infans" meaning "without words"). Critical theory, following Marx, has always stressed the way in which being precedes consciousness or, as Gramsci (1971) put it, that we have both a practical (implicit in our activity) and a theoretical consciousness. So, both critical theory and psychoanalysis stress how articulated thought always tends to lag behind practice and action. Hoggett and Clarke (in this book) have criticised cognitivist conceptions of emotions such as compassion and envy for the way in which they deny such emotions an independent role. It follows that we see value in conceiving of emotion, thought and action as separate but overlapping spheres none of which are synonymous with meaning, but all of which contribute to the meaningfulness of experience. We would like to offer the following framework as a useful device for thinking about their relatedness.

Much human activity is primarily unreflexive and is expressed through what Gramsci terms "practical consciousness". This is the action embodied in the individual activities of everyday life and in the uncoordinated, dispersed and spontaneous activities stretched across time and space of untold thousands of actors through which history is largely made. As Raymond Williams (1977) noted, it is through these activities that language evolves, settlements take shape, taste develops, manners form and dissolve and so on. Reflexive agency in contrast is purposeful in a more consciously organised sense. Through such agency individuals seek to shape their own life course. Such agency is also the consequence of the interaction between the practical consciousness of people and the interventions of social movements, the mass media, parties and political activists, interventions which shape what Gramsci terms a "theoretical consciousness". Passion inheres in both forms of agency but, we suggest, the passion which guides unreflexive agency refers primarily to the realm of the senses, to gut reactions, to unarticulated and more somatic forms of feeling.

We are drawing attention to the powerful role of pre-discursive but nevertheless organised structures of experience, something Williams (1977, p. 132) calls "structures of feeling". According to Williams, "we are talking about characteristic elements of impulse, restraint and tone; specifically affective elements of consciousness and relationships" (ibid.). In other words, at this pre-discursive level our attention is drawn to form and style rather than content, to the implicit rather than explicit, to the coming-into-being rather than to the precipitates of the already existing, to "what is actually being lived, and not only what it is thought is being lived" (p. 131). Williams specifically links this to emergent and pre-emergent social phenomena such as new class formations coming into being, or the ways in which new forms of the organisation of production (such as globalisation) manifest themselves at first through what he calls "changes of presence". Thompson (in this book) grapples with the same issue when looking at the way in which Honneth seeks to conceptualise the experience of injustice. Honneth seeks to understand how the lived everyday experience of the injustices of class, race, gender and so on is at first made manifest at this largely pre discursive level, something Bourdieu (1999) captures in terms of "social suffering". Social suffering can therefore be thought of as the practical consciousness of injustice. The question Thompson wrestles with is this: does this suffering orientate actors towards particular forms of action and understanding; in other words, is there an intelligence inherent to these inchoate feelings of anger, frustration and resentment or not?

Our sense is that at the moment we have to say that we do not know. Thompson concludes that what seems clear is that an enormous amount appears to depend upon the way in which these experiences are "framed", what resources for resistance are available to the group in question, what probability of success awaits such resistance and so on. As the chapter by Demertzis indicates, such questions appear to determine whether the experience of perceived injustice gives articulation to collective resentment or to ressentiment, towards a counter-hegemonic struggle for recognition or towards populism. But we cannot rule out the chance that these unformed feeling states do in fact orientate us towards some possibilities rather than others. After all, to return to the scenario of the out-of-control car, the affective arousal it produces does not predispose me towards daydreaming, yawning or thinking about a desired cup of tea. Similarly, social suffering may predispose actors towards some kinds of political signals rather than others, something we might think of in terms of a "psychological readiness". In other words we can agree that there is no necessary reason why social suffering should lead to progressive protest but this does not rule out the possibility that it nevertheless makes some kinds of response more likely than others. So whilst injustice may fuel class anger and resentment or spiteful and vengeful attacks on minorities it is unlikely to lead to hopefulness about one's future or a sense of pride in the achievements of one's group nor is it likely to fuel compassion for the perpetrators of this injustice.

The same issues have been debated within psychoanalysis. For Freud "desire" (the primary affect) is essentially "objectless"; in other words the object of the affect, that to which it attaches itself, is the most contingent aspect of it (Freud, 1915). For Freud our passions lead us like a wild horse on whose back we cling precariously. From this perspective it is only when such inchoate feelings have been given form and shape by finding expression discursively that they can be properly thought of as emotions. Object-relations analysts however see a much closer tie between passion and its object; indeed for the Kleinians, desire is structured by the unconscious phantasies (good breast/bad breast, etc.) that surround it and permeate it. Rather than the unbound energy of the horse we have something more akin to the structured energy of the guided missile (Lagache, 1964).

What is at stake in these debates is the relative autonomy of passion. Take anxiety for example. We have hinted that anxiety may be integral to the structure of feeling of contemporary modernity, to "risk society" as Beck (1992) has put it. So as modernity possibly reaches its apogee is it feasible for us to imagine flows of anxiety which suddenly inundate and flood financial markets or erupt across cities? A kind of electric energy equally capable of fuelling panics about paedophiles as it is the apocalyptic fantasies of Christian or Islamic fundamentalists. Or is it mistaken to imagine the existence of powerful feelings somehow operating freely and beyond the discursive anchorings provided by the media, governments and corporations? In making such distinctions we feel the need to reiterate that if it is to be of value the distinction between pre-discursive and discursive feelings is one of "more or less" rather than "either/or". There is always some degree of articulation in even the most inchoate feelings and, on the other hand, within the most refined emotion unknown passions will lurk.

We also need to recognise the existence of feelings which are largely unarticulated because of resistances to articulation. The following example was given by the psychoanalyst and political activist Marie Langer (1989); it draws from her experience of work in Nicaragua after the fall of the Somoza dictatorship.

> We call (this) frozen mourning. In 1982, in a therapeutic group in Leon, a handsome woman of about forty complains about her marriage. Her husband, who used to be a very good companion, has in recent years become irritable, jealous and alcoholic. He reproaches her and insults her for her evening outings even though he knows that she is a good woman and goes out to do political tasks. We carefully ask what might have happened and where and when this change occurred. Thus we touch upon a painful experience that took place only days before the fall of Somoza. This couple and their children were Sandinistas. One night the Guardia broke into the house and, pointing towards the eldest son, shouted: "This is the one". And they killed him in front of their eyes. At the time it was dangerous to cry or dress in mourning. The mother controlled her pain as much as she could and lay down in her son's bed; since then she has not returned to the marital bed. We could explain to her that through her political activity she kept alive the memory of her son, but that her attempt to repress the grief and give life to the dead son by sleeping in his bed was senseless: paralysing her and destroying her marital life. In a sense her husband's jealousy was justified.

In this instance an individual life was given orientation by powerful feelings that the actor herself was only fleetingly aware of. Such feelings give organisation and meaning to lives, so much so that to problematise them threatens the moral and epistemological order that the individual has created for himself or herself. For this reason individuals do not always reach eagerly for ideas which would provide them with a more reflexive understanding of their circumstances.

Similarly with groups, some things are simply too painful to think about. As those working to bring about reconciliation in South Africa, the former Yugoslavia and elsewhere have discovered, perpetrators of political violence are often in a state of deep denial about what they have done. By denying certain thoughts to consciousness the perpetrator of violence is able to stave off what would otherwise be a catastrophic blow to their moral system. In Bosnia and elsewhere most acts of political violence were not undertaken by psychopaths but by ordinary people in thrall to powerful group emotions and imaginings. To the extent that they deploy denial they betray a tacit awareness of what they have done. Their capacity to "feel nothing" is itself a particular kind of affect, "affectlessness" being a mood state well known to modern psychiatry. It provides its own distinctive orientation to the world, an active "feeling nothing" which at one level can be understood as a form of emotional intelligence which aims to bring about psychic survival.

In these examples the feelings that individuals and groups experienced are embodied neither in forms of practical consciousness nor in reflexive agency. The feelings are geared towards the avoidance of reality (the reality of political violence) rather than towards facing and acknowledging reality. The woman is overwhelmed by grief and yet she cannot name it, face it and therefore "feel" it. She appears to have a feeling without being aware of it, and this feeling gives structure and meaning to her life, but in ways that she did not intend and which are ultimately destructive for her and those she loves. Her husband's jealousy seems incomprehensible, and so the fact that she sleeps in another man's bed seems to have no significance for her. For both victims and perpetrators the memory of the violence involved is too much to bear, it becomes unthinkable. To follow Freud we could say that the "thing presentation" (the raw emotional experience) becomes split off from the "word presentation" (the symbolisation of experience) or, following Alford in this book, we could say that neither the victim nor the perpetrator has the capacity to imagine, dream or think their experience.

To summarise, the relations between feeling, thought and action are complex and varied. Powerful feelings can exist which are largely unthought but which are expressed and embodied in action. This action can be the partly habitual and partly improvisational practices of everyday life or it can be the "acting out" of feelings which cannot be worked through and symbolised – if individuals or groups cannot symbolise experience they may be doomed to repeat it.

The problem of methodological individualism

In contrast to the concept of "interest", the focus of rational choice theory, Jasper offers emotion as an alternative building block of political life. But Jasper also notes that any attempt to move from concepts of the individual actor, guided by interests or emotions, to concepts of the social and political poses the question, how do we get from the individual to the social, from the micro to the macro, without reducing the latter to the former? This is the problem of methodological individualism.

Sara Ahmed (2004) notes that psychologistic accounts of the emotions typically assume that an emotion "belongs" to the individual and is somehow located inside him or her. The question then becomes how does something "inside" get "outside", how does my anger become your or our anger? Psychoanalysis addresses this problem through the concept of projective identification – for example, I "put" the unbearable sadness inside me into you through a subtle and largely unconscious process of affective communication. Interestingly enough this unidirectional concept of projective identification is undergoing criticism and reappraisal from emerging relational and intersubjective currents within psychoanalysis itself (Benjamin, 2004).

Ahmed also notes the existence of what she calls an "outside in" account of the emotions in which emotions are seen essentially as properties of social and cultural practices which somehow then "get inside" individuals. For example, Hochschild (1983) outlines the ways in which social systems develop "feeling rules" which influence what can and cannot be felt. Also, psychoanalytic understandings of the group such as Bion's (1961) insist that groups have emotional structures – hope, paranoia, faith – which are irreducible to the properties of their individual membership.

But whilst Ahmed's distinction between psychologistic and sociologistic accounts of the emotions can be useful in reality, many existing models are highly complex. Hochschild, for example, acknowledges the role of bodily, psychodynamic and social-interactionist influences and yet also situates the emergence of "emotion work" in the context of broader changes towards post-industrial forms of society. Rather than construing emotion as if it was an individual property or possession, contributors to this book have largely argued for a position which sees emotion as a relational phenomenon. Barbalet, for example, draws upon Kemper's (1978) model of relations of hierarchy and solidarity to situate feelings such as shame. Clarke analyses the place of organised envy as a powerful but hidden dimension in racism. But in saying that such emotions are relational we mean more than the fact that they involve movements of "towardness" or "awayness" (Ahmed, p. 8) in relation to their objects. As Ahmed demonstrates through her more detailed analysis of hate (pp. 49–54) emotions are constituted complex patterns of real and imagined relationships involving (real and imagined) actors occupying distinct positions. Indeed much of contemporary psychoanalysis is strongly relational in which feelings are constituted by complex "object relations". Both love and hate move us towards the object of our feeling whereas disgust and fear move us away, but love seeks to preserve the object whereas hate seeks to destroy it; guilt, on the other hand, perceives the object to be already destroyed or damaged. But we can go further than this. Say X has nursed a grievance, we know not from where, over many years. There is a good probability X will carry this grievance over into other situations. Friends and colleagues may begin to become aware of this as they get to know X; for example, they may notice how X can suddenly take offence at others, accusing them of wrongs of which X feels to be the victim. The point is that X's sense of grievance requires the existence of another whose real or imagined wrongdoings provide X with the grounds for his complaints. We use the example of grievance simply to illustrate that any emotion requires a set of actors to play different, and sometimes quite complex, parts – this is what we mean by the relational nature of the emotions. In political life there may be very valid grounds for nursing a grievance in this way, for "keeping the wounds open" as the Mothers of the Disappeared in Argentina put it (Holst-Warhaft, 2000). To reiterate, we should be wary about making hasty distinctions between what is rational and what is irrational.

In this book we have also offered a number of ways of thinking about the social organisation of feeling at the macro-level. Hoggett, for example, outlines the way in which "compassion fatigue" is an integral aspect of neo-liberal responses to modernisation. Demertzis provides a fine-grained analysis of ressentiment as an organised feeling specific to a particular social group within post-war Greece. Our view is that passion adheres to all social forms. It directly influences the experience of a historical period, of processes of social and economic change, the experience of city life in particular places and periods, the experiences of specific social groups such as black people or gays and so on. We are still at the early stages of developing social scientific understandings of the human passions. One thing that is required is the development of a more morphological approach which might, for example, analyse the dynamic qualities of organised emotions. Are there recurrent configurations to be discerned in the passionate relations between groups, structured games if you like? For example, what about relations of mutual recrimination or recurring cycles of humiliation and revenge? Can we begin to discern cycles of envy and reparation at work between political leaders and the constituencies they organise? These kinds of questions seem beyond our means to answer at the moment.

Emotional relations and emotional communication

Returning to Sara Ahmed, she stresses the limitations of both psychologistic and sociologistic models of the emotions, insisting that emotions are something which neither "I have" nor "we have"; moreover simply adding them together to build a model which is both psychological and sociological is no improvement. In declaring that "my model refuses the abbreviation of the 'and'" (p. 10) Ahmed appears to be arguing for a psychosocial model which sees the emotions as constitutive of subjectivity itself, and specifically of those boundaries we use to mark off inner from outer, I from we and we from them. The crucial question, according to Ahmed, is not "what are emotions" but "what do emotions do"? And one of the key things they do, she argues, is they move and circulate. Ahmed considers Le Bon's (1952) idea of contagion, the original model of emotional circulation, but suggests it presumes some movement from outside (the crowd or mass) in (to an individual member of the crowd). Ahmed (pp. 44–49) seeks to advance beyond this model by using the idea of "affective economies" so that the circulation of affect becomes analogous to the circulation of commodities, but her analysis remains at a high level of abstraction.

Interestingly enough the psychoanalyst R. D. Hinshelwood developed a similar line of thinking in the late 1980s. In two articles (Hinshelwood, 1986, 1989) he explores processes of reification, fetishism and circulation in psychoanalysis and Marxism and in particular considers the Kleinian concept of projective identification as the psychical equivalent of alienation. Traditionally psychoanalysis has seen projective identification as the process by which X communicates something about his affective state to Y by making Y feel something of what he is feeling – the process is unreflexive, the affect being embodied in gesture, tone and action. Based on his observations of groups and institutions Hinshelwood suggests that Y in turn may pass on to a third the affect that X has passed to him, and so on. As he puts it, "my thesis is that an essential ingredient of a social network is that bits of experience, affects, emotions, feeling-states, are moved around" (Hinshelwood, 1989, p. 77). Unsurprisingly Hinshelwood refers to this as "the affective network" (p. 78). Hinshelwood suggests that the parallel with alienation comes from the fact that the bits of experience that are circulated refer to feeling-states that actors wish to disown. But then this would lead us to assume that all flows of affect across bodies, that is all collective emotion, are in some respects alienated. This seems unnecessary. We could simply say (following Bion's (1962) model of containment) that a feeling was too strong for X to contain and so it overflowed. To use the example of grief we can see how the feeling is often too powerful for an individual to bear (ie. to contain): a close friend may pick up some of this grief and be similarly affected by it but we do not say that in this instance the circulation of affect is in some way alienated. So affective networks may comprise alienated affect (most of the worst forms of political violence over the past century have been committed by groups who perceive themselves to be the victims of another group's aggression) or they may not (when Nelson Mandela dies there will presumably be global displays of mass grief which will make the outpourings upon the death of Princess Diana seem puny, yet only by a perverse stretch of the imagination will we be able to say this was alienated).

Given the importance of the concept of social network to a whole range of sociological and political investigations – social movement theory, actor network theory, policy networks, inter-organisational networks and so on – the idea that pre-existing social networks may be conduits for affect and, perhaps even more interesting, the idea that circulations of affect may also be constitutive of social networks (alongside other factors), that is the idea of affective networks, could potentially prove to be a powerful concept with real empirical applicability.

Emotions, institutions and power

The previous two sections have drawn us increasingly towards relational and systemic analyses of emotion. Perhaps such forms of analysis provide the basis for another field of investigation – the relation between affects, emotions and organisations, particularly the institutions of government. In what ways do institutions both shape and get shaped by collective feelings and sentiments, including contradictory and ambivalent sentiments (Hoggett, 2005)? Again there are a number of developments that could be drawn upon – the idea of organisations as social defences against anxiety (Menzies Lyth, 1960) and the accumulating studies of "emotional labour" (Smith, 1992) for example. For government this presents issues of internal organisation, systems and practice as well as questions of policy. These kinds of questions are particularly important as governments struggle increasingly to cope with threats to national security posed by the new terrorism and the consequences of global warming (Sunstein, 2005).

The emphasis upon organisations and institutions is also a necessary corrective to the belief that emotions are something that the masses have as opposed to the elites. How, for example, do emotions affect the political decisions of ruling elites in western democracies, decisions such as the invasion of Iraq (Hoggett, 2005)? How do political or corporate elites "do aggression" in today's globalised and flexibilised economy (a theme which haunts the pages of Sennett's (1998) investigation of corporate life)? These kinds of question enable us to examine the role of the emotions in the exercise of power and might usefully be turned upon a range of hegemonic institutions, including universities themselves. And perhaps particularly universities, for after all where else is the myth of calm and dispassionate communities of reason so unquestioned?

Bibliography

Adorno, T. (1991). "Freudian Theory and the Pattern of Fascist Propaganda". *The Culture Industry*. London: Routledge. pp. 114–135.

Ahmed, S. (2004). *The Cultural Politics of Emotion*. Edinburgh: Edinburgh University Press.

Alexander, J., Eyerman, R., Giesen, B., Smelser, N. and Sztompka P. (2004). *Cultural Trauma and Collective Identity*. Berkeley: University of California Press.

Alexander, J. C. and Lara, M. P. (1996). "Honneth's New Critical Theory of Recognition". *New Left Review*, No. 220, pp. 126–136.

Alford, C. F. (1989). *Melanie Klein and Critical Social Theory*. Berkeley: Yale University Press.

——. (1994). *Group Psychology and Political Theory*. New Haven: Yale University Press.

——. (2001). *Whistleblowers: Broken Lives and Organizational Power*. Ithaca, N.Y.: Cornell University Press.

——. (2005). *Melanie Klein and Critical Social Theory*, reprint edition. New Haven: Yale University Press.

Anderson, B. (1991). *Imagined Communities*, revised edition. London: Verso.

Arendt, H. (1965). *Eichmann in Jerusalem: A Report on the Banality of Evil*, revised and enlarged edition. New York: Viking Press.

——. (1973). *The Origins of Totalitarianism*, new edition with added prefaces. New York: Harvest Books.

——. (1990). *On Revolution*. New York: Penguin Books.

Aristotle. (1991). *The Rhetoric*, ed. and trans. H. C. Lawson-Tancred. London: Penguin.

——. (2000). *The Nicomachean Ethics*, ed. Roger Crisp, Cambridge: Cambridge University Press.

Armon-Jones, C. (1986). "The Thesis of Constructionism", in R. Harré (ed.) *The Social Construction of Emotions*. Oxford: Blackwell. pp. 57–82.

Atran, S. (2003). Genesis of Suicide Terrorism. *Science*, 299 (7 March), pp. 1534–1539.

Bacon, F. (1905). "The Advancement of Learning", in John M. Robertson (ed.) *The Philosophical Works of Francis Bacon*. London: George Routledge and Sons. pp. 42–176.

Bagehot, W. (1964). "Introduction to the Second Edition". *The English Constitution*. London: C.A. Watts and Co. pp. 270–297.

Barbalet, J. M. (1996). "Social Emotions: Confidence, Trust and Loyalty". *International Journal of Sociology and Social Policy*, 16(9–10), pp. 75–96.

——. (1998, 2001). *Emotion, Social Theory and Social Structure: A Macrosociological Approach*. Cambridge: Cambridge University Press.

——. (2002). "Secret Voting and Political Emotions". *Mobilization*, 7(2), pp. 129–140.

Barrows, K. (2002). *Envy*. Cambridge: Icon Books.

Barry, B. (1970). *Sociologists, Economists and Democracy*. London: Collier-MacMillan.

Barton, R. E. (1998). " 'Zealous Anger' and the Renegotiation of Aristocratic Relationships in Eleventh and Twelfth Century France", in B. H. Rosenwein (ed.) *Anger's Past: The Social Uses of an Emotion in the Middle Ages*. Ithaca, N.Y.: Cornell University Press.

Bauman, S. (1989). *Modernity and the Holocaust*. London: Polity.

Bauman, Z. (1982). *Memories of Class: The Prehistory and After-life of Class*. London: Routledge.

Beck, U. (1992). *Risk Society: Towards a New Modernity*. London: Sage.

Benford, R. and Snow, D. (2000). "Framing Processes and Social Movements: An Overview and Assessment". *Annual Review of Sociology*, 26, pp. 11–39.

Benjamin, J. (2004). "Beyond Doer and Done to: An Intersubjective View of Thirdness". *Psychoanalytic Quarterly*, LXXIII, pp. 5–46.

Bentley, A. F. (1949). *The Process of Government: A Study of Social Pressures*. Evanston, Ill: Principia Press.

Berezin, M. (2002). "Secure States: Towards a Political Sociology of Emotions", in J. Barbalet (ed.) *Emotions and Society*. Oxford: Blackwell Publishing/The Sociological review. pp. 33–52.

Berlant, L. (ed.) (2004). *Compassion: The Culture and Politics of an Emotion*. New York/London: Routledge.

Betz, H.-G. (2002). "Conditions Favoring the Success and Failure of Radical Right-Wing Populist Parties in Contemporary Democracies", in Y. Mény and Y. Surel (eds) *Democracies and the Populist Challenge*. Hampshire: Palgrave. pp. 197–213.

Bion, W. (1961). *Experiences in Groups*. London: Tavistock Publications.

——. (1962). *Learning from Experience*. London: Tavistock.

——. (1970). *Attention and Interpretation*. London: Tavistock.

——. (1984). *Second Thoughts: Selected Papers on Psycho-Analysis*. New York: Jason Aronson.

——. (1989). *Learning From Experience*. London: Karnac.

Bittner, R. (1994). "Ressentiment", in R. Schacht (ed.) *Nietzsche, Genealogy, Morality: Essays on Nietzsche's Genealogy of Morals*. Berkeley: University of California Press. pp. 127–138.

Blight, J. G. (1990). *The Shattered Crystal Ball: Fear and Learning in the Cuban Missile Crisis*. Savage, Md.: Rowman and Littlefield.

Bourdieu, P. (1992). *The Logic of Practice*. Cambridge: Polity Press.

Bourdieu, P. *et al.* (1999). *The Weight of the World: Social Suffering in Contemporary Society*. Cambridge: Polity Press.

Bowlby, J. (1978). *Attachment*. Harmondsworth: Penguin.

Briggs, J. L. (1970). *Never in Anger: Portrait of an Eskimo Family*. Cambridge: Cambridge University Press.

Brooks, D. (2002). "The Culture of Martyrdom". *The Atlantic Monthly*, 289(6), pp. 18–20.

Brown, W. (1995). *States of Injury: Power and Freedom in Late Modernity*. Princeton: Princeton University Press.

Brown, J. and Richards, B. (2000). "Introduction to the Psychoanalytic Sociology of Emotion". *Psychoanalytic Studies*, 2(1), pp. 31–33.

Calhoun, C. and Solomon, R. (eds) (1984). *What Is an Emotion? Classic Readings in Philosophical Psychology*. Oxford: Oxford University Press.

Campbell, A., Converse P. E., Miller W. E. and Stokes D. E. (1960). *The American Voter*. New York: Wiley.

Canovan, M. (1999). "Trust the People! Populism and the Two Faces of Democracy". *Political Studies*, XLVII, pp. 2–16.

Charalambis, D. (1989). *Clientelism and Populism: The Extra Institutional Consensus in the Greek Political System*. Athens: Exandas Publications.

Chasseguet-Smirgel, J. (1994). "Brief Reflections on the Disappearance in Nazi Racial Theory of the Capacity to Create Symbols", in A. K. Richard and A. Richards (eds) *The Spectrum of Psychoanalysis*. Madison, Connecticut: International Universities Press.

Chaucer, G. (1958). "The Parson's Tale". *The Canterbury Tales*. London: Dent.

——. (1993). *The Canterbury Tales: A Complete Translation into Modern English*, trans. Ecker, R. and Crook, E. Palatka, Florida: Hodge and Braddock Publishers.

Chong, D. (1991). *Collective Action and the Civil Rights Movement*. Chicago: University of Chicago Press.

Clarke, S. (1999a). "Splitting Difference: Psychoanalysis, Hatred and Exclusion". *Journal for the Theory of Social Behaviour*, 29(1), pp. 21–35.

——. (2001). "From Aesthetics to Object Relations: Situating Klein in the Freudian Uncanny". *Free Associations*, 8(4), pp. 547–560.

——. (2002). "On Strangers: Phantasy, Terror and the Human Imagination". *Journal of Human Rights*, 1(3), pp. 1–11.

——. (2003a). "Psychoanalytic Sociology and the Interpretation of Emotion". *Journal for the Theory of Social Behaviour*, 33(2), pp. 145–163.

——. (2003b). *Social Theory, Psychoanalysis and Racism*. London: Palgrave.

——. (2004). "The Concept of Envy: Primitive Drives, Social Encounters, and Ressentiment". *Psychoanalysis, Culture and Society*, 9(1), pp. 105–117.

Clarke, S. and Bird, J. (1999b). "Racism, Hatred, and Discrimination Through the Lens of Projective Identification". *Journal for the Psychoanalysis of Culture and Society*, 4(2), pp. 158–161.

Clarke, S. and Hoggett, P. (2004). "The Empire of Fear: the American Political Psyche and the Culture of Paranoia". *Psychodynamic Practice*, 10(1), pp. 89–106.

Clarke, S. and Moran, A. (2003). "The Uncanny Stranger: Haunting the Australian Settler Imagination". *Free Associations*, 10(2), pp. 165–189.

Clore, G. L., Schwarz, N. and Conway M. (1994). "Affective Causes and Consequences of Social Information Processing", in R. S. Wyer and T. K. Srull, (eds) *Handbook of Social Cognition*, 2nd edn, Hillsdale, N.J.: Erlbaum. pp. 323–418.

Collins, R. (2001). "Social Movements and the Focus of Emotional Attention", in J. Goodwin, J. M. Jasper and F. Polletta (eds) *Passionate Politics: Emotions and Social Movements*. Chicago: University of Chicago Press. pp. 27–44.

——. (2004). *Interaction Ritual Chains*. Princeton, N.J.: Princeton University Press.

Connolly, W. (1991). *Identity/Difference: Democratic Negotiations of Political Paradox*. Ithaca: Cornell University Press.

Craib, I. (1995). "Some Comments on the Sociology of Emotions". *Sociology*, 29(1), pp. 151–158.

——. (1997). "Social Construction as a Social Psychosis". *Sociology*, 31(1), pp. 1–15.

——. (2001). *Psychoanalysis: A Critical Introduction*. London: Polity Press.

Crawford, N. C. (2000). "The Passion of World Politics: Propositions on Emotion and Emotional Relationship". *International Security*, 24, pp. 116–156.

Dalal, F. (2002). *Race, Colour and the Processes of Racialization: New Perspectives from Group Analysis, Psychoanalysis and Sociology*. New York: Brunner-Routledge.

Damasio, A. (2000). *The Feeling of What Happens: Body and Emotion in the Making of Consciousness*. London: Heinemann.

Davis, J. M. (2003). *Martyrs: Innocence, Vengeance and Despair in the Middle East*. New York: Palgrave Macmillan.

de Rivera, J. (1977). *A Structural Theory of the Emotions*. New York: International Universities Press.

Derryberry, D. (1991). "The Immediate Effects of Positive and Negative Feedback Signals". *Journal of Personality and Social Psychology*, 61, pp. 267–278.

Durkheim, E. (1970). *Suicide: A Study in Sociology*. London: Routledge and Kegan Paul.

Eckstein, H. (1988). "A Culturalist Theory of Political Change". *American Political Science Review*, 82(3), pp. 789–804.

Ekman, P. (1972). *Emotions in the Human Face*. New York: Pergamon.

Elias, N. (2000). *The Civilizing Process*, revised edition. Oxford: Blackwell.

Elshtain, J. B. (1995). *Augustine and the Limits of Politics*. Nortre Dame, Indiana: University of Nortre Dame Press.

Elster, J. (1999a). *Alchemies of the Mind: Rationality and the Emotions*. Cambridge: Cambridge University Press.

——. (1999b). *Strong Feelings*. Cambridge: MIT Press.

Epstein, B. (1991). *Political Protest and Cultural Revolution: Nonviolent Direct Action in the 1970s and 1980s*. Berkeley: University of California Press.

Evans, D. (2004). *Emotion: The Science of Sentiment*. Oxford: Oxford University Press.

Fanon, F. (1968). *Black Skin White Masks*. London: MacGibbon and Kee.

Fieschi, C. (2004). *Fascism, Populism and the French Fifth Republic: In the Shadow of Democracy*. Manchester: Manchester University Press.

Filias, V. (1976). *Sociological Essays*. Athens (in Greek): Boukoumanis Publications.

Fineman, S. (2000). *Emotions in Organisations*. London: Sage.

Flax, J. (1993). *Disputed Subjects*. London/New York: Routledge.

Fonagy, P., Gergely, G., Jurist, E. and Target, M. (2002). *Affect Regulation, Mentalization and the Development of the Self*. New York/London: Other Books.

Foster, R. (1999) "Recognition and Resistance: Axel Honneth's Critical Social Theory". *Radical Philosophy*, No. 94, March/April, pp. 6–18.

Frank, R. H. (1988). *Passions within Reason: The Strategic Role of the Emotions*. New York: W. W. Norton.

Fraser, N. (2003). "Distorted Beyond all Recognition: A Rejoinder to Axel Honneth", in N. Fraser and A. Honneth (eds) *Redistribution or Recognition? A Political-Philosophical Exchange*. London: Verso.

Freud, S. (1915). "The Instincts and their Vicissitudes". *The Standard Edition of the Complete Psychological Works of Sigmund Freud*. London: Hogarth Press. Vol. 14, pp. 109–140.

——. (1920). *Beyond the Pleasure Principle*, trans. James Strachey (1961). New York: W. W. Norton.

——. (1930). "Civilization and Its Discontents". *The Standard Edition of the Complete Psychological Works of Sigmund Freud*. London: Hogarth Press. Vol. 21, pp. 57–145.

Fromm, E. (1942). *The Fear of Freedom*. London: Routledge.

Gambetta, D. (1993). *The Sicilian Mafia: The Business of Private Protection*. Cambridge, MA: Harvard University Press.

Gamson, J. (1995). "Must Identity Movements Self-Destruct? A Queer Dilemma". *Social Problems*, 36, pp. 390–407.

Ganor, B. (2000). "Suicide Terrorism: An Overview". http://www.ict.org.il/articles/articledet.cfm?articleid = 128.

Garrett, H. E. (1941). *Great Experiments in Psychology*, revised and enlarged edition. New York: Appleton-Century.

Gay, P. (1993). *The Cultivation of Hatred*. New York: W. W. Norton.

Giddens, A. (1984). *The Constitution of Society*. Oxford: Polity Press.

Goleman, D. (1996). *Emotional Intelligence: Why It Can Matter More Than IQ*. London: Bloomsbury.

Gomes, P. J. (2004). *Strength for the Journey: Biblical Wisdom for Daily Living*. San Francisco: Harper.

Goodwin, J. (1997). "The Libidinal Constitution of a High-Risk Social Movement: Affectual Ties and Solidarity in the Huk Rebellion". *American Sociological Review*, 62, pp. 53–69.

Goodwin, J., Jasper, J. M. and Polletta, F. (2001). *Passionate Politics: Emotions and Social Movements*. Chicago: University of Chicago Press.

Goodwin, J., Jasper, J. M. and Polletta F. (2004). "Emotional Dimensions of Social Movements", in D. A. Snow, S. A. Soule and H. Kriesi (eds) *The Blackwell Companion to Social Movements*. Oxford: Blackwell. pp. 413–432.

Gould, D. (2001). "Rock the Boat, Don't Rock the Boat, Baby: Ambivalence and the Emergence of Militant AIDS Activism", in J. Goodwin, J. M. Jasper and F. Polletta (eds) *Passionate Politics: Emotions and Social Movements*. Chicago: University of Chicago Press. pp. 135–157.

——. (2005). "The Shame of Gay Pride in Early AIDS Activism", in Valerie Traub and David Halperin (eds) *Gay Shame*. Chicago: University of Chicago Press.

Gramsci, A. (1971). "The Philosophy of Praxis", in *The Prison Notebooks*. trans. Quintin Hoare and Geoffrey Nowell Smith. London: Lawrence and Wishart.

Greenspan, S. I. and S. G. Shanker. (2004). *The First Idea*. New York: Perseus Books.

Griffiths, P. E. (1997). *What Emotions Really Are: The Problem of Psychological Categories*. Chicago: University of Chicago Press.

Griffiths, P. J. (2004). "Orwell for Christians". *First Things*, December, No. 148, pp. 32–40.

Habermas, J. (1970). *Toward a Rational Society*. Boston: Heinemann.

Harré, R. (ed.) (1986). *The Social Construction of Emotions*. London: Blackwell.

Hassan, N. (2001). "An Arsenal of Believers". *The New Yorker*, 19th November. pp. 36–41.

Hedström, P. and R. Swedberg. (eds) (1998). *Social Mechanisms*. Cambridge: Cambridge University Press.

Heise, D. R. (1979). *Understanding Events: Affect and the Construction of Social Action*. Cambridge: Cambridge University Press.

Hennessy, A. (1969). "Latin America", in Ionescu G. and Gellner E. (eds) *Populism. Its Meanings and National Characteristics*. Hertfordshire: Garden City Press, pp. 28–61.

Hinshelwood, R. D. (1986). "A Dual Materialism". *Free Associations*, 4, pp. 36–50.

——. (1989). "Social Possession of Identity", in B. Richards (ed.) *Crises of the Self*. London: Free Association Books.

——. (1989). *The Dictionary of Kleinian Thought*. London: Free Association Books.

——. (1994). *Clinical Klein*. London: Free Association Books.

Hirschman, A. (2003). *The Passions and the Interests*. Salonica Paratirites (in Greek).

Hochschild, A. (1979). "Emotion Work, Feeling Rules, and Social Structure". *American Journal of Sociology*, 85(3), pp. 551–575.

——. (1983). *The Managed Heart: The Commercialization of Human Feeling*. Berkeley: University of California Press.

Hoggett, P. (2000). "Hatred of Dependency", in *Emotional Life and the Politics of Welfare*. Basingstoke: Macmillan. pp. 159–180.

——. (2005). "A Service to the Public: The Containment of Ethical and Moral Conflicts by Public Bureaucracies", in P. Du Gay (ed.) *The Values of Bureaucracy*. Oxford: Oxford University Press.

——. (2005). "Iraq: Blair's Mission Impossible". *British Journal of Politics and International Relations*, 7, pp. 418–428.

Hoggett, P. and Thompson, S. (2002). "Towards a Democracy of the Emotions". *Constellations*, 9(1), pp. 106–126.

Holmes, M. (2004). "Politicizing the Sociology of Emotion and Anger in Feminist Politics". *European Journal of Social Theory*, 7(2), pp. 209–227.

——. (2004). "The Importance of Being Angry: Anger in Political Life". *European Journal of Social Theory*, 7(2), pp. 123–132.

Holst-Warhaft, G. (2000). *The Cue for Passion: Grief and its Political Uses*. Cambridge, MA: Harvard University Press.

Honneth, A. (1994). "The Social Dynamics of Disrespect: On the Location of Critical Theory Today", *Constellations*, 1(2), pp. 255–269.

——. (1995). *The Struggle for Recognition: The Moral Grammar of Social Struggles*. Cambridge: Polity.

——. (2002). "Grounding Recognition: A Rejoinder to Critical Questions". *Inquiry*, 45(4), pp. 499–520.

Horkheimer, M. and Adorno, T. (1947, 1994). *Dialectic of Enlightenment*. New York: Continuum.

Hutchinson, D. S. (1995) "Ethics", in J. Barnes (ed.) *The Cambridge Companion to Aristotle*. Cambridge: Cambridge University Press.

Inglehart, R. (1977). *The Silent Revolution: Changing Values and Political Styles among Western Publics*. Princeton, N.J.: Princeton University Press.

Ionescu, G. and Gellner, E. (eds) (1969) *Populism. Its Meanings and National Characteristics*. Hertfordshire: Garden City Press.

James, W. (1902). *The Varieties of Religious Experience*. London: Longmans, Green and Co.

Jasper, J. M. (1997). *The Art of Moral Protest: Culture, Biography, and Creativity in Social Movements*. Chicago: University of Chicago Press.

——. (1998). "The Emotions of Protest: Affective and Reactive Emotions in and around Social Movements". *Sociological Forum*, 13, pp. 397–424.

——. (2004). "A Strategic Approach to Collective Action: Looking for Agency in Social Movement Choices". *Mobilization*, 9, pp. 1–16.

——. (2006a). *Getting Your Way: Strategic Dilemmas in Everyday Life*. Chicago: University of Chicago Press.

——. (2006b). "Motivation and Emotion", in R. Goodin and C. Tilly (eds) *Oxford Handbook of Contextual Political Studies*. Oxford: Oxford U**niversity Press. pp. 157–171.

Jasper, J. M. and J. Poulsen. (1993). "Fighting Back: Vulnerabilities, Blunders, and Countermobilization by the Targets in Three Animal Rights Campaigns". *Sociological Forum*, 8, pp. 639–657.

Jenkins, J., Oatley, K. and Stein, N. (eds) (1998). *Human Emotion: A Reader*. London: Blackwell.

Joffe, W. (1969). "A Critical Review of the Envy Concept". *International Journal of Psycho-Analysis*, 50, pp. 533–545.

Joseph, B. (1989). "Envy in Everyday Life", in M. Feldman and E. Bott Spillius (eds) *Psychic Equilibrium and Psychic Change*. London: Tavistock/Routledge. pp. 181–191.

Jurist, E. (1994). "Review of Axel Honneth, *Kampf um Anerkennung*". *Constellations*, 1(1), pp. 171–180.

Karapostolis, V. (1984). *Consuming Behavior in Greek Society 1960–1975*. Athens: National Center of Social Research (in Greek).

——. (1985). *The Impenetrable Society*. Athens (in Greek): Polytypon Publications.

——. (1987). *Symbiosis and Communication in Greece*. Athens (in Greek): Gnosis Publications.

Kemper, Th. (1987). "How Many Emotions are there? Wedding the Social and the Autonomic Components". *American Journal of Sociology*, 93(2), pp. 263–289.

——. (ed.) (1990) *Research Agendas in the Sociology of Emotions*. New York: State University of New York Press.

——. (1991). "An Introduction to the Sociology of Emotions", in K. Strongman, (ed.) *International Review of Studies on Emotion*. Vol. 1, New York: John Wiley. pp. 301–349.

Kemper, T. D. (1978). *A Social Interactional Theory of Emotions*. New York: Wiley.

Kemper, T. (2001). "A Structural Approach to Social Movement Emotions", in J. Goodwin, J. M. Jasper, and F. Polletta (eds) *Passionate Politics: Emotions and Social Movements*. Chicago: University of Chicago Press. pp. 58–73.

Kernberg, O. (1980). *Internal World and External Reality*. New York: Jason Aronson.

——. (1995). "Hatred as a Core Affect of Aggression", in S. Akhtar, S. Kramer, and H. Parens (eds) *The Birth of Hatred: Developmental, Clinical and Technical Aspects of Intense Aggression*, Northvale, N.J.: Jason Aronson. pp. 53–82.

Kierkegaard, S. (1957). *The Concept of Dread*, trans. Walter Lowrie. Princeton: Princeton University Press.

Klein, M. (1952, 1997). "The Mutual Influences in the Development of the Ego and Id". *Envy and Gratitude and Other Works 1946–1963*. London: Vintage. pp. 57–60.

——. (1957, 1997). "Envy and Gratitude". *Envy and Gratitude and Other Works 1946–1963*. London: Vintage. pp. 176–235.

——. (1975a). "Early Stages of the Oedipus Conflict", in *Love, Guilt and Reparation and Other Works 1921–1945*. New York: Free Press. pp. 186–198. [Volume 1 of the Writings of Melanie Klein]

——. (1975b). "Envy and Gratitude". *Envy and Gratitude and Other Works 1946–1963*. New York: Free Press. pp. 176–235. [Volume 3 of *The Writings of Melanie Klein*]

——. (1975c). *Narrative of a Child Analysis*. New York: Free Press. [Volume 4 of *The Writings of Melanie Klein*]

Kolinsky, E. (2004). *After the Holocaust: Jewish Survivors in Germany After 1945*. London: Pimlico.

Kundera, M. (1990). *Immortality*. New York: Grove Weidenfeld.

Kurzman, C. (1996). "Structural and Perceived Opportunity: The Iranian Revolution of 1979". *American Sociological Review*, 61, pp. 153–170.

Laclau, E. (1977). *Politics and Ideology in Marxist Theory: Capitalism, Fascism, Populism*. London: Verso.

Laclau, E. (2005) "Populism: What's in a Name?", in F. Panizza (ed.) *Populism and the Mirror of Democracy*. London: Verso.

Lagache, D. (1964). "Fantasy, Reality and Truth". *International Journal of Psychoanalysis*, 45, pp. 180–189.

Langer, M. (1989). "Psychoanalysis Without the Couch". *Free Associations*, 15, pp. 60–66.

Lazarus, R. S. (1999). "Hope: An Emotion and a Vital Coping Resource against Despair". *Social Research*, 66, pp. 653–678.

Le Bon, G. (1952). *The Crowd*. London: Ernest Benn.

Le Doux, J. (2002). *Synaptic Self: How Our Brains Become Who We Are*. London: Macmillan.

Lewis, H. B. (1971). *Shame and Guilt in Neurosis*. New York: International Universities Press.

Likierman, M. (2001). *Melanie Klein: Her Work in Context*. London: Continuum.

Lively, K. J. and Heise D. R. (2004). "Sociological Realms of Emotional Experience". *American Journal of Sociology*, 109, pp. 1109–1136.

Lofland, J. (1982). "Crowd Joys". *Urban Life*, 10, pp. 355–381.

Lomax, E. (1996). *The Railway Man*. London: Vintage.

Lyman, P. (1981) 'The politics of anger'. *Socialist Review*, 11, pp. 55–74.

Lyrintzis, Ch. (1984). "Political Parties in Post-Junta Greece: A Case of 'Bureaucratic Clientelism?' ", in G. Pridham (ed.) *The New Mediterranean Democracies: Regime transition in Spain, Greece and Portugal*. London: Frank Cass. pp. 99–118.

——. (1987). "The Power of Populism: The Greek Case". *European Journal of Political Research*, 15, pp. 667–686.

——. (1993). "PASOK in Power: From 'Change' to Disenchantment", in R. Clogg (ed.) *Greece, 1981–89: The Populist Decade*. New York: St. Martin's Press. pp. 26–46.

Macchiavelli, N. (1950). "The Prince", in Max Lerner (ed.) *The Prince and Discourses*, New York: Modern Library. pp. 1–98.

Madsen, D. and Snow P. G. (1991). *The Charismatic Bond: Political Behavior in Time of Crisis*. Cambridge: Harvard University Press.

Malakunas, K. (2001). "Israel Launches Major Retaliation for Jerusalem Suicide Bombing". *Middle East Times*. August 10.

Marcus, G. E. (2000). "Emotions in Politics". *Annual Review of Political Science*, 3, pp. 221–250.

——. (2002). *The Sentimental Citizen: Emotion in Democratic Politics*. Philadelphia: Pennsylvania State University Press.

Marcuse, H. (1961). *Eros and Civilization: A Philosophical Inquiry into Freud*. New York: Vintage Books.

May, C. P., Kane M. J. and Hasher L. (1995). "Determinants of Negative Priming". *Psychological Bulletin*, 118, pp. 35–54.

McGowan, J. (1998). *Hannah Arendt: An Introduction*. Minneapolis: University of Minnesota Press.

McNeill, W. H. (1995). *Keeping Together in Time: Dance and Drill in Human History*. Cambridge: Harvard University Press.

McPhail, C. (1991). *The Myth of the Madding Crowd*. New York: Aldine de Gruyter.

Mead, G. H. (1934). *Mind, Self and Society*. Chicago: University of Chicago Press.

Meltzer, B. and Musolf, G.-R. (2002). "Resentment and Ressentiment". *Sociological Inquiry*, 72(2), pp. 240–255.

Meltzer, D. (1978). *The Kleinian Development*. Perthshire, Scotland: Clunie Press. [3 parts in 1 volume]

Mendus, S. (ed.) (2000). *Feminism and Emotion: Readings in Moral and Political Philosophy*. London: Palgrave Macmillan.

Menzies Lyth, I. (1960). "A Case Study in the Functioning of Social Systems as a Defence Against Anxiety". *Human Relations*, 13, pp. 95–121.

Merton, R. (1957/1968). *Social Theory and Social Structure*. New York: Free Press.

Mestrovic, S. (1997). *Postemotional Society*. London: Sage.

Meyer, J. W. and B. Rowan. (1977). "Institutionalized Organizations: Formal Structure as Myth and Ceremony". *American Journal of Sociology*, 83, pp. 340–363.

Mill, J. S. (1960). "Considerations on Representative Government". *Utilitarianism, Liberty, Representative Government*. London: J. M. Dent and Sons. pp. 175–193.

Miller, A. (1983). *For Your Own Good: Hidden Cruelty in Child-Rearing and the Roots of Violence*. New York: Farrar, Straus, Giroux.

Minogue, K. (1969). "Populism as a Political Movement". *Populism. Its Meanings and National Characteristics*, pp. 197–211.

Moore, B. (1978). *Injustice: The Social Bases of Obedience and Revolt*. New York: MacMillan.

Morgan, R. and D. R. Heise (1988). "Structure of Emotions". *Social Psychology Quarterly*, 51, pp. 19–31.

Morsbach, H. and Tyler, W. J. (1988). "A Japanese Emotion: *Amae*", in R. Harré (ed.) *The Social Construction of Emotions*. Oxford: Blackwell. pp. 289–307.

Mouffe, C. (2000). *The Democratic Paradox*. London: Verso.

Mouzelis, N. (1985). "On the Concept of Populism: Populist and Clientelist Models of Incorporation in Semi peripheral Polities". *Politics and Society*, 14(3), pp. 329–348.

Mudde, C. (2004). "The Populist Zeitgeist". *Government and Opposition Ltd*, pp. 541–563.

Nelson, D. (2004). "Suffering and Thinking", in L. Berlant (ed.) *Compassion: The Culture and Politics of an Emotion*. New York/London: Routledge.

Nietzsche, F. (1970). *Genealogy of Morals*. Athens (in Greek).

Nussbaum, M. C. (2001). *Upheavals of Thought: The Intelligence of Emotions*. Cambridge: Cambridge University Press.

——. (2004). *Hiding from Humanity: Disgust, Bodies and the Law*. Princeton: Princeton University Press.

Nygren, T. E. (1998). "Reacting to Perceived High- and Low-Risk Win-Lose Opportunities in a Risky Decision-Making Task: Is it Framing or Affect or Both?". *Motivation and Behavior*, 22, pp. 73–98.

Oatley, K. and Jenkins, J. (1996). *Understanding Emotions*. Oxford: Blackwell.

Ortony, A., Clore, J. L. and Collins, A. (1988). *The Cognitive Structure of Emotions*. Cambridge: Cambridge University Press.

Orwell, G. (1949). *Nineteen Eighty-Four*. New York: Signet.

——. (1953). "Why I Write". *Such, Such Were the Joys*. New York: Harcourt Brace Jovanovich. [original 1946]

Ost, D. (2004). "Politics and the Mobilization of Anger". *European Journal of Social Theory*, 7(2), pp. 229–244.

Overy, R. (2004). *The Dictators: Hitler's Germany, Stalin's Russia*. London: Allen Lane.

Pagels, E. (1995). *The Origins of Satan*. New York: Random House.

Paxton, P. (2002). "Social Capital and Democracy: An Interdependent Relationship". *American Sociological Review*, 67, pp. 254–277.

Piven, F. and Cloward, R. (1988). *Poor People's Movements: Why They Succeed, How They Fail*. New York: Random House USA Inc.

Polletta, F. and J. M. Jasper. (2001). "Collective Identity and Social Movements". *Annual Review of Sociology*, 27, pp. 283–305.

Portman, J. (2000). *When Bad Things Happen to Other People*. London: Routledge.

Putnam, R. D. (2002). *Bowling Alone: The Collapse and Revival of American Community*. New York: Simon and Schuster.

Rawls, J. (1971/1991). *A Theory of Justice*. Oxford: Oxford University Press.

Richards, B. (2000). "The Anatomy of Envy". *Psychoanalytic Studies*, 2(1), pp. 65–76.

Rieff. P. (1961). *Freud: The Mind of the Moralist*. New York: Harper and Row.

Ringmar, E. (1996). *Identity, Interest and Action: A Cultural Explanation of Sweden's Intervention in the Thirty Years War*. Cambridge: Cambridge University Press.

Roger, J. (2003). "Social Solidarity, Welfare and Post-emotionalism". *Journal of Social Policy*, 32(3), pp. 403–421.

Rokkan, S. (1966). "Mass Suffrage, Secret Voting and Political Participation", in Lewis A. Coser (ed.) *Political Sociology*. New York: Harper. pp. 102–31.

Rorty, R. (1993). "Human Rights, Rationality, and Sentimentality", in S. Shute and S. Hurley (eds) *On Human Rights: The Oxford Amnesty Lectures, 1993*. New York: Basic Books. pp. 111–134.

Rosenfeld, H. (1988). "A Clinical Approach to the Psychoanalytic Theory of the Life and Death Instincts: An Investigation into the Aggressive Aspects of Narcissism", in E. Bott Spillius (ed.) *Melanie Klein Today*. Vol. 1, London: Routledge. pp. 239–255.

Sabini, J. and Silver, M. (1986). "Envy", in R. Harré (ed.) *The Social Construction of Emotions*. London: Blackwell. pp. 167–183.

Sabini, J. and Silver, M. (1998). "The Not Altogether Social Construction of Emotions: A Critique of Harré and Gillett". *Journal for the Theory of Social Behaviour*, 28(3), pp. 223–235.

Sartre, J.-P. (1939, 2002). *Sketch for a Theory of Emotions*. London: Routledge.

Sartre, J.-P. (1964). *Nausea*, trans. Lloyd Alexander. New York: New Directions.

Sennett, R. (1998). *The Corrosion of Character*. London/New York: W. W. Norton.

Scheff, T. J. (1980, 1990). *Microsociology: Discourse, Emotion and Social Structure*. Chicago: University of Chicago Press.

——. (1994). *Bloody Revenge*. Boulder, Colo.: Westview Press.

——. (1997). *Emotions, the Social Bond, and Human Reality: Part/Whole Analysis*. Cambridge: Cambridge University Press.

——. (2001). "Male Emotions and Violence". *Journal of Mundane Behavior*, 2, pp. 9–11.

Scheler, M. (1961). *Ressentiment*. Glencoe: Free Press.

——. (1992) *On Feeling, Knowing and Valuing*. H. Bershady (ed.). Chicago: University of Chicago Press.

Scherer, K. R. (1984). "On the Nature and Function of Emotion: A Component Process Approach", in Klaus R. Scherer and P. Ekman (eds) *Approaches to Emotion*. Hillsdale, NJ: Lawrence Erlbaum Associates. pp. 295–317.

Schmitt, C. (1932/1976). *The Concept of the Political*. New Brunswick, N.J.: Rutgers University Press.

Schwartz, N. and Bless H. (1991). "Happy and Mindless, but Sad and Smart? The Impact of Affective States on Analytic Reasoning", in Joseph P. Forgas (ed.) *Emotion and Social Judgments*. New York: Pergamon. pp. 55–71.

Segal, H. (1989). *Melanie Klein*. London: Karnac Books.

Seligman, M. E. P. (1975). *Helplessness: On Depression, Development, and Death*. San Francisco: W. H. Freeman.

Senault, J-F. (1671). *The Use of Passions*. London.

Senechal de la Roche, R. (1996). "Collective Violence as Social Control". *Sociological Forum*, 11, pp. 97–128.

Sennett, R. and Cobb, J. (1972). *The Hidden Injuries of Class*. New York: W.W. Norton and Company.

Shils, E. (1956). *The Torment of Secrecy: The Background and Consequences of American Security Policies*. London: Heinemann.

Shklar, J. (1990). *The Faces of Injustice*. New Haven, CT: Yale University Press.

Shott, S. (1979). "Emotion and Social Life: A Symbolic Interactionist Analysis". *American Journal of Sociology*, 84(6), pp. 1317–1334.

Simmel, G. (1950). *The Sociology of Georg Simmel*. ed. and trans. Wolff, K. New York: Free Press.

——. (1969). *Conflict and The Web of Group-Affiliations*. New York: Free Press.

——. (1971). "The Metropolis and Mental Life", in Donald N. Levine *On Individuality and Social Forms*, Chicago: University of Chicago Press. pp. 324–339.

Smith, A. (1976). *The Theory of Moral Sentiments*. Oxford: Oxford University Press.

Smith, P. (1992). *The Emotional Labour of Nursing*. Basingstoke: Macmillan.

Snow, D. and Benford, R. (1988) "Ideology, Frame Resonance and Participant Mobilization". *International Social Movement Research*, Vol. 1, pp. 197–219.

Solomon, R. C. (1998). "Emotions", in E. Craig (ed.) *Routledge Encyclopaedia of Philosophy*. London: Routledge. Retrieved 27 May 2005 from http://www.rep.routledge.com/article/VO12.

——. (2002). "Back to Basics: On the Very Idea of 'Basic Emotions' ". *Journal for the Theory of Social Behaviour*, 32(2), pp. 115–155.

Sombart, W. (1913/1998). *The Bourgeois*. Athens (in Greek).

Steiner, J. (1993). "Review: Narcissistic Object Relations and Pathological Organizations of the Personality", in *Psychic Retreats*. London: Routledge. pp. 40–53.

Stewart, A. (1969). "The Social Roots", in *Populism. Its Meanings and National Characteristics*, pp. 180–196.

Steuerman, E. (2000). *The Bounds of Reason: Habermas, Lyotard and Melanie Klein on Rationality*. London/New York: Routledge.

Stohl, M. (ed.) (1983). *The Politics of Terrorism*. 2nd edition. New York: Marcel Dekker.

Stohl, M. and Lopez, G. A. (eds) (1984). *The State as Terrorist: The Dynamics of Governmental Violence and Repression*. Westport, Connecticut: Greenwood Press.

Strawson, P. F. (1974). *Freedom and Resentment and Other Essays*. London: Methuen and Co. Ltd.

Stryker, S., Owens, T. and White, R. (eds) (2000). *Self, Identity and Social Movements*. Minneapolis/London: University of Minnesota Press.

Summers-Effler, E. (2005). "The Emotional Significance of Solidarity for Social Movements Communities", in Helena Flam and Debra King (eds) *Emotions and Social Movements*. London: Routledge. pp. 135–149.

Sunstein, C. (2005). *Laws of Fear: Beyond the Precautionary Principle*. Cambridge: Cambridge University Press.

Swanson, D. and Mancini, P. (1996). "Introduction", in D. Swanson and P. Mancini (eds) *Politics, Media, and Modern Democracy*. Westport/Connecticut: Praeger.

Szczurek, T. (2005). *Pursuit of Passionate Purpose: Success Strategies for a Rewarding Personal and Business Life*. New York: Wiley.

Taggart, P. (2000). *Populism*. Buckingham: Open University Press.

Taguieff, P.-A. (1995). Political Science Confronts Populism: From a Conceptual Mirage to a Real Problem. *Telos* N, 103, pp. 9–36.

Tarrow, S. (1989). *Democracy and Disorder: Protest and Politics in Italy, 1965–1975*. Oxford: Oxford University Press.

The Runnymede Trust. (1997). *Islamophobia: A Challenge for Us All*.

Thernstrom, M. (1996). "Diary of a Murder". *The New Yorker*, June 3, pp. 62–71.

Timpanaro, S. (1975). *On Materialism*. London: New Left Books.

Titmuss, R. (1968). *Commitment to Welfare*. London: George Allen and Unwin.

——. (1971). *The Gift Relationship*. London: Pantheon Books.

Turner, J. (1987). "Analytical Theorizing", in A. Giddens and J. Turner (eds) *Social Theory Today*. Cambridge: Polity Press, pp. 156–194.

Volkan, V. D. (1988). *The Need to Have Enemies and Allies*. Northvale, N.J.: Aronson.

Volkov, V. (2002). *Violent Entrepreneurs. The Use of Force in the Making of Russian Capitalism*. Ithaca, N.Y.: Cornell University Press.

Walicki, A. (1969). "Russia", in *Populism. Its Meanings and National Characteristics*, pp. 62–96.

Weber, M. (1970). "Politics as a Vocation", in H. H. Gerth and C. Wright Mills (eds) *From Max Weber*. London: Routledge.

——. (1978). *Economy and Society*, Vol. 1. Berkeley: University of California Press.

——. (1991). *The Protestant Ethic and the Spirit of Capitalism*. London: Harper Collins.

Whitebrook, M. (2002). "Compassion as a Political Virtue". *Political Studies*, 50, pp. 529–544.

Wiles, P. (1969). "A Syndrome, Not a Doctrine: Some elementary theses on populism", in *Populism. Its Meanings and National Characteristics*. pp. 166–179.

Williams, R. (1977). *Marxism and Literature*. Oxford: Oxford University Press.

Williams, S. and Bendelow, G. (1996). "Emotions and 'Sociological Imperialism': A Rejoinder to Craib". *Sociology*, 30(1), pp. 145–153.

——. (1998). "Modernity and the Emotions: Corporeal Reflections on the (Ir)rational". *Sociology*, 32(4), pp. 747–769.

——. (2001). *Emotion and Social Theory*. London: Sage Publications.

Winnicott, D.W. (1947). "Hate in the Countertransference", in *Through Paediatrics to Psycho-Analysis*. London: Hogarth Press (1975). pp. 194–203.

——. (1965). "The Theory of the Parent-infant relationship", in *The Maturational Processes and the Facilitating Environment*. Madison, CT: International University Press. pp. 37–55.

——. (1978). "Hate in the Counter-Transference", in *Through Paediatrics to Psycho-Analysis*. London: Hogarth Press.

Woodward, K. (2004). "Calculating Compassion", in L. Berlant (ed.) *Compassion: The Culture and Politics of an Emotion*. New York/London: Routledge.

Worsley, P. (1969). "The Concept of Populism", in *Populism. Its Meanings and National Characteristics*, pp. 212–250.

Young, I. M. (1997). "Asymmetrical Reciprocity: On Mutual Respect, Wonder, and Enlarged Thought". *Constellations*, 3(3), pp. 340–363.

Young, R. M. (1994). *Mental Space*. London: Process Press.

Young-Bruehl, E. (1982). *Hannah Arendt: For Love of the World*. New Haven: Yale University Press.

Zizek, S. (1989). *The Sublime Object of Ideology*. London: Verso.

Zurn, C. (2000). "Anthropology and Normativity: A Critique of Axel Honneth's 'Formal Conception of Ethical Life'". *Philosophy and Social Criticism*, 26(1), pp. 115–124.

Index

189